# The Complete Gardener

by
Brian Walkden

ENIGMA

*Right : Helenium autumnale pumilum magnificum, an easily grown perennial with bright yellow daisy-like flowers. Overleaf: a well-designed garden is a useful extension to the home as well as a source of pleasure all the year round.*

**Edited by Linda Fox**
**Designed by Barbara Howes**

Published by Marshall Cavendish Books Limited, 58 Old Compton Street, London W1V 5PA

Printed in Great Britain

First printing 1978

ISBN 0 85685 341 0

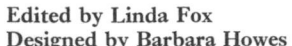

# Introduction

Gardening is an activity in which most of us indulge at some time in our lives. For some it is an all-absorbing hobby, and for others the weekly chore of mowing the lawn is quite sufficient effort! Most of us fall somewhere between the two extremes: we love flowers but don't always know their names, and although we long for a superbly laid out and planted garden, we don't quite know where to start.

*The Complete Gardener* fills the gap with plenty of factual information, photographs and useful step-by-step diagrams. It discusses all the things that the glossy gardening catalogs leave out, like which plants are frost-tender or just difficult to grow; which food crops give you the best return for your money; and how to make your own garden compost for nothing out of kitchen and garden waste. It takes you right through the process of creating a garden tailored to your personal needs and tastes, from the exciting initial planning stage, through making your choice of plants that will suit your climate and locality, down to the basics of finding out your soil type, keeping the garden fertile, and recognizing and controlling garden pests.

Today's garden should be an extension of the home. It should be a place for recreation and relaxation, a place which looks attractive all the year round without requiring a vast amount of time and money for maintenance. The beautiful gardens that we admire are not created without some initial effort and expense, but the challenge is not beyond the capabilities of even a complete newcomer to gardening. Whether you are a complete novice or an enthusiast, you will find in this one volume all you need to create and maintain *your* ideal garden.

# Contents

# Planning your garden

# Planning your garden

This is the really exciting part of making a garden. The first thing to appreciate, however, is the fact that no hard and fast rules can be applied, although of course one can have a reasonably clear plan of campaign. Obviously a great deal depends on personal requirements, and a tremendous amount will depend on the site itself. Basically one should always endeavour to plan the work and the layout so that the minimum amount of labor is involved and consequently the amount of time required is reduced to the minimum.

There is so much on the actual site itself to influence any plan. For example, what is the shape of the garden? If it is square or rectangular then planning is much easier than for a site which is irregular, such as a tapering site. Then there is the problem of the actual contours. If the site is level, work will be much easier, but if the area is undulating or has steep slopes much more of a challenge is involved and greater ingenuity required. There is one important tip here, however, and this applies to the planning of a garden which has steep slopes or banks. It is much better and easier to work *with* the contours rather than against them. In other words, it would be wiser to use a steep bank as a rockery feature or even to incorporate a water garden where a cascading waterfall course can be incorporated in the steep slope of the bank, thus creating a most natural effect.

It is obvious however that much of garden planning is a very personal business, since you will obviously want to incorporate those features that you particularly like. It is also a personal matter with regard to finance because garden making these days is not a cheap undertaking, and perhaps the planning of a new garden or the reorganization of an existing one is best done over a period of a few years so that the outlay is reduced to more reasonable proportions.

*Below: a fountain can be accommodated in the smallest garden. This unusual fountain makes a striking focal point, while primulas and bulbs provide color. Below right: stone walls have been used to create different levels in this small garden. This type of design is very expensive initially, but the finished garden requires minimum upkeep.*

You must also consider the amount of time you may have, or may be prepared to allow, for the general running or maintenance of your garden. The very busy household, for example, may require the most labor saving garden possible, so that only a few hours each week or weekend are necessary to keep it at a good level of cultivation. One must appreciate the fact that the more soil there is left exposed the more weeding will have to be done. One can cover soil as much as possible by paving, which will prevent weed growth and which will be virtually maintenance free. Of course paving or any stone work is quite expensive, but the outlay could be considered as an excellent investment in time and labor saving. On the other hand a very large area or the greater proportion of a garden can be put down to turf. Once a week mowing will be all that is necessary for the greater part of the year but even so this is relatively time and labor consuming—and do not forget that there will be all those edges to keep neat and trim.

There are of course many other permutations of garden design. There is the flower lover's garden, where a large proportion of the layout is devoted to many types of flowers and flowering trees and shrubs. There is the utility garden, a most important feature in these years of self sufficiency. Here the plan is to incorporate a food production area which can be devoted to vegetables or to a combination of vegetables and fruit. Some glass or plastic protection is helpful for food crops and you should plan for a greenhouse and a few frames if possible.

A general survey of the site could reveal that there are many areas where some food or fruit crops could be used or gathered from situations which may escape the average gardener's notice. Why not, for example, make use of warm walls, especially south-facing walls, where a lean-to greenhouse could be established or where certain fruits could be grown such as figs, vines, or espalier loquats where the climate permits? Nor should you overlook those valuable fences or walls against which many fruits can be trained, such as raspberries and brambles, as well as vegetables such as beans.

There is much to be said for having privacy and shelter in the garden: privacy from neighbors, and shelter from cool prevailing winds which can be damaging to many plants. This is facilitated by the planning for and the planting of trees and/or shrubs. Shade is invaluable and so welcome during hot, dry summers, and a suitably placed tree or shrub can cast welcome shadow when one wants to sit out in the garden during the height of the summer.

A garden should be a place to relax in as well as a place to enjoy the beauty of fragrance and color. Although plants will provide that restful atmosphere there is much to commend the inclusion of special features such as patios, terraces and even water. The terrace or patio will provide a restful place for sitting out or for eating meals in the open air, and of course the terrace or patio fitted with a barbecue and lighting can extend the enjoyment of the garden well into the evenings during the warmer weather and can quickly become a great social area.

Few features provide such tranquillity as water, and a garden pool with a sparkling, dancing fountain or even with the addition of a cascading waterfall will provide relaxation and will cool the area around the feature during hot weather. There is no reason at all why one cannot become ambitious enough to think about a swimming pool in the garden. Here the feature can be combined with a terrace or patio which provides a cleaner surface around the water area where one can sit and relax after an enjoyable swim. Although this type of feature is relatively expensive, the above-ground type of swimming pool would suit the budget-conscious gardener, and for more luxury the in-ground or below-ground types are superb.

The shape of the garden as mentioned earlier on is a planning point which must be very carefully considered at the outset. One of the problems of the long, narrow garden is the fact that it can become uninteresting unless planned very carefully. It is surprising, however, what a difference can be made if, instead of using straight beds and paths which only extend the length, paths and beds are allowed to widen and curve gracefully. This gives an illusion of a broader, more interesting garden, and if

*This garden combines many of the features of good design. It centers around an attractive water feature and a well-chosen piece of statuary. Dense shrubbery to the right of the pool creates an intriguing concealed corner.*

# Planning your garden

*A formal garden pool needs plenty of plants to soften the severity of the design. Here a statue is positioned to one side and rock plants are allowed to spill across the formal paving.*

the gardener goes to the additional trouble of dividing a long garden into sub-sections, each with a different layout, the long narrow garden can be quite transformed, and an even more fascinating layout created than one might have imagined originally. There is a great deal to commend the use within reason of curving lines, whether these are for lawns, paths or borders. There is a lot to be said also for island beds which can break up the monotony of a very broad garden or a large garden. There is no reason why some beds cannot jut out into the lawn like peninsulas. This type of planning creates fascinating pockets or areas which are always intriguing to investigate especially by friends who come to stay.

The use of these sweeps and curves has the effect of softening the contours or outlines of a garden. Another method of creating interest in a difficult site such as a long narrow garden is to arrange borders to come out at various angles from the boundaries of the garden. This creates the illusion of a shorter and broader garden. You can also deceive the eye through the careful positioning of focal points. There are several ways in which this can be done. A nice piece of statuary can be positioned and offset to one side of the garden and the view from the house is taken toward this feature so that the focus is placed upon it. Instead of a statue a beautiful specimen tree or shrub could be used, and in some cases even structures can be employed: for example, an attractive summer house or even an attractive greenhouse, such as the round types, which can be ornamental as well as useful.

A lot can be done with lawn shapes. Why have a square or rectangular lawn where one can be created with attractive sweeps or curves in it? In a long garden a lawn can be made to wander down the length of the garden, twisting or bending here and there to follow around various beds, borders or shrubberies. Of course one has to be careful in this type of planning to make sure that the irregular outline of the lawn does not make it too difficult to cut. Another example of a natural blending or smoothing out of outlines is in the case of a terrace where the paving slabs are let into the lawn in a reasonably irregular formation, so that there are no hard lines where one feature begins and another ends.

Another great planning aid is the use of color. One can have a garden which is a blaze of color using brightly colored plants such as dahlias, roses, etc., but there is the converse idea of having tranquillity in the forms of subtler shades where a more restful approach is achieved. For example, borders can be planned to have restful grays and greens in them so that this color is emphasized and only a few areas here and there are allowed to have some brighter colors to create an interesting contrast. Many of the conifers, for example, can be used to provide quite an amazing range of greens from a deep green to the very palest. For sheer coolness there is nothing to match an area of garden which is predominantly green or silver or a combination of both. Previously mentioned were the various conifers and there are other delightful

*Dry stone walls are used to retain different levels in a sloping garden. In places, aubrietas trail down the walls, softening the effect.*

# Planning your garden

*Above : these two restful color schemes are based on gray and green foliage effects. On the left Bugle, Helichrysum, Stachys and Houseleeks form the basis of the planting scheme ; on the right Cineraria, Euphorbia and Senecio are planted for striking contrasts in color, form and texture.*

border plants such as the Hostas, Eryngium, Verbascum, Centaurea, *Echinops ritro, Cineraria maritima, Senecio laxifolius,* and finally *Santolina chamaecyparissus.*

If you are elderly or infirm your garden planning or rearrangement should be undertaken with a view to making maintenance as easy as possible. For example, raised beds are invaluable to reduce stooping, and the level of the soil in some borders can be brought to waist level or thereabouts. The use of labor saving ground cover plants has much to commend it as this will avoid the necessity of stooping to weed.

There are two other very important considerations to bear in mind when you are planning or renovating a garden. These are soil and aspect. The type of soil varies considerably from region to region and in fact soil can vary somewhat within a small area also. Depth of soil must be considered. A good depth means that a wider range of plants can be grown, whereas sparse coverage will present its own problems, and deep rooted plants could be difficult to establish. The variation in the actual soil type must be considered also. The heavy sticky clays require much more physical attention than the lighter soils, but the latter can prove difficult because they dry out quickly and may well need countless amounts of organic matter incorporated so that they retain every vestige of moisture, especially in hot dry summers.

Aspect or position in relation to the sun is also important. The area immediately to the north of an obstruction such as a building, high wall or fence is unlikely to receive much direct sunlight except perhaps in high summer and this means that even more careful selection of plants is necessary, with the emphasis on those which will grow well or at least reasonably well in shade. To the south of the garden there will be areas which could receive plenty of sunlight and a very dry area could be a problem, but there could be also places which receive shade during part of the day and this must be considered also. If the garden is high up and exposed to strong cold winds this must be considered too and planning must incorporate the use of windbreaks or at least some method of providing shelter from these cold winds in the form of fencing, walling, hedging or even trees and tall shrubs. Some gardens may be low-lying and all or part of the garden may be badly drained and damp. An improvement in soil conditions is vital here. Low-lying ground is also prone to frost damage or persistent frost because cold air tends to fall to the lowest point or level of ground. Obviously here would be a case for careful choice of plants so that tender plants are not positioned or grown in these circumstances.

## Putting pencil to paper

There is a lot to be said for putting pencil to paper when you reach the stage of the actual planning of the layout. Making a scale plan, no matter how simple, is a tremendous aid to organizing a garden since it helps one to visually appreciate proportions and roughly how the garden is going to look. Proportions are very important, and by planning to scale on paper one can adjust the plan by erasing lines with an eraser and amending areas here and there until eventually a satisfactory layout is achieved.

The type of scale will depend on the area of the ground to be planned, but an approximate scale of 1/8th in. to a foot is generally adequate. In other words if the length of the plot were some 64 feet, the length of the area on paper would be 8in. The nearest metric equivalent is a scale of 1:50, in which 1 cm is equivalent to 0.5m. You can make larger plans simply by using another proportional scale such as $\frac{1}{4}$ in to the foot (1cm = 0.25m). In this case the same garden just mentioned would be some twice the length on the paper, and this obviously gives much more room for detailed planning. The area or outlines or boundaries of the site should be drawn out to scale, and then it is a good idea to make scale drawings of features such as a terrace, a greenhouse, a lawn, vegetable plot, etc., which can be cut out and arranged on the outline plan. Draw on any existing features which are to be retained. In this way one can immediately visualize or appreciate the scale of things. For example it is a simple matter to trim, say, the lawn area until a satisfactory proportion has been achieved.

Using this jigsaw sort of idea one can cut out irregular areas such as a wavy edge to a flower border, or even cut out an irregularly shaped lawn, and immediately one can appreciate how the idea would look if actually carried out. The proportion of flower garden to utility garden can be ascertained in this way also. Once the various sizes, proportions and positions of the desired features have been determined they can then either be drawn in on the outline plan or glued into position and suitably captioned. As the work proceeds it is important to mark in important measurements so that these can be transferred to the actual site by measuring out with some tape and marking out the positions with canes or other suitable means. It may well be that even when the plan has been transferred to the plot by marker canes etc. one may wish to adjust on site by moving the canes here and there until finally the finished layout has been agreed upon. It is a good idea also to stand inside the house and view the layout from the living room windows, because a good or attractive view from the house is so important, and this rough and ready means of positioning of features can be most helpful. Naturally it goes without saying that someone with an artistic aptitude could sketch out three-dimensional drawings so that an even more accurate picture would be achieved.

## Planning for minimum upkeep

It is probably true to say that the majority of gardeners, especially new ones and young married couples, prefer to have a layout which is very simple and labor and time saving. One must appreciate the fact that if one is away from the home for most of the day it is difficult to maintain a garden of complex design satisfactorily. One might well say that 'the plainer the better' is a good motto to follow. The simple layout could also be one of the cheapest to construct.

What in fact is a simple minimum upkeep garden? What is meant by a minimum

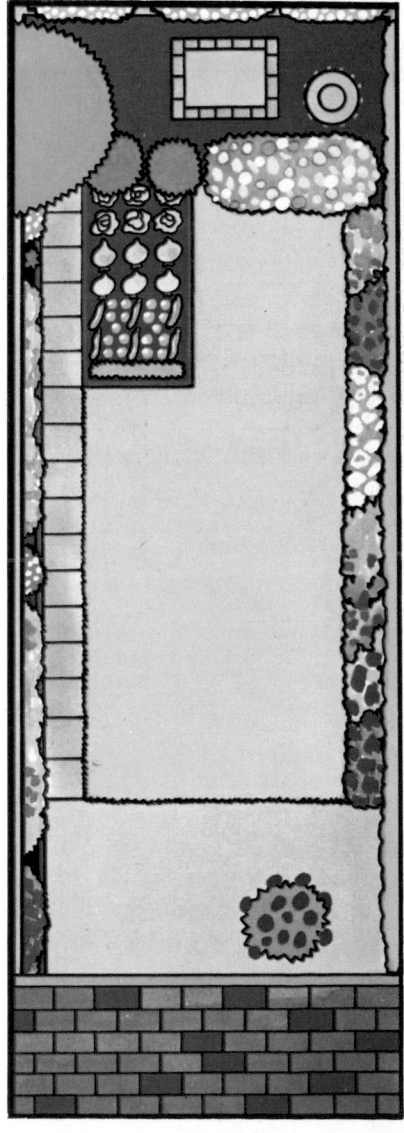

*Plan and elevation for a typical rectangular garden, incorporating a small utility area and a vegetable plot.*

upkeep design? Taking the back garden first, it could be an area devoted chiefly to lawn with small or narrow flanking borders on either side for flowers, with perhaps one or two focal points of small trees or shrubs. To reduce the care and attention the borders could consist of ground cover plants which smother weeds or they could consist of shrubs which, once well established, will fulfil the same purpose. Possibly also just outside the house, especially if there are French windows to the property, a small paved area would be useful for sitting out purposes and to cover the ground and prevent weed growth. The front garden again could consist of a reasonable lawn area if there is room but if the site is quite small a tiny lawn would be irritating to cut and maintain and it could well be that most of the area could be attractively paved. To add color and interest containers could be used and planted up with attractive flowering plants, or areas could be left here and there in the paving where plants could be established such as rock plants which require minimum attention.

A minimum upkeep garden should not have hedging which requires a great deal of labor and time devoted to it to keep it neat and trim. Instead there is a good case for the use of wooden fencing which, if well preserved before erection, should last for many seasons. Fencing can be obtained in various heights from about 1m (3ft) up to about 2m (6ft). In many instances the tallest fence will not be necessary, and adequate privacy and especially shelter can be achieved if 1.25m (4ft) high fencing is erected.

It is true to say, however, that in order to produce a minimum upkeep garden a little more expense is involved because one is likely to be dealing with expensive materials such as paving and fencing, but any expense should be looked upon as an excellent investment over the years. There are several other interesting points to observe when planning a minimum upkeep garden. For example, the lawn itself should be considered, and if it is to be subjected to a lot of hard wear during the season (for example if the family has several children) then it would be more labor saving to use a hardwearing grass mixture than to have a quality lawn mix which would need regular care and attention to maintain it in good order. Modern seed mixes enable the gardener to have a lawn of good appearance which at the same time wears well.

Take the flower borders themselves. Here it would be sensible to select plants, say, in the herbaceous border which are virtually self-supporting or low-growing so that there is minimum need for staking and tying. More permanent flower planting makes sense also. Although annuals are very pretty plants they have to be raised from seed every year so probably it would be better, particularly where time is precious, to plant beds with more permanent subjects which virtually look after themselves each season. In other words, perennial plants, which grow up every year, would be better than the annuals which require yearly attention. Another advantage is the fact that herbaceous or hardy plants increase in size every year so that one is covering the ground more and more as the seasons pass by.

Probably the labor saving garden could do without its utility section such as the vegetable plot for there too is an area which would need regular attention to weeding, feeding, training, harvesting, resowing and replanting throughout the gardening year. Of course in these days of self sufficiency—and in order to reduce household expenditure—one might be tempted to have a small plot devoted to just a few vegetables which would not require too much time to keep in good order.

The temptation to install a greenhouse may have to be resisted also, for to get the best value from a greenhouse it should be filled with plants for most months of the year. This necessitates regular attention especially during the growing season when watering and feeding is required.

### Making a garden from scratch
This is a real challenge and a most exciting one too. The amount of work involved and the way in which it is tackled will depend very much on the size of the garden

and also on its condition. This is particularly pertinent as far as the new estate is concerned where unfortunately so much rubble and junk can be left behind by the builders.

Sometimes, however, some of the rubble can be useful. Collected systematically it can be used, for example, for the base of paths and drives or the foundations of the greenhouse or garden shed. It can even be used to raise areas of ground to make special features such as a rock garden where excellent drainage is required and provided by the rubble. In a wet and badly drained site rubble can be used for the construction of rubble drains or dry wells. A herringbone fashion layout of trenches is excavated to a depth of at least 38–46cm (15–18in), the parallel side drains running into a main central drain which is deeper than the others, and this main drain is taken to the lowest part of the garden where it terminates into a deep sump or drainage pit which is at least 1m (3ft) deep. This pit is filled nearly to its top with rubble. The bottom 15cm (6in) or so of the other drains should be lined with rubble and the soil returned. Care must be exercized to see that drainage water does not spill or empty from the sump into neighbors' property.

Another problem with a new site is the fact that some of the top soil may have been removed for some reason or other, or it may have been placed in parts of the garden only, while other areas are left with just a shallow top layer of good soil. Wherever possible the whole site should be covered with a reasonable depth of good soil, and a minimum depth of 30cm (12in) is essential.

Where the soil is of relatively poor quality or if it is impossible for some reason or other to import more soil to achieve greater depth then it is important to consider carefully the method of creating a lawn. In this situation it is more sensible to purchase turves than to attempt to sow grass seed. At least with the sods one has the plus factor of about 2.5–4cm (1–1½in) of soil already there and in this way it is possible to establish quite a good lawn quickly on a relatively poor area of ground. As far as plants are concerned, on a poor site it may be necessary to dig out special planting areas for larger subjects such as trees or shrubs and fill in with better quality soil. Another idea is to build small retaining beds a foot or so higher than the surrounding ground and fill these up with better soil. Raised beds are a particularly good solution where drainage is poor.

It is quite likely of course that the site is not pleasantly flat and easy to deal with, so any variations in height such as steep banks should be carefully noted and a plan made to either retain these with colorful or textured walling or to make features such as rockeries or even waterfalls. In some cases of course it may be possible to do a lot of levelling so that an overall gentle slope is achieved or at least one or two levels can be achieved, these being linked by walling and attractive paving or stepping stones. Do try to plan so that there is minimum work involved in moving soil about the site. Remember too that the more level the site the easier it is to maintain.

## The small garden

Many new gardens in estates and development areas are unfortunately quite small these days. This is due to the fact that the cost of land is extremely high and builders or developers try to cram in as many units as possible per acre. Even so, with careful planning it is surprising what can be accommodated in a confined area, and it is quite a fascinating task to try and juggle your available space around to include as many features as possible. Obviously, correct proportion is of paramount importance in the smaller garden, and one must be particularly careful in the choice of trees and shrubs so that only those which are very slow-growing or which attain only a modest height and spread when they are fully mature are planted. Beds will have to be kept small in proportion to the amount of lawn which is created, and even features like terraces and pathways will have to be kept down to the minimum. One distinct advantage of a small garden is the fact that, with a simple layout, it can be a garden which requires the absolute minimum of upkeep.

*Opposite: two types of boundary screen for the minimum upkeep garden are interwoven wooden fencing and concrete grille blocks.*

*Below: the minimum upkeep garden should incorporate plenty of ground cover plants. The top picture shows Euonymus radicans variegatus, a useful trailer with variegated leaves, and below it is one of the pretty Epimediums, sub-shrubby plants which do well if planted under trees.*

In the small garden it is quite a good idea to consider the use of small containers in which attractive displays of flowering plants can be arranged. You can even re-produce large garden features on a miniature scale by making a sink garden or a tiny rock garden.

One of the other problems of the small garden is its lack of privacy as so many housing units are built virtually on top of each other. It is important therefore to give special consideration to the provision of some privacy, and if fencing or hedging seems too expensive then why not construct a small sitting out area which is sheltered and partly concealed by, say, an L-shaped screen wall feature? Carefully sited (probably close to the house itself) this idea will give a great deal of privacy from neighboring windows. Even one or two carefully situated trees or shrubs can afford some measure of privacy further down a garden and at the same time they will provide welcome shade in hot sunny weather. The siting of buildings in the smaller garden could present some problems as they are obviously going to occupy valuable growing space. Even so, high priority should be given to a garden shed in which garden tools and perhaps garden chairs can be stored in a safe dry place. Modern shed designs include interesting ranges of small sheds occupying only a few square feet, and one of these could fit into most small garden schemes. Even if the owner desires a greenhouse there are many small or mini-greenhouses available, some of which can be used as lean-to designs against a suitable warm wall of the house.

### Facelift for an old garden

Of course you are in a different situation if you are tackling an old or neglected garden for the first time. Here your plan of campaign should be geared to assessing the site to begin with to see whether or not there are any or many plants which are worth keeping. Probably there are some shrubs and trees well established and these should be examined carefully to see whether they are healthy and worth retaining and also (if small enough) whether they could be moved to another site to suit your new planting scheme. If, however, you find that there are some old trees which you do not wish to retain, then these will have to be cut down and removed. Great care is needed if one is tackling the removal of a large tree, and in many cases it is well worth getting the services or at least an estimate from one of the tree specialists or arborists in your area. Felling a large tree can be a dangerous business as some of the branches can be extremely heavy and unwieldy. There is also the special care one must take to ensure that no damage to neighboring property or persons is incurred during the work. Usually the topmost part of a tree is sawn through first of all after many of the

*Below: derelict garden before and after renovation. The original layout has been retained, so the new garden loses none of its old-fashioned charm.*

side branches have been cut off. It is necessary in most cases to attach ropes to the part being cut off so that the limb can be guided to the ground by placing the rope over another strong branch and lowering it down like a hoist. The tree is gradually cut down length by length, and an electric or gasoline-driven chainsaw is probably the only tool which can tackle this thick hard growth. The biggest problem comes when the root system is removed and this can entail a considerable amount of hard long labor. It may be possible, however, to leave the stump in the ground and try to kill it by boring a large number of deep holes in it and filling these up with either saltpeter or sulfuric acid. Afterwards the holes are sealed with putty and the stump allowed to rot through the action of these chemicals. Great care is necessary when using these preparations as they are very caustic. It takes several months (approximately six to eight) before most of the wood is rotted away and then it should be a reasonably easy matter to chop the trunk out. If the root system has to be dug out then a deep wide trench has to be excavated several feet away from the main trunk and the roots cut away as they are discovered.

With smaller trees and shrubs there is less of a problem, and those which are very badly overgrown, weak or diseased are best rooted out and burnt. Where specimens are good enough to retain but require moving to a more suitable position this work is best done when the plants are dormant which is in the late autumn and winter. The root system should be dug out with as large a ball of soil attached as

*Above : the lines of an old lean-to greenhouse are softened by imaginative planting. At the front of the bed Ajuga reptans multicolor encroaches on the path.*

*Left : an established herbaceous border like this one gives an air of permanence to the garden. Neglected beds and borders can be replanted if necessary in an old garden.*

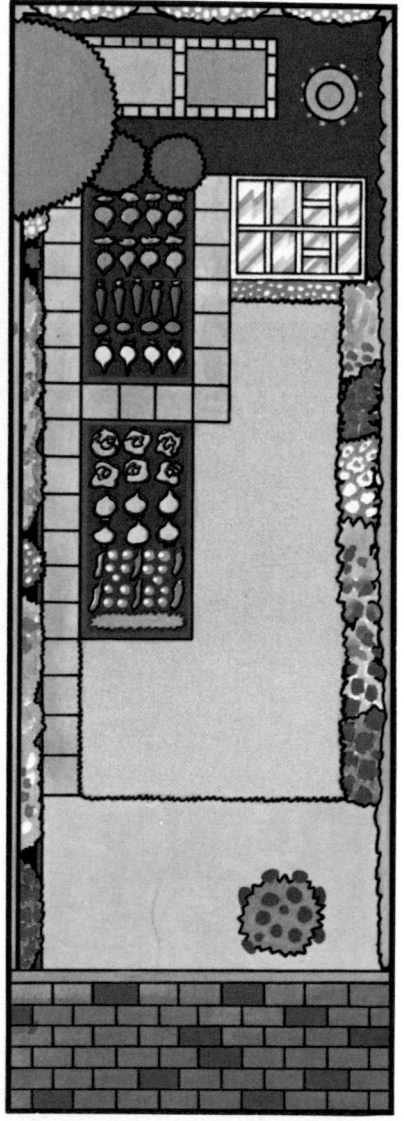

*A large older garden can be replanned to include valuable space for growing fruit and vegetables for the kitchen.*

possible and without too much damage to the roots. The new site must be prepared beforehand by excavating a hole larger than the spread of the roots and making sure that plenty of moist peat is worked in and that drainage is good. When moving the specimen it is wise to contain the soil and roots in a large canvas sheet or tarpaulin. This prevents roots drying out badly and also retains as much of the soil around the roots as possible. Once the tree is in position, the roots should be spread out and the soil returned carefully around the roots and firmed with the feet. It may be necessary to provide a temporary stake and tie so that the plant can re-establish itself without too much wind disturbance of the root system through the swaying of the tree itself. It is also important to keep an eye on watering. Under no circumstances should the soil be allowed to dry out.

In an old garden there may be the problem of neglect, and there may be a lot of weeds and even grass to cut down before one can really appreciate the exact layout and scheme of things in the garden itself. Usually in an old garden the main problems could be that there are too many paths, or that beds and borders are filled with plants which either are not to your liking or which have outgrown their usefulness and require replacing with new healthy stock. Care should be taken when plants are being examined and removed to see that choice old varieties are not destroyed. Quite often in very old established gardens there are some varieties of plants which are no longer available from nurseries, and these should be treasured.

Replanting beds and borders with more modern varieties of plants, whether these be trees and shrubs or herbaceous or annual plants, will certainly give a facelift to the old garden. It could be that beds need replanning or resiting because they may be far too wide and occupy far too much room; it is also possible that the lawn may need rejuvenating either by careful feeding and maintenance or even by drastically digging up and remaking from seed or turf. The amount of facelift required will obviously depend on personal opinion. You may find that you can take to the old layout with just a few minor alterations here and there, but a bigger facelift could entail a great deal of work. However, you do have one big advantage, which is that unless the garden has been neglected for a long time the soil itself should be reasonably easy to recultivate. Another common problem with an old garden is the fact that many of the trees and shrubs are quite mature and may well be growing into each other badly. A lot can be done by thinning out and removing branches here and there, although in some cases it may be necessary to remove the odd tree or shrub altogether to give more space. The overgrown condition of trees and shrubs can also exclude a lot of valuable light and sunlight from the garden, and drastic thinning will do much to improve the growing conditions within the garden by allowing this valuable light to enter.

Weeds will probably be another difficulty, as they quickly take hold, particularly if the house has been vacant for some time, so a priority task must be the cleaning up of the beds and borders. A lot depends on the state of neglect and the time of year you move in. For example, if there is an overgrown perennial border it will be wise to wait until the autumn when most plants have died down. Then carefully lift the plants and heel them in conveniently near by, digging over the whole site and removing as many of the weeds and weed roots as possible as work proceeds. This drastic clearing out pays dividends as one can then replant the perennial plants in clean soil, incorporating fertilizer or garden compost as necessary. At the same time many of the plants themselves may need dividing up as they are too large, and this will give you the opportunity to replan and remake one of the important main features of your garden.

In an old garden the pathways may not be in very good condition. These may be renovated by relaying using the same materials, but it may well be that completely new paths and foundations will have to be created. This will give the owner the opportunity to redesign the route of paths, perhaps altering their width too if necessary, and also to brighten them up by the introduction of patterning with various sizes of slabs, or by using colored stone.

Quite often the old garden presents a problem as far as the boundaries are concerned, where probably a hedge has got out of hand and needs cutting back to shape or even replacing where it has died down or gaps have occurred. It may be also that old fencing needs attention, especially the supporting posts which may have loosened or even rotted.

A lot depends too on the time of the season you take over an old garden. If you are fortunate enough to take over during the summer months you will be in a position to appreciate the amount of color (or the lack of it) and, if notes are made, then you will be in a position to improve the general appearance by replanting. Of course an autumn takeover is, likewise, convenient because most plants will have died down and can be removed or replaced—but of course one cannot appreciate the existing features of the garden as there will be no floral or leaf displays. One possible advantage in the taking over of an old garden is the fact that the borders may have sweeping or graceful curves as opposed to the popular straight lines and edges of more modern gardens. A lot depends also on the size of the garden and it is often a good idea to plan the facelift in easy stages, dealing with sections each year until the whole garden has been changed to your particular satisfaction. One has the advantage of course that most plants, especially the trees and shrubs, will be well established and there could be less of a problem providing privacy, shelter from winds and shade during hot weather. Many old gardens have an atmosphere or character of their own and you may well feel inclined to retain this friendly atmosphere and work within the broad lines of the original layout rather than try to change the whole site dramatically. One must also appreciate the important fact that an old garden will probably belong to an old house, and the house itself will probably have its own character which should relate to the landscape of the garden. New planning must take this into consideration.

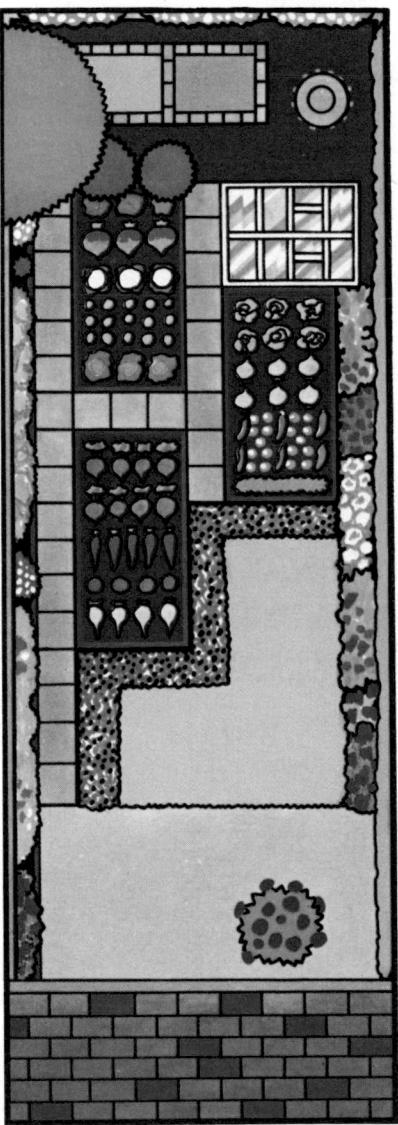

The size of older gardens is a definite advantage if you wish to grow your own fruit and vegetables, and the two plans and elevations shown here illustrate how a food production area can be incorporated into a typical long, narrow garden. On the left a sizeable area of the garden is lawned, but the garden on the right takes self-sufficiency a stage further, incorporating three vegetable plots which allows a three-year rotation of crops to be practised. The vegetable garden is screened from the sitting-out area by a hedge, and in both gardens the utility area behind the greenhouse has been screened off.

### The city dweller's garden

A city garden has its own peculiar problems. These are chiefly the lack of light, lack of privacy, the vortex and cold draughts caused if the garden is surrounded by tall buildings, poor quality soil, and very restrictive space generally. There could be slight problems with smoggy atmosphere and, in addition, there is the hidden problem of damage by cats and birds, especially the pigeon. Another problem is the transportation of materials from the front of the house to the garden if it is situated at the rear, and quite often materials like soil, plants, even paving may have to be taken through the house itself.

Like the problems of the small, new garden, however, all these restrictions are an exciting challenge to the new owner. The first thing to do is to decide on what you want to have, or at least hope to have, in the garden. It is of paramount importance to plan as simple a layout as possible because in most cases one cannot be too ambitious. It may take a little time, for example, before one can see how certain plants progress in a given environment, and there may be failure now and again until the right type or variety is used. Quite often the city garden is surrounded by walls, many of which can be quite high, and these can be put to good use. If they are sited in a reasonably sunny situation they can be covered or clothed with attractive climbing or trailing plants such as roses, Wisteria, Clematis, etc. Failing this, and if permission is obtainable, strong hooks or supports can be attached to the walls from which attractive

*This plan includes even more space for fruit and vegetables; and the whole area is screened off by a neatly clipped hedge.*

*The curvature, different levels and planting scheme of this city garden are all designed to make the most of a site which does not receive a great deal of sun.*

hanging baskets or plant containers can be hung filled with some gay plants. Many of these can be fragrant so that, sited near the windows or French windows of the town house, their perfume will delight the occupants especially during the evenings.

The walls of a city garden can be covered attractively with wooden trellis suitably preserved to prevent rot, or some of the modern steel designs which are covered in plastic can be attached. If the ground is enriched with adequate amounts of composted vegetable waste, peat or—ideally—rotted manure, climbing shrubs can be planted directly in the soil. If, however, the ground is paved or concreted then plants could be grown in large containers filled with good soil. It is possible to buy large capacity plastic tubs, and old beer or water barrels are even more attractive.

Ideally one should not clutter up the city garden and, as recommended earlier on, the layout should be as open and as simple as possible. To achieve this effect it is wise to have the center of the garden either paved or with a grass area. It is usually better and easier to establish a lawn in a city garden from turf rather than seed because turf is already established and seed can be eaten or badly disturbed by birds and cats etc. There is also the point that turf will establish itself quite well even if the original soil is very impoverished whereas more painstaking soil preparation is required for seeding and quite a lot of enrichment would be necessary before a lawn from seed would be successful. If the situation is really difficult, however, it is better to concentrate on paving the main area of the city garden. There are many attractive materials for this purpose, but usually plain flagstone is ideal as it provides a restful, stately appearance. If a gayer atmosphere is required, paving of different sizes and textures would produce pleasing patterns, and of course there is the possibility of colored paving to add atmosphere to the finished layout. In any case a small area should be devoted to paving so that there is an area for sitting out on and for eating meals outdoors.

Color is welcome in a city garden, and this can be provided by use of attractive urns or containers which can be filled with easy-to-grow annual flowers, both hardy and half hardy types. If the containers are large enough there is no reason why a few more permanent subjects such as herbaceous plants, or even dwarf shrubs such as azaleas, etc., cannot be accommodated. To overcome the problem of impoverished soil the construction of raised beds is recommended, provided that there are reasonable facilities for bringing in imported soil to the back garden. This will provide greater depth of soil and makes a very attractive feature, especially if the walling used is of a colored, textured design. In the longer type of town garden divisions can be made using screen walling blocks to provide interesting pockets in the garden, or to provide useful shade and privacy for a sitting out area. If you have the problem of a solidly paved area with only small areas of very poor quality soil, it is a good plan to provide an interesting focal point or feature such as a pool with fountain. This is easily constructed with raised walling in which a preformed basin, or even tough plastic sheeting, can be introduced to hold the water. A few plants can be inserted around the edge of the pool feature, and of course the pool itself will contain many attractive and colorful water plants including the various water lilies. A fountain will add the finishing touch and will provide a perfect focal point as well as having a cooling influence on the surrounding area. Goldfish can also be introduced to add movement, color and interest. The construction of such a small formal pool is quite simple, and the initial expense will be repaid many times over, for no other feature can contribute so much to the charm and personality of your garden.

A pleasantly designed city garden deserves to be used as much as possible and there is no reason why its enjoyment cannot be extended to the evenings, and even late evenings, if some lighting is introduced. There are several designs of lighting kits which are specially formulated for outdoor use, and these are easily affixed to walls or can be placed in the ground by their special ground spikes. If need be—to enhance a social evening or a party for example—colored lights can also be introduced.

The sink garden should not be forgotten as this can form a very attractive feature in a city garden, and many different types of alpine plants can be established quite easily. It is a feature which would be most in keeping with a paved area and with a garden which is surrounded by walling. Do not forget also that a great deal of use can be made of window boxes which can be situated in the house windows and even along the edges of pathways and on the terrace itself.

Another attractive feature could be an archway or covered walk constructed from either pergola poles or from thick square timber, especially cedar wood. The covered archway or walk can be clothed with attractive climbing and trailing plants such as roses, honeysuckle, Wisteria, etc., and this would give character and depth to the city garden itself.

*The city garden should be a restful retreat, and this corner with its pool and pleasant greenery provides just the right atmosphere for sitting outside on hot days and long summer evenings.*

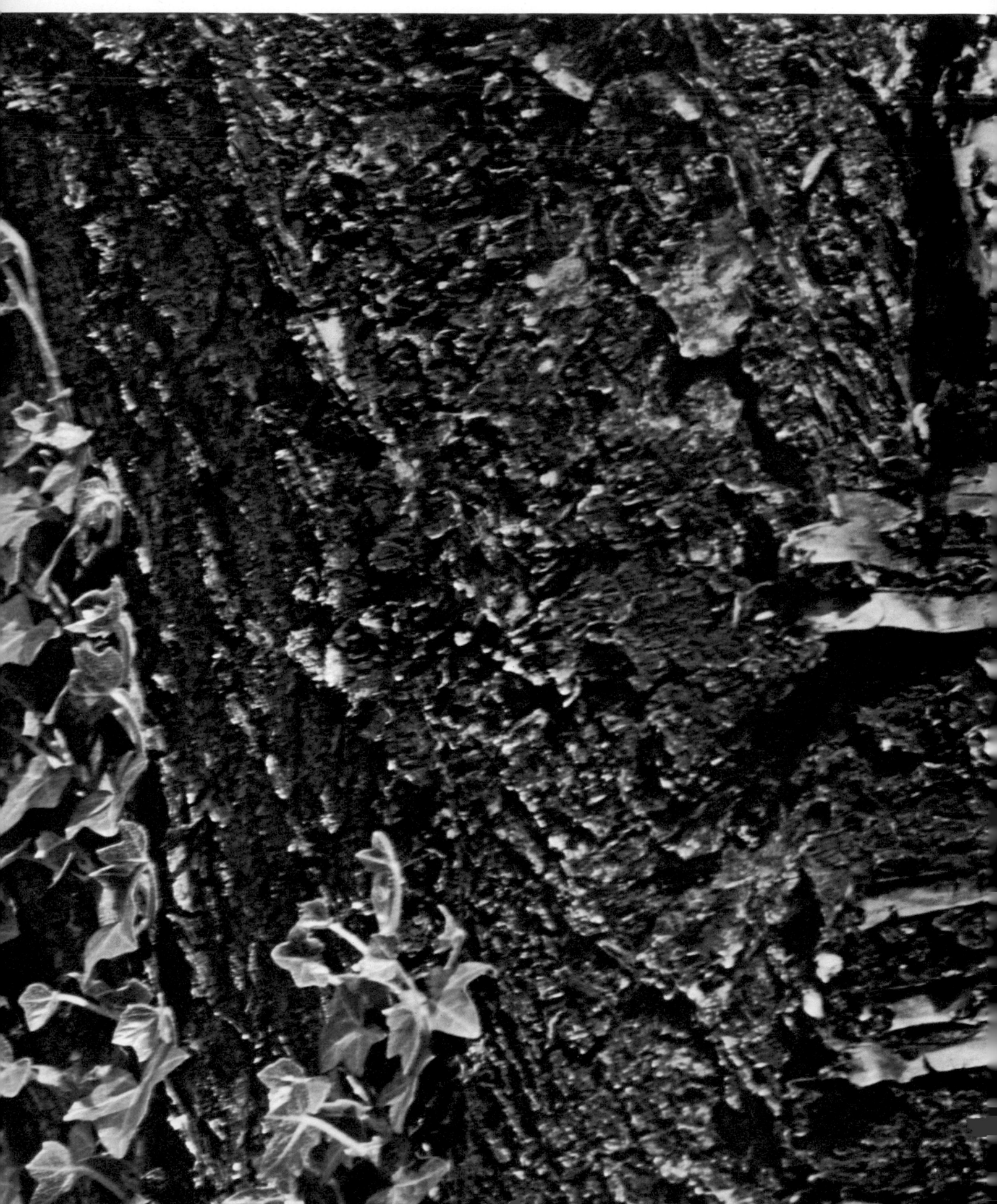

# LAWNS

Without any doubt the lawn is the most important feature in a garden. It forms the background to all the other features and makes a perfect foil for the colorful plants which are arranged in beds around it. An expanse of green is also a very restful feature, and the lawn provides a sitting out area where the householder can relax and enjoy his or her garden. It may be the first feature the new gardener tackles, and in fact it is a good idea to treat the construction of the lawn as the highest priority when a new garden is being created.

The following can be only a general guide to the whole subject of lawn-making, but the important thing to remember is that painstaking care in the initial planning and preparation will be well rewarded. Careful leveling of the site will ensure that there are no bumps or hollows to impede the regular task of grass-cutting, and if you can incorporate changing levels and curved edges in your design this will add immeasurably to the interest of your garden in the years to come.

**Seed or turf?**  This always poses a problem for the new gardener. Basically there is a simple answer. If you want a lawn quickly so that it can be used within a few days then turf is the answer. If, however, you want a high quality lawn with a much finer and more eye-catching appearance then seed is the answer, but seed takes longer than turf to establish. Having said this, though, there has been constant development in the breeding of grass seed and now we have the situation where some blends or mixtures will germinate very rapidly and produce a good coverage of grass within a few weeks of sowing.

Good quality turf is now available from many garden centers and nurseries and it

*A high quality lawn can be produced from seed. Here the split level adds interest to a formal garden layout.*

is surprising how, with attention to feeding and watering, the turf can be brought to top condition. In fact, many of the finest lawns are established from purchased turf in a very short time. It completely avoids the danger of seeds washing away or being eaten by birds. Likewise, there is little danger of the weeds getting ahead of the grass.

A good supplier of turf will cut the sods or pieces of turf accurately, and usually there is about 2.5cm (1in) of soil attached to the root systems. This can be an advantage where the soil on site is of poor quality or of shallow depth, since at least one is purchasing some extra soil when one purchases turf. Another advantage of purchasing turf is that the grass is usually growing in approximately the same conditions and type of soil that you have in your own garden, and establishment is quite rapid.

Large quantities of turf are usually delivered rolled, and it is a material which is quite heavy to handle, especially if it is wet. However, it is now being grown by specialists and is sure to be weed-free and composed of the finest types of grasses.

Grass seed is quite a different proposition because one has a personal control over the quality and final appearance of the grass itself. One will find various mixtures available in local garden shops or garden centers for special purposes and conditions. Grass seed mixtures contain a blend of different types of grass, and an appreciation of the different mixes of grass seed is helpful.

For the best quality ornamental lawn the Bents or Agrostis seeds and the Fescue or Festuca are good. They are dwarf growing and produce fine leaves when established. There are in fact only four species of the Bent or Agrostis, but these have many types or strains produced through many years of constant research and breeding. The commonest of the species is the Browntop or *Agrostis tenuis*. This particular grass seed is incorporated in mixtures which produce the best quality lawns. In the Fescues these are several species which are used but the most popular is the Red Fescue or *Festuca rubra*.

In most grass seed mixtures which are sold to the gardener there are several different types of grasses incorporated to produce an ideal blend. Many of the mixtures have special names, but usually the finest quality grass is known as 'park' mixture and is likely to have the following specifications: Kentucky bluegrass, one or more varieties, 60%; a fine-leaved fescue such as Chewings, and perhaps a little fine-leaved ryegrass.

*Below left : the site for a new lawn is often weedy and may be full of builder's debris. The debris must be removed before the work of clearing the site can start. Below: perennial weeds must be removed during the initial digging over of the site.*

# Permanent planting

Then there are the standard types of mixtures which give a good covering quite quickly and will withstand hard wear—for example where children are playing. The specifications vary but might include the following ingredients: 36% Alta Fescue, 20% fine-leaved perennial ryegrass, 20% Creeping Red Fescue, 12% Kentucky bluegrass, 6% rough stalked Meadow grass and 6% Highland Bent. South of the Mason-Dixon line these mixtures become less and less common as one goes south. There the emphasis is on the Bermuda grasses, Zoysias, Centipede, Carpet, St. Augustine and Bahia grasses. Many of these are planted with stolons. In the arid Plains a great deal of interest is now developing in the native grasses such as Buffalo, the Blue Stems, etc.

One of the fascinations of the lawn grass mixtures is that it is possible to have a blend of seed to suit almost all sorts of situations. In fact, it should be possible to contact some of the local seed companies and arrange for them to supply a special blend for a particularly difficult situation. As an example of how versatile grass seed mixtures are, one may want a blend of grasses which will produce a good hard-wearing lawn in a shaded situation such as an area beneath some trees. Here, provided the soil can be kept reasonably well watered, a mixture of grass seed can be produced to ensure a good coverage of grass in a rather unfavorable situation. A specification for this purpose could include the following blends: 20% Kentucky bluegrass, 30% Creeping Red Fescue, 35% rough stalked Meadow grass and 15% wood meadow grass or a fine-leaved perennial ryegrass.

## Making a lawn from turf

First of all one needs to be able to calculate the number of turves which will be repuired for the site. This is quite easy to do if one takes into consideration the length of the turf and its width. For example, take a site 10m (30ft) wide and 3m (10ft) in length. If the turves were placed across the width 10 turves would be required to go across the 10m (30ft) (10 × 1m (3ft) lengths). Along the length of the lawn there would be 10 rows each 30cm (12in) wide, i.e. the width of the turf. Therefore one would require 10 × 10 which is 100 turves for an area 10m × 3m (30ft × 10ft). The same principle can be used for calculating the quantity of turves required whatever the dimensions of the turves and the area to be covered.

The turf will be delivered to a convenient site in front of your house, either on the tree strip, on the driveway or on the lawn itself. In any case one must get the turves in as quickly as possible to prevent a hazard to man or turf, and it is wise to be organized with a helper or two to take delivery and start laying the lawn immediately. Turves are very heavy and a large number of turves on a truck represent quite a heavy load; therefore you will find that drivers will be very reluctant to drive their heavy truck over paving or sidewalks in case they crack them. Therefore you must expect your turf to be dropped outside your house and you will have to wheel it into the back garden. This must be taken into consideration when you are making a choice between seed or turf. If you are requiring a large number of turves the work of taking the delivered turves in can be quite considerable.

The turves should never be allowed to stand for more than about a day, otherwise they quickly start to become yellow and if left too long, can be spoiled completely. On the site, turves should be placed in small areas along the line of the work so that one does not have to trample up and down the area too much. Work starts by laying whole turves across the site, butting them or placing them close together and firming them with the back of the spade as work proceeds. Make sure that each turf is in close contact with the ground and wherever necessary some soil will have to be added or taken away to ensure a level finish. Turves should be bonded like bricks in a wall; in other words, no vertical joint in one row should fall opposite a joint in the preceding row. To achieve this it may be necessary to cut the first turf in the next row in half so that this bonding is achieved. As work proceeds the turves should be placed close to each other so that no gaps occur, and after a few rows have been

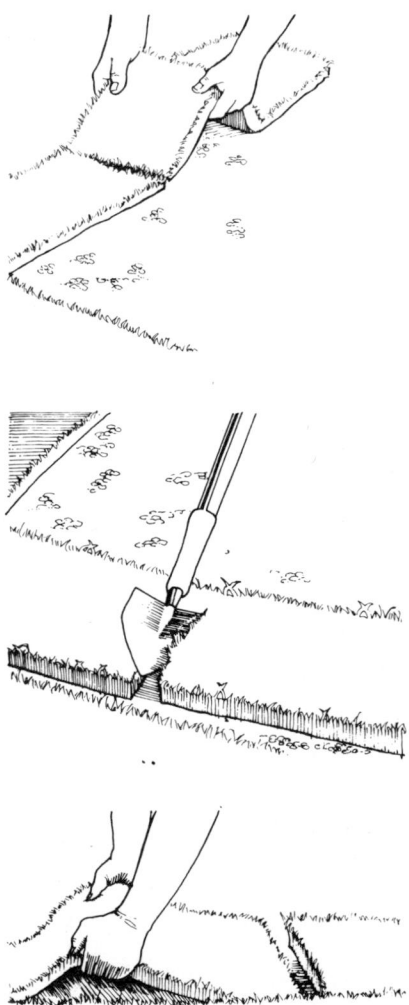

*Below: laying a lawn from turf. The first row of turves is usually laid along one edge of the site, and the next row is staggered so that no vertical joint falls opposite the joint in the preceding row. An edger is used to cut the turves when necessary.*

laid the joints between should be filled in with a little fine sifted soil. This helps to make the sections knit or bond together more quickly and, should dry weather prevail, it prevents the turves drying out and the joints opening up. Work from a plank of wood if possible, placing the plank on the turf already laid and working forward into the site all the time. Never use odd bits and pieces of turf at the edges because these will break away and it will be very difficult to get them to root and become established. In any case, in the early stages it would be dangerous to have such loose pieces of turf at the edges. If a large area of turf has to be laid this will obviously be done in easy stages, but do keep an eye on the weather conditions and make sure that the turf already laid is watered suitably with a sprinkler in dry weather. Once the site has been completed the turves can be given a light—and it must be only a light—rolling to bond them down. On heavy soils this should be omitted.

After about two weeks the grass should have begun to root into the site, and the first mowing can be given with the blades on the mower set high; in other words only the top of the grass should be cut off or 'tipped'. This advice applies to spring and early summer laid turf; autumn turf should not be cut unless of course a mild autumn is experienced and the grass is exceptionally vigorous.

Where the lawn is to have a curved or waving edge the outline can be finally cut out after the turf has been laid using an edger or a garden spade. To avoid wastage, a mark on the site using sand or a trickle of bonemeal, or even a very fine trickle of lime, can be placed down to mark the outline of the edge. As turves are laid at the edge, sufficient turf should overlap the marks to allow the area to be cut out easily and neatly with the cutter. It is not necessary to allow, say, half a turf to overlap the edge. Only a few inches may be necessary in many cases.

## Sowing grass seed

This operation should be carried out when there is very little or no wind, otherwise it will be rather difficult to scatter the seeds evenly over the site. The amount of seed required can be calculated quite easily if one takes the average sowing rate at about 45g of seed per sq. m (1½oz per sq. yd); this works out at approximately 450g (1lb) of seed for every 8.5 sq. m (10 sq. yd) of ground to be sown. To calculate the complete area one multiplies the length of the site by the width of the site in meters or yards, and the total will give the area in square meters or square yards.

Many gardeners are worried about the possibility of birds eating the seeds, but some of the modern grass seed mixtures are pre-treated with a bird repellent preparation, and this is obviously the best type to use if available. It is important to sow the seed as evenly as possible so that an even coverage of grass results. There are several ways in which this can be done. The very experienced gardener can actually go down the site broadcasting the seed just as the old farmers used to sow their wheat. The best method, however, is either to use a spreader which is pushed along the site distributing the grass seed at the correct rate, or to mark out the site in meter or yard width strips with a garden line; the strips are then subdivided into square meters (square yards) with wooden sticks and seed is sown square by square, moving the sticks forward to mark out the next area. After a strip has been sown the line is moved over to form the next strip and the sticks are used once again to subdivide the strip.

When each square meter (square yard) or so has been sown in this fashion it is a good plan to cover the seed by raking the surface lightly with the garden rake. This must be done very lightly, only allowing the teeth to bite into the surface some 1–2cm (½–¾in) deep. Good coverage is achieved if the rake is used first one way and then at right angles to the first raking. Another system, where plenty of soil can be spared, is to make up a mound of finely sifted loam which can be used to scatter over the sown area thus covering the seed to the required depth. The site, when completed, should not be rolled, but it is advisable to put one or two criss-cross lines of black thread over the area or to use a suitable bird scarer to prevent the attentions of birds,

*Below: the site for making a lawn from seed is dug and leveled. Light soils should be trodden to firm. After a light raking the area is marked off into squares for even seed distribution.*

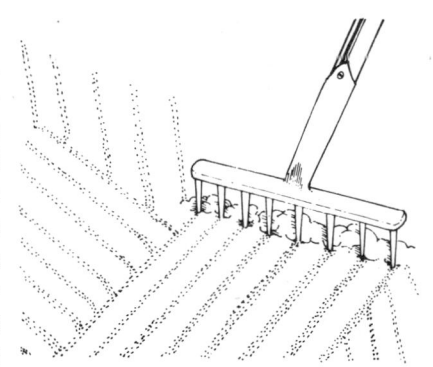

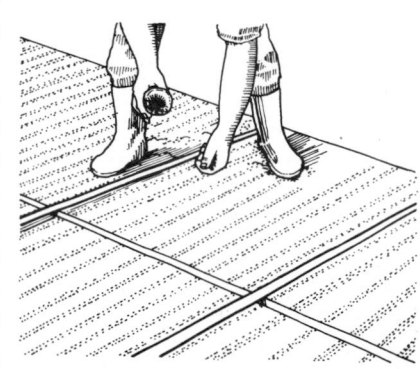

even if the seed has been pre-treated. Many birds like the soft prepared surface of a lawn site and in warm weather tend to have dust baths, thus disturbing the seed badly. This can cause bad patches.

A lot will depend on weather and soil conditions as to when the newly sown area will be ready for its first cut, but generally this will be about seven weeks after sowing and, as with turf, the grass must only be topped and not mown close. Usually when the grass is about 7.5cm (3in) high is the ideal time to carry out this first light cutting. Gradually, as the grass becomes established, the mower blades can be set lower to give a progressively closer cut. Careful attention must be paid to watering, and in dry weather the sprinklers must be used to ensure good and quick germination. On a new site quite a few weed seedlings will grow, and these should be carefully pulled out before they can become established. Later on, once the grass becomes established, many of the weed seedlings (especially the annual ones) will be smothered.

### Looking after the established lawn

In the earlier days it may well be necessary to do something about the odd patches here and there where, for some reason or another, part of the turf has not taken and has died, or where there are patches of ungerminated grass after seed sowing. In either case the area should be lightly forked over and new seed scattered and covered. It will not be long before the bald or patchy area is covered over with some nice new grass.

**Mowing** Many gardeners are uncertain about how frequently a lawn should be mown. No hard or fast rules can be given, as much will depend on the type of grass grown and the type of soil, on weather conditions and, finally, on the amount of feeding it receives. Generally speaking, the average lawn is cut once a week but at some times of the year a twice a week cut may have to be given. Regular mowing will encourage a thicker growth or sward of grass. Grass can be mown fairly close if the weather is nice and moist, but if dry weather prevails the grass should be mown with the cutting blades set a little higher. In the early days of mowing it is important to go over the site with a brush or fine rake to remove any stones which may be lying beneath the surface of the grass; these stones, of course, would damage the blades of the mower. The start of the mowing season will again depend on weather conditions, but usually lawns are ready for a first cut in March or April and cutting can go on well into the autumn, as late as October in many cases. In exceptionally mild areas or winters lawns can even be mown during December, but there only light topping is given.

*Below: a small lawn sown from seed can be lightly clipped over with shears when it is ready for its first cut. Below right: however carefully the site has been prepared, perennial weeds such as the dandelion, daisy and yarrow are likely to make their appearance along with the new grass. Treatment consists of pulling out individual weeds, or using an appropriate selective weedkiller.*

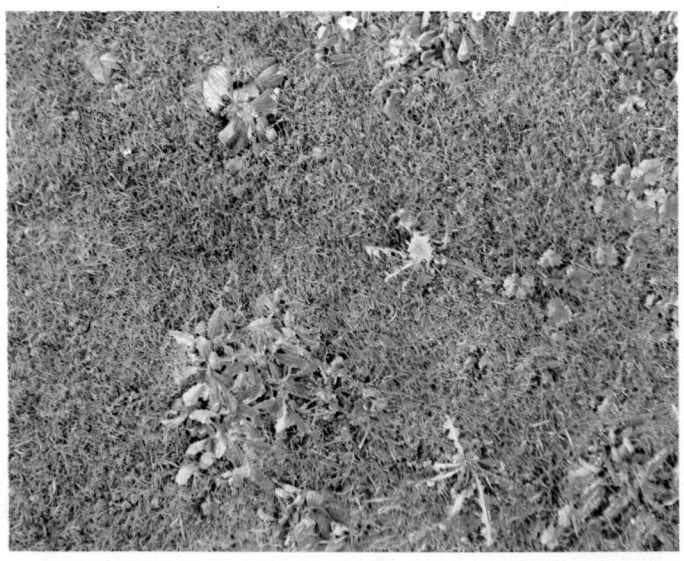

The type of mower to use is a matter of personal preference, but it is as well to bear in mind the following facts. For the best quality cut or finish there is no doubt that the reel mower is the one to use. The rotary type of cutter gives the gardener the best of both worlds, as it were, because this mower will cut long or short grass equally well. It will not give as fine a finish as the reel mower but nevertheless it gives a very satisfactory one for most general purposes. The rotary will also cut off the tough stalks of grass which are often missed by the reel mower.

**Edging**   A lawn is only as neat as its edges, so edging or trimming the edges of the lawn is a most important operation. This is done either with a half moon lawn edger, or a long handled shear-type edger can be employed. For larger areas of lawn it may be as well to consider the use of mechanical aids such as a gasoline operated edge trimmer.

**Watering**   Another vital operation is keeping the lawn watered, and where there are no hose restrictions a sprinkler is the ideal equipment to use for this purpose during very dry weather. On larger lawns the oscillating types are ideal, as they have a very large throw or spread of water, and they can be adjusted to water certain areas, allowing you to work close by on flower borders without getting wet.

**Raking and spiking**   The lawn likes a good scratching! This means going over the area with a lawn rake, which is sometimes known as a broom rake. The system is to rake out as much of the dead growth, or 'thatch' as it is called, from beneath the surface, and also to rake out any moss which is growing there. There are two periods in the year when this treatment should be given; the first is in the spring and the

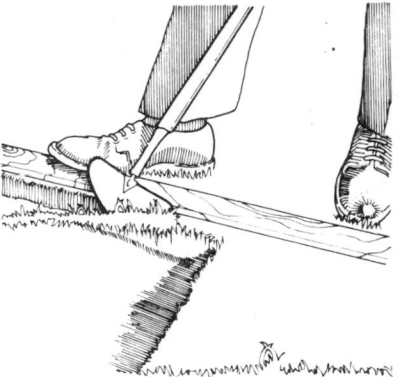

*Above : two methods of edging a lawn. The lawn edger should be used to make a sharp, straight edge when you are making the edges of an established lawn neat and level, or edging a new lawn for the first time. Long-handled edging shears can be used for routine maintenance of the lawn edges.*

*Left : a lawn rake is a most useful tool for clearing moss and dead growth from the lawn in spring and the fall.*

# Permanent planting

*Below: a topdressing is applied, distributed with a rake or 'lute', and surplus brushed off.*

second is in the early autumn, around late September.

The lawn also needs to breathe easily and aeration is necessary. This operation, also known as 'spiking', is carried out in the early autumn, and means that the lawn surface is pierced with numerous holes. The depth of these will depend on the equipment used. Mechanical lawn aerators are available which are pushed or wheeled over the area, and the teeth or tines bite into the lawn creating these drainage or aeration holes. There are also special lawn aerators which have hollow tines, which are pushed more deeply into the surface to a depth of about 10cm (4in) and a plug or core of soil is taken out. Afterwards the area can be given a dressing of sharp sand and peat which, if worked in with a stiff brush or the back of the rake, will enter these holes and keep them open for good drainage. Where the lawn is used a great deal and the soil is heavy it is often helpful to give a light spiking in the late spring and during the summer. The latter operation is very useful in dry weather because this means that when artificial watering is given the moisture gets down to the roots very quickly.

**Feeding** The lawn also appreciates feeding, and a top dressing of a soil and peat mixture is very useful. This can be applied to a depth of about $\frac{1}{2}$cm ($\frac{1}{4}$in) and then rubbed or worked in well with a stiff brush or the back of the rake. It can be applied in the autumn, and is made up as follows: 3 parts fine loam or soil, 1 part sharp sand and 1–1$\frac{1}{2}$ parts fine peat. Mix well together before application. As well as this sort of top-dressing the lawn needs fertilizers. There are two main types: a spring lawn dressing which is specially formulated to encourage rapid growth of the top or the grass itself, and an autumn dressing, where the feed is prepared specially to encourage root formation rather than leaf or top formation. The idea of this is to encourage the lawn to produce a good vigorous root action during the late autumn so that it is ready for the busy season ahead. If lush top growth were encouraged this would weaken the lawn and in severe winter weather the grass would suffer. There are many different brands available today, and one can make up one's own very useful mixture for revitalizing weak lawns. However, this takes some care and is not advisable unless you have a very large area to treat since so many excellent commercial preparations are available specially formulated for the purpose. Normally one or two applications are given during the spring, each one being applied at the rate of 90–120g per sq. m (3–4oz per sq. yd) or according to instructions.

In the autumn another important operation would be to remove the autumn fall of leaves. On a small lawn this can be easily undertaken with the use of a leaf or lawn rake, but on the larger scale it will pay the gardener to invest in one of those leaf removal or sweeping machines which consist of a large brush which revolves backward and throws the leaves into a suitable collecting bag at the rear of the machine. By mowing from the center, rotary mowers will also throw the leaves into shrub borders or wooded areas. For large areas leaf blowers are available, and vacuum machines are also made.

**Weeds and their control** There are several weeds which are commonly found in lawns, but fortunately, with modern chemicals and preparations, their control is fairly straightforward and most effective. One of the common lawn weeds is the dandelion. This has serrated thin leaves and yellow flower heads. The best control is to carefully treat the patches with a recommended weedicide. Several treatments may be necessary. Another weed is plantain; this is a perennial like the dandelion, which means it appears year after year unless it is dealt with. This particular weed has broad aspidistra-like leaves, though not quite as large. It is controlled by the same types of weedicide as the dandelion. Another weed is yarrow, again a perennial, with ferny foliage and a bunched white flower head. It can be controlled by mowing the lawn closely and feeding with sulfate of ammonia fertilizer at rates not exceeding 15g per sq. m ($\frac{1}{2}$oz per sq. yd).

The annual bluegrass is a weed which unfortunately seeds very freely. It is a form of rather fine grass, and the best way to control is to returf the small affected areas and to feed the lawn well so that the better quality grasses smother this interloper. Another common weed is the creeping buttercup, which has a long creeping stem which quickly invades large areas of the grass. It has bright yellow flowers and is very close-growing. It can be controlled with the dandelion spray. Daisies are a common weed although one must admit that they can look rather attractive especially in an old fashioned garden setting. The control is to apply the same medicine. Self heal is another perennial weed which has purplish flowers and oval pointed leaves. Control may possibly take several applications. Cinquefoil is another common weed, perennial again. This has pretty serrated leaves in five leaf formation per stem with bright yellow flowers, and is low-growing. Again, it is best controlled using a recommended weedicide.

The mouse ear chickweed can invade lawns, especially those on new ground. it is a plant with small leaves and white insignificant flowers. It is difficult to kill but can be controlled with special materials. There is also the common chickweed with broader, larger leaves and this again can be controlled by the same chemical. If the lawn is made up of acid soil it is more than likely that the weed Sheep sorrel will make its appearance. This has peculiar dart-shaped leaves, and control is by frequent applications of weedkiller or by liming very acid soils. Speedwell is another pest of a weed in lawns, with little bright blue flowers. It tends to creep around and can affect large areas of lawn if not controlled quickly. It is advisable to use the grass catcher on the mower because it will root from small sections cut off by a mower. Chemical control, however, can eliminate it if applied in early spring. It can be checked somewhat also by the use of lawn sand. Another common weed is pearlwort, which has masses of little yellow flowers and tends to spread in small groups. The control is the approved weedkiller and avoiding mowing the lawn closely. Another trouble which can affect lawns is that of moss. Proprietary moss killers can be used, or lawn sand, to get rid of this moss, though where the moss is burned out it will leave patches which will have to be resown. One can make up one's own mixture for lawn sand if the following ingredients are obtained: sulfate of ammonia 3 parts by weight, sulfate of iron 1 part by weight, fine silver sand 20 parts by weight. The ingredients are mixed well together and applied at about 120g per sq. m (4oz per sq. yd) during the dry weather in the spring and summer. It will burn out broad-leaved weeds and mosses and stimulate the finer grasses.

Another problem that can occur with a lawn is that you may discover patches of yellow and dying grass, and this is caused by fusarium patch, which is a disease. The application of an approved control according to the makers' instructions will prevent this trouble in future and sulfate of iron at 7.5g to 2.25 liters ($\frac{1}{4}$oz to half a gallon) of water watered on per square meter (square yard) will also do the trick. Another important safeguard against this disease is to keep the lawn well aerated.

**Pests of the lawn**   Fortunately the lawn is not troubled with too many pests. If you are making a new lawn on a new or badly neglected site it is quite likely that one of the troublesome pests could be wireworm. This pest attacks the roots of plants as well as grasses and can cause patches of dead grass to appear. The control is to use a state-approved treatment. If you suddenly see mounds of soil on the lawn and areas of lawn which suddenly sink in lines then it is a sure sign that the area has been infested with moles. These creatures tunnel just under the ground, bringing some of their very fine soil to the surface in mounds. They are not easy creatures to control, but there are proprietary traps or mole pellets which one can obtain from garden shops to try and effect control, or make the moles move on elsewhere. In the Northeast, Japanese beetle grubs eat the roots and kill the grass, while chinch bugs suck the juice from the blades. You should consult your local dealer for advice and approved materials with which to deal with these pests.

*Below: moles can cause havoc in country areas, throwing up molehills on lawns and causing subsidence with their tunneling.*

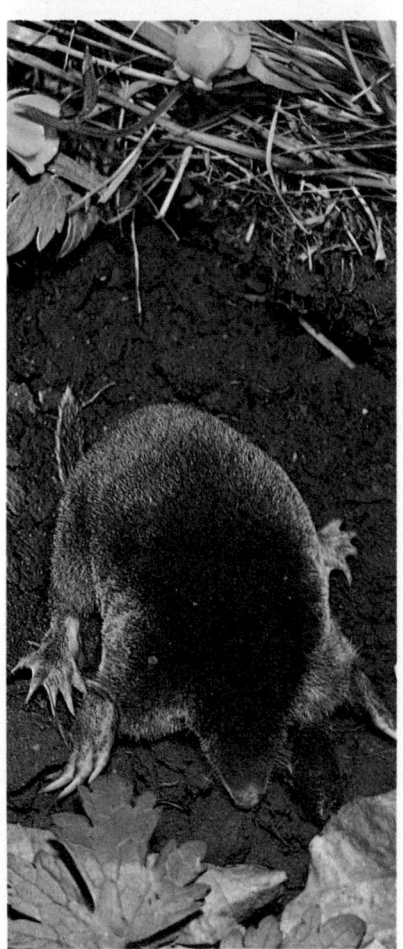

*A border of mixed shrubs selected for both flower and foliage color makes a decorative feature which will provide interest all year round.*

AUTUMN COLOUR
The following trees and shrubs are especially valuable for their autumn foliage, flowers or berries. See General Lists for fuller information.

Acer (Maple) T & S
Amelanchier T
Cotinus (Smoke Tree) S
Hamamelis (Witch Hazel) S
Malus (Crab Apple) T
*Ribes aureum* (Flowering Currant) S
Sorbus (Rowan) T
*Viburnum opulus* varieties S

T: Tree    S: Shrub    C: Climber

These are perhaps the most important plants in the garden. Important because they form the character of the layout and, selected wisely, they will provide interest in so many ways right through the gardening year. A garden laid out with low growing plants could be relatively uninteresting; just add a tree and shrub here and there and the whole character of the garden changes dramatically. The variation in heights and forms of these wonderful plants provides the gardener with a means of adding tremendous interest to his garden layout. Trees and shrubs are long term plants because they will grow for very many years and they are therefore excellent investments. There are, however, several practical points to consider when the selection is being made.

One of the most important decisions to make is whether the plants are to be evergreen or deciduous or both as far as the planting scheme goes. What are evergreen and deciduous plants? An evergreen, as its name implies, is a plant which has leaves all through the year including the autumn and winter, whereas deciduous plants shed all their foliage in the autumn, just leaving the bare skeleton as it were of the plant. Even so, the framework or skeleton in many cases can be a most attractive feature. Some plants, although they shed their foliage, will produce a welcome display of flowers during the drab winter months in the warmer climates.

Another very important consideration is the fact that one should look well ahead when a tree or shrub is being selected. Do not forget that eventually many of these subjects can attain great heights and spreads and it could be most embarrassing and in fact rather dangerous to have, for example, a tree in the garden which in many years time can be a considerable nuisance because it grows to a very great height with encroaching root systems too. The selection of trees and shrubs, particularly the former, must take this into consideration, especially when the garden is on the small scale. This consideration of ultimate height and spread must also be related to the planting distances and many mistakes are made where trees and/or shrubs are planted far too close together, and eventually some drastic thinning unfortunately has to take place. Nothing looks worse in fact than trees or shrubs grossly entangled in each other because they have been planted too close.

Trees and shrubs can be used for so many purposes. They can for example be used to act as a windbreak, or one or two specimens can be sited in a suitable part of the garden to provide shade when one is sitting out. Trees and shrubs can be used to blot out unsightly views from the house. Many shrubs are ideal for use against walls or fences to break up the hard outline, and of course a shrub border carefully planted can be one of the most labor and time saving features one can create in one's garden.

The selection of the plants must take into consideration other factors also. There is the type of soil and its depth. Some shrubs, for example, are not happy or will not grow at all in very limy or chalky conditions. The actual planning of a shrub border or garden will depend to a very great extent on the amount of room available. Where space is limited it might be a good idea to select only one or two specimens for their particular beauty of form, foliage or flower display. Where there is much more room, however, a wider range of subjects can be established and a long or reasonably continuous display of color can be achieved by carefully planting varieties which follow each other or follow the seasons in their flowering or display times.

There is a lot to be said for keeping one's eye open in one's travels. On journeys visiting friends, or when one is going on holiday, it is an excellent idea to look at various gardens to appreciate the use of various planting schemes. On one's very doorstep there are many beautiful parks, and here one can take more time to digest the way in which trees and shrubs are used to provide special effects or to overcome situations and planting problems. In many cases the specimens are clearly labelled and it is an excellent idea therefore to take notes of types and varieties. If you have a local park you can see the range of types which will grow in your locality, in your own soil conditions, and in your own weather conditions too.

There are of course peculiar or individual situations according to the locality of one's garden. It could be that the garden is exposed to strong winds, or the garden may be particularly sheltered or shady, and of course there is the peculiar or special problem of the seaside garden where trees and shrubs could be subjected to very strong winds, gale force at times, with the additional hazard of salt-laden air. This chapter has some useful tables listing trees and shrubs for various purposes, and special types and varieties are suggested to suit these various problem situations. Local or reasonably local garden centers can often supply a useful range of trees and shrubs which should do well in one's own area.

## Planting trees and shrubs

First of all it is important to prepare the site carefully in readiness for planting. The soil around the planting area or site should be well broken up by deep forking or digging, and during this operation plenty of well rotted manure or composted vegetable waste should be worked in. The many prepared or concentrated manures are useful too during this important initial site preparation. These special manures are ready bagged, easy to apply, and contain valuable amounts of plant food. They also provide valuable organic matter.

Bear in mind that good drainage is important for all trees and shrubs, and if the site is particularly heavy or poorly drained the condition must be improved by breaking up the subsoil and by opening up the soil particles by the addition of generous amounts of the organic matter, plus sharp sand or very well weathered ashes or cinders. This sort of material should be gritty, and this helps to improve drainage and aeration.

There is a lot to be said also for preparing individual positions or stations for the plants by taking out a hole wider than the spread of the roots and forking up the base

SHRUBS FOR THE ROCK GARDEN
There are many low-growing shrubs which will lend variety and interest to the rock garden. The following is just a selection: see General List for further details on each type.

*Acer dissectum* varieties S
Azalea (evergreen varieties) S
  (see Rhododendron)
Cistus (Rock Rose) S
Cytisus species (Brooms) S
Daphne varieties S
Erica (Heather) S
*Euonymus radicans* S
Hebe S
Lavandula (Lavender) S
Potentilla S
Santolina varieties S

*Erica vulgaris makes a low evergreen hedge and likes acid soil.*

# Permanent planting

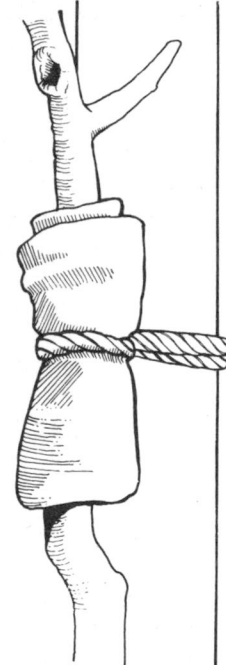

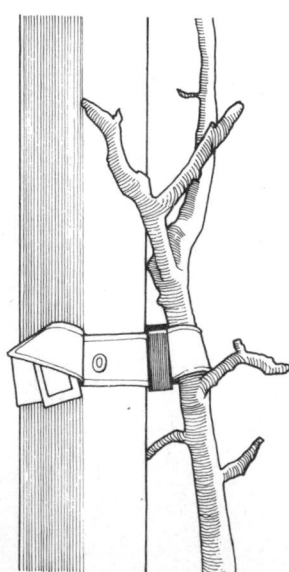

and also working in any of the food materials previously mentioned. On poor ground this is very important, but if time permits it is still a good idea to prepare most of the area overall by deep digging and by including the food materials. Tree and shrub planting is a long term investment; one has to appreciate the fact that eventually the roots will spread out of their planting area and will forage into the surrounding ground. If this is of a poor nature the tree or shrub can be retarded because the ground is relatively infertile. Therefore it is always a good idea to look ahead and prepare a wider band or area of soil as a good investment for future years' progress.

On a new site it is advisable to allow the cultivated area to settle a little before trees or shrubs are planted. This will also give weeds, especially the annual weeds, time to show themselves, and these can be killed off by hoeing before planting takes place. This is very important on new sites where quite often the ground is full of weed seeds.

The number of trees and/or shrubs which can be planted in any given area will depend on their ultimate size, which means their eventual spread as well as height. It is vital therefore that this information is ascertained and taken into account in any planting schemes. The distance between shrubs, for example, can be estimated approximately by allowing at least half the total of their eventual spread. Planting distance, and especially siting, is very important where trees are concerned. It is useful to have as an aid an up-to-date catalog from one of the leading tree and shrub nurseries because here quite often the probable height of a tree, say about 20 years after it has been planted, is indicated by the side of the tree and its variety. As an example of height let us take a look at the Acers or Maples. There are some varieties which are quite reasonable in height such as the Japanese *A. palmatum* which can grow to a height of about 6m (20ft). If however the variety *Schwedleri* is selected this can easily attain a height of 27m (90ft). Trees are often available in different types such as standard, half standard, feathered tree, young tree, short standard and bush tree.

The **standard tree** according to variety will have a single stem clear of branches about 1.5–2m (5–6ft) from ground level. Above this will be formed a head to give an overall height depending upon the species of the tree. This type of tree is very useful as it makes an excellent specimen or even a focal point in the garden, and it is a tree reasonably free of branches under which one can move around quite easily. This is very handy of course when one has to cut grass beneath such a tree.

The **half standard tree**, according to variety, may have a stem clear of branches about 1.25–1.5m (4–5ft) from ground level and its head or framework of branches above this will give the tree an overall approximate height of 1.75–2.5m (6–8ft). Here much lower head room is available but this could be a useful tree for providing low and close shade in a sitting-out area.

A **feathered tree** is a specimen which has a single stem but the side growths or branches are left on the stem from near ground level. Within this group of trees there are several types, such as the erect tree with branches pointing upwards, and there is the beautiful pendulous tree or weeping tree where the branches cascade down towards the ground. There are some **young trees** which should be grown in containers or pots to facilitate transplanting. Some trees such as the Eucalyptus do not move quite so easily as other trees and therefore this system is advisable. They are usually available only as small specimens but will of course, with good soil preparation and subsequent care, grow into magnificent specimen trees. The **short standard** is usually a shrub which has been grown specially with a single stem clear of branches to about 1m (3–4ft) from the ground, thus forming a small tree. An example of this type of plant is the Syringa.

The **bush tree** has a clear stem only some 0.5m (1–2ft) above ground level. There are not many specimens which come into this category, but the half standard tree and short standard and bush tree are particularly useful types for the smaller gardens.

Once the selection of trees and shrubs has been made and the plants have arrived their positions can be marked out simply by inserting a cane stick or piece of wood in the appropriate position in the borders. Quite often a little preplanning on paper such as is later suggested for the annual and herbaceous borders is a good idea so that good groupings and associations can be arrived at accurately. The type of root system each specimen has will depend upon where it was bought or ordered.

Some specimens may arrive as virtually bare stems, perhaps packed in moss or straw, and these can establish quite well, but there could be more failures owing to the fact that these roots can become damaged in transit or they can have dried out badly on arrival, or even before arrival. Those grown in containers can be planted within reason at practically any time of the season except when weather or soil conditions are bad, such as in times of frost or snow or extremely heavy rainfall. Plants grown with roots contained in burlap or plastic, or where the roots arrive bare, can often be planted in October or April if they are evergreen types. If deciduous, the best planting time is in late October or early spring. In many cases, especially with regard to the trees, a strong stake or support should be inserted in the planting hole before the tree is placed in position. The stake should be driven in firmly and just off-center of the hole. It is a good plan in fact to temporarily place the tree in position and work out the exact placing of the stake, so that the stake will support the stem or trunk firmly without causing damage. This is especially important in the smaller types of tree where branches could interfere with the placing of the stake.

Once the hole has been excavated wider than the ball of soil or spread of roots the area should be given a thorough watering, and this should be allowed to soak in

*Top, left to right: heeling in is a temporary measure when it is inconvenient to plant out newly arrived specimens in their permanent quarters. First dig out a narrow trench and place the young trees or shrubs at an angle against one side of it. Replace the earth and firm with the feet. Move them to their permanent positions as soon as possible.*

*Opposite: trees must be staked and tied firmly to their supports, either with a homemade tree tie (top) or with one of the commercial tree ties now available.*

*Below: young trees and shrubs often arrive with a balled root encased in plastic or burlap.*

for an hour or so before planting finally takes place. It is also a good plan to check the actual plant itself and give this a good watering before planting occurs. Where a container grown tree or shrub is being planted, the depth to plant is just fractionally below the top of the existing container of soil. Where a bare-rooted tree or shrub is being planted or one which has had its ball of soil encased in plastic or burlap, the depth of planting is either to the top of the ball of soil or to the original soil mark on the stem of the plant. In the case of large specimens a helper is advisable to hold the plant as the soil is carefully returned over the roots or around the soil ball. Obviously it is easier planting a container grown plant as this is relatively self supporting. In the case of a bare rooted tree or shrub the roots should be very carefully teased or opened out and arranged evenly over the base of the hole and then some fine soil carefully trickled over and firmed with the feet. If any broken or damaged roots are noticed these are best cut off cleanly with a sharp pair of shears. Return the soil carefully over the roots or around the soil ball, firming as work proceeds, until finally the site is covered level with the surrounding soil. Tie the plant carefully to its supporting stake, using a proprietary tree or shrub tie which is pliable and which will not therefore harm or chafe the bark of the plant. Many of these are also adjustable so that they can be altered as the trunk of the tree expands with age.

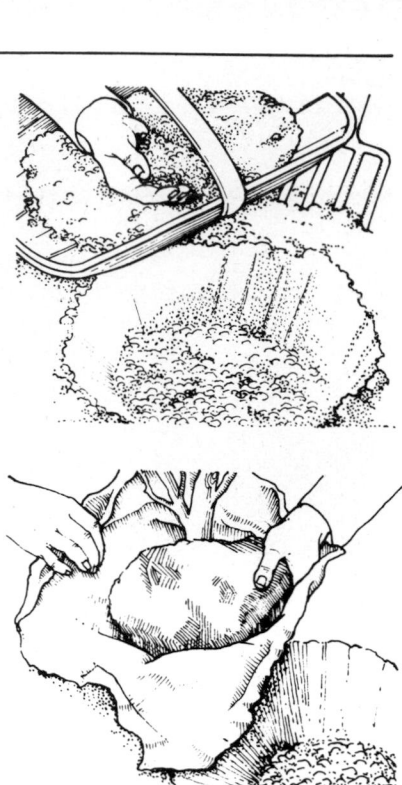

If a tree, or especially a shrub, is to be planted near a wall, then care must be taken to see that the site is well watered beforehand as these situations are often dry. The siting of a tree near property or walls or fences must be very carefully considered as there can be damage caused by the roots of the plant itself, especially to the foundations of property in the case of vigorous trees. Wherever possible it is best to keep trees and vigorous shrubs well away from these situations.

Do not forget to make sure that the label on the plant is securely tied so that the reference for future years is always available even if the planting plan has been mislaid. It is important to pay particular attention to aftercare. If the weather should be dry for some time after planting then it is essential that the planting area is kept well watered so that there is no danger of the roots or the ball of soil drying out. Make sure that a thorough flooding of water is applied, preferably with a hose, allowing the water to soak throughly into the subsoil. A great deal of moisture loss or evaporation can be prevented if the area around the base of the tree is given a mulch or covering with materials such as well rotted manure, peat or even leaves after this initial watering.

It is surprising how severely retarded a newly planted specimen can be if it is not protected during severe weather. In the case of small specimens it may be possible to slip a large tough plastic bag over the plant during these periods. The plastic can be temporarily wrapped round and tied in place, or a temporary screen of burlap or sacking can be tacked to several wooden supports which in turn are driven into the ground near the plant, enclosing the plant and protecting it from cold searing winds. If plenty of straw can be obtained then the plant (obviously a small one) can be enclosed with wire netting suitably supported with wooden or metal stakes and the interior filled in with straw, thus enclosing the small plant and protecting it from severe weather. These protections must be removed of course when the severe weather has passed.

## Planting in containers

It is quite possible of course that there may not be the room or situation for a shrub in the garden borders themselves. If one has a city garden which has no soil facilities, or very few, then it is a good plan to consider the use of large containers. They should be selected as big as possible so that the plant roots have ample room in which to grow and spread, otherwise very poor starved specimens will result. There is one peculiar advantage of restricting shrubs to a certain extent which is that many tend to flower more prolifically in these circumstances. It is important of course that only certain types of plants are selected for this purpose and the list in this chapter

*Above: planting a shrub. First, an ample hole is excavated and a little compost or gritty material to aid drainage may be placed in the bottom of the hole. Check for correct depth of planting with a stick placed across the hole. Tread returned soil firmly.*

*Above : even in a paved yard shrubs can be grown in suitable containers. On the left, wooden tubs are planted out with shrubs surrounded by summer bedding plants. On the right, an old half barrel painted white makes the ideal container for a hydrangea.*

will include suitable suggestions. Usually a container some 60–75cm (2–2½ft) wide and at least 45cm (18in) deep is essential for most specimens. As many of the shrubs suggested attain a height of only 1.2–1.5m (4–5ft) then these containers will be adequate. Many barrels these days are unfortunately made of plastic but if one is fortunate enough to obtain some old oak barrels these are excellent. Large ones can be sawn in half, thus making two very adequate shrub containers.

Growing in containers means adequate drainage, and the containers must have suitable drainage holes provided. If these are not present they must be made. The bottom of the container should then be covered with an inch or two of gravel, making sure that the layer of gravel is thick enough to protect the drainage holes from being blocked by soil. Some coarser soil should then be placed over the drainage material, and very small pebbles and chippings can be used to improve drainage. The most suitable type of soil mix is one that is water-retentive yet drains well and is fairly rich. One can make up one's own mixture using good quality soil at the rate of 4 parts of soil, 2 parts of peat, 1 part sharp or coarse sand. To each bushel of this mixture add about 15–50g (½–2oz) of general or complete balanced fertilizer such as is sold for growing vegetables. The best type of soil is a fibrous loam which has plenty of organic matter in it. Under no circumstances dig out or acquire poor subsoil which is relatively infertile. For planting in containers the best type of specimen plant is that which has been grown in a container, or which has a good ball of soil attached when purchased or received from the nursery. Make sure the soil is well watered beforehand and then place a little amount of soil in the bottom of the container, pack round with more soil, firm, add more soil and finally fill up to within 2.5cm (1in) of the top of the container. This gap is important as it allows for watering.

# Permanent planting

## Propagating shrubs

Many shrubs can be propagated or increased by cuttings. This of course saves a great deal of money and it is a very nice way to increase the stock of favorite specimens. There are several different ways in which shrubs can be increased. These are by hard root cuttings, semi-hard wood cuttings, heeled cuttings, soft wood cuttings, leaf bud cuttings, and layering.

**Hard wood cuttings**   These are generally taken in late autumn and early winter. Hard wood cuttings are probably the easiest way of propagating many of the shrubs and trees. The type of wood or growth to select is that which has just completed its first season of growth and has in fact become, as its name implies, hard and woody. The best type of growth to select is healthy, vigorous shoots, stems of the current year's growth. As many as are required should be cut off with a pruner, cutting them about 30cm (12in) long. Then each cutting should be cut cleanly just below the bud or joint at its base. Where leaves are attached to the stems a few of these should be carefully removed an inch or so above the prepared cut. It does help to encourage rooting if the ends of the prepared cutting are dipped in hormone rooting powder or liquid just before they are inserted in the soil. The best position for the cuttings is in a sheltered north border or in a frame. A shallow trench or slit is taken out with a spade about 10–13cm (4–5in) deep and the bottom 2.5cm (1in) lined with some sharp sand. Each cutting is then gently pushed into the sand for about 1cm (½in) and the cuttings arranged along the trench about 8–10cm (3–4in) apart between each cutting. The soil is then carefully returned to the slit or trench and firmed with the feet. Keep an eye on the soil and if dry weather prevails make sure that the trench is given a good watering. It will be necessary to firm the soil occasionally during the winter, especially after hard weather when the soil tends to lift through the action of frost. About a year after insertion most of the cuttings should have taken root and can then be lifted carefully, with a good ball of soil attached to the small root system, and the cutting planted out where it is to grow.

**Semi-hard wood cuttings**   Some plants root more easily if semi-hard wood cuttings are selected. These are the current year's growth which have made reasonably hard or mature wood but not quite as mature as the hard wood types. The period in which these cuttings can be taken is from about mid July to late August. Shoots should be selected and cut about 20cm (8in) in length, usually from the side shoots of the current season's growth, and a cut should always be made just below a leaf bud or joint. Next, the top or tip of the cutting should be treated by cutting off the soft section or stem so that the final prepared cutting is only about 8–10cm (3–4in) in length. The prepared cuttings are then inserted in the slit trench, or one or two can be placed round the inside edge of a large pot or container filled with a suitable rooting medium. Again it is advisable to dip the bottom, prepared ends of each cutting in a hormone powder or liquid preparation. Some shrubs will not root readily even if they are semi-hard, but in some cases if a sliver of bark or stem is allowed to remain at the bottom of each cutting the rooting takes place quite easily. This type of cutting is called a heel cutting and the way to prepare it is as follows. A selected semi-hard length of stem or branch should be cut off and then as many of the little side shoots or branches as necessary can be taken off. In order to provide a heel with each shoot or cutting, the selected shoot should be partly cut off with a knife from the main stem. Just before the cut goes right through the knife should be removed and the growth pulled away from the stem. By doing this a piece of the bark or skin will be removed also, and this heel or sliver can be trimmed at its pointed end by cutting off the tip. The end of the cutting is then dipped in powder or liquid rooting preparation and inserted as for the other types of cutting.

One of the most successful ways of rooting semi-hard wood cuttings or heel cuttings is to set them in containers of sharp sandy soil or a special rooting medium and

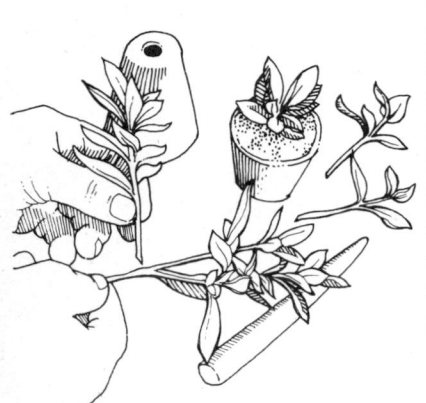

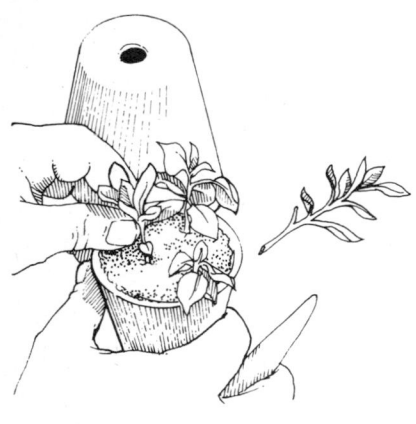

*Below : hard wood and semi-hard wood cuttings can be taken from many shrubs. Rooting can be assisted by dipping the ends of the prepared cuttings in hormone rooting powder or liquid.*

then place them in a frame or even in a greenhouse where warmth and humidity can be provided. Mist propagating units, where overhead standpipes with nozzles emit frequent bursts of a very fine mist-like spray of water, are ideal for quick rooting. If a large number of cuttings is required it is a good idea to make up a special propagating bed on the greenhouse bench or staging and insert large numbers of cuttings in this. A temperature of about 15–18°C (60–65°F) is ideal, and this can be provided quite easily with soil warming cables. Some shade is necessary in the greenhouse or the frame during hot sunshine. Rooted cuttings can eventually be potted out singly into suitable small pots and the plants gradually hardened off by placing them in the frame, with the frame lights gradually opened up to admit more air, until eventually they are ready for planting outdoors in their permanent quarters.

**Soft wood cuttings** Several shrubs can be propagated easily from very soft growth known as soft wood, and soft wood cuttings are prepared by taking suitable growths in June or July. These should be selected from young non-flowering shoots and should be cut about 10cm (4in) in length. The bottom pair of leaves should be carefully removed and the stem cut through with a sharp knife or razor immediately below a leaf joint. The end should be dipped in a mild hormone rooting preparation, and several cuttings can be inserted around the inside edge of a 10–13cm (4–5in) pot. The medium should be sand, perlite, a mixture of sand and peat, or any medium which contains a high proportion of gritty material such as sand. Cuttings should be inserted firmly and then placed in a frame and given some shade from hot sunshine. Keep an eye on watering. When rooted they can be tapped out of their pot and potted up singly into small containers. They are gradually hardened off so that they can go out in the open garden in their permanent quarters.

**Leaf bud cuttings** Another less common but interesting method of increasing shrubs is by leaf buds. These are selected from cuttings taken from semi-hard lateral growths in August or September. You will notice that there is a small bud in the axil of the leaf stem and the main stem. The appropriate growth should be cut about 2cm (¾in) below the leaf stem, leaving about three-quarters of the stem, and the stem immediately above the bud should be cut close back to it. What one is left with therefore is the leaf with a short piece of leaf stem attached to a short piece of main stem in which there is a bud. The prepared cutting of leaf bud is then inserted in a mixture of peat and sand in a pot so that the leaf axil just shows above the surface of the medium. Several of these prepared leaf buds can be accommodated in a large 15cm (6in) pot. It is important that the mixture is firmed gently but firmly around each leaf bud stem. The prepared leaf buds should be given a light watering. A plastic bag can then be placed over the pot, and the pot kept in a greenhouse or frame in shade. Several months later (approximately seven or eight) the prepared leaf buds should have rooted. The plants can be carefully tapped out of the container, carefully separated and potted out singly in small 9–10cm (3½–4in) pots. They can be placed in the garden frame, hardening them off very gradually until the following late spring or summer, when the rooted plants are planted out in their permanent growing quarters.

**Layering** Another fascinating method of propagation is a very natural one called layering. This is carried out simply by allowing stems or growths of some shrubs to lie in close contact with the soil where the covered portion of the stem will eventually root. A flexible branch is selected and bent down into a prepared area of soil which consists of some moist peat and sharp sand mixed into the existing soil. Any number of individual pockets of prepared soil can be made, according to the number of shoots that require layering. The shoot should be pegged down or wired into its prepared site about 30cm (12in) from its tip. A bent pin or wire is ideal for inserting into the soil, and the hooked end can be arranged over the stem to keep it in close

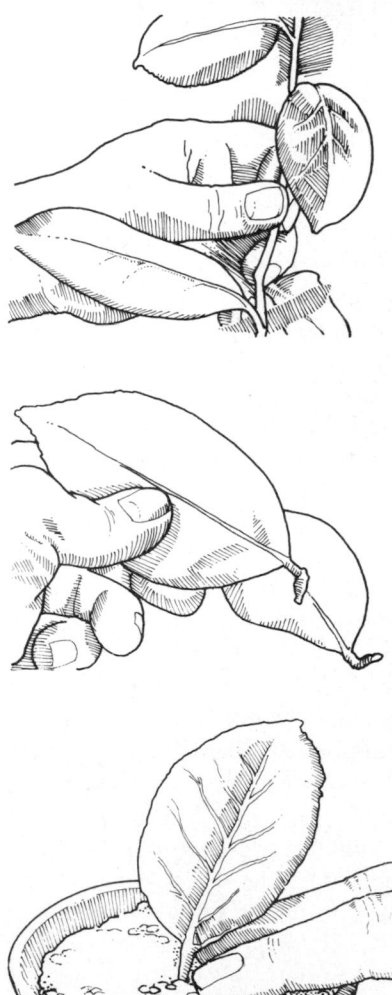

*Below: leaf bud cuttings are the ideal way to propagate plants such as camellias. The prepared cuttings are inserted in a mixture of peat and sand, and a clear plastic bag tied over the pot will maintain the humidity and assist rooting.*

# Permanent planting

contact with the prepared site. Once in position some more prepared soil is returned until the area is completely covered, and it is then firmed with the feet. To encourage rooting, the stem underneath where it will be buried in the soil is given a little nick with a knife, or a short lengthwise cut is made to produce a tongue. From this cut area the roots will eventually form. It will help if the area is dusted with the hormone rooting powder just before the prepared stem is inserted and pegged in place. About 12 months after treatment the layered portion should have formed roots, the stem can be cut away from its parent plant and the new plant carefully lifted with a spade with as much soil adhering as possible and planted out in its permanent growing quarters elsewhere in the garden.

### Pruning trees and shrubs

Many shrubs will grow and progress quite happily without much, if any, pruning; but usually pruning is a good idea not only to keep the shrub within bounds but also to occasionally remove dead or badly placed wood. In many cases pruning has the beneficial effect of encouraging stronger, healthier growth to form, which eventually will produce good flowering displays. Pruning becomes a major operation only when one has to tackle sadly neglected shrubs and trees, and then it is chiefly a matter of cutting out—fairly drastically in many cases—the dead or diseased wood. Many overgrown specimens need thinning out so that air and sunlight can pass through the branches, and some judicious thinning of branches is therefore necessary to open up the center of the plant.

All cuts should be made to sound, healthy, vigorous growth, and where branches are badly crossing these should be removed. If large limbs or branches have to be cut out, their cut surface should be painted over afterwards with a tree wound dressing which will prevent the entry of diseases. All dead or diseased wood must be burned afterwards.

There are many shrubs however which need pruning according to the way in which they flower. In other words, the season for pruning depends on whether that particular shrub flowers on last year's wood or on new growth. Plants which flower on growth made the previous year—in other words on last year's wood—include such popular specimens as Deutzia, Weigela, Buddleia, and Prunus. This group of shrubs should be pruned every season as soon as they have finished their flowering. Though some may bloom and be pruned in winter, the usual time is late spring. The growth which has carried the flowering display should be pruned back to about three shoots or buds from the place where it arises from the main stem. Growths from the new shoots will produce the flower display for the following season.

Shrubs such as Ceratostigma, Santolina, and Ceanothus produce their flowering display on growth that has been produced in the current season. They are pruned by cutting out all the previous year's growths or shoots to about 3 buds or shoots from their base. This will encourage the production of good new growth for the flowering display. Many shrubs can be pruned very severely and a good example is the other type of Buddleia known as *B. davidii*. This is commonly known as the Butterfly Bush because it attracts hosts of butterflies. This shrub can have all its old growth cut right back even to the ground in the North, and during the following season vigorous new growth will take place, culminating in a lavish flower display on the new wood, with blooms of high quality.

Many gardeners like to spare the knife or pruners from their trees and shrubs. Even if only occasional cutting out of diseased, weak or badly placed growth is practised, it is surprising how well the flowering display can be maintained, but it is as well to appreciate the fact that some shrubs produce better displays if attention is paid to the cutting out of old wood or the preserving of new wood according to the type.

There are a few shrubs which should not be pruned at all. These include many of the conifers, which are in any case extremely slow-growing, and the short-lived Brooms (Cytisus).

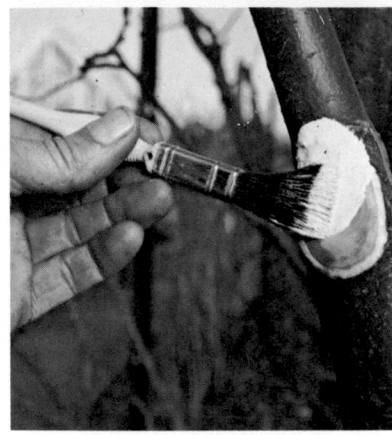

*Top: pruning cut made just above the bud. Above: painting a large cut with sealing compound. Below: Maples are lovely in the fall.*

**Acer** (*Maple*)   These are especially attractive because of their foliage. They will thrive in most types of soil but certainly do not like badly drained or wet soils. If large trees are required the following species are worthy of note. *A. negundo* has a bushy type of head and is quite a vigorous grower. The tree grows to a height of about 18m (6oft) or more, so it needs plenty of room. The variety *Drummondii* has beautiful variegated green leaves with cream margins. It grows 12m (4oft) or more high. Another beauty is *Leopoldii* which has yellowish pink leaves beautifully speckled white. Height is about 16m (5oft) plus. A very striking section of the Acers are the snake-bark varieties which have very attractive striped bark. The species *A. capillipes* has reddish young bark which turns brown and is streaked with white. The young growths are red and it has attractive autumn tints in its foliage. The species *A. rufinerve* is a particularly beautifully shaped tree and has very conspicuous white striated bark. It grows to a height of about 12m (4oft) and is excellent for autumn color.

Where a small to medium Acer is required there are several very beautiful types to select from. For example there is the species with green and white bark called *A. pennsylvanicum*, commonly known as the striped maple or moosewood, which grows to a height of 6–9m (20–3oft). The popular Japanese Maple *A. palmatum* grows usually about the same height. It has scarlet to purple-red leaves in the autumn and in the summer the lobed leaves are green or reddish.

**Ailanthus** (*Tree of Heaven*)   A fast growing tree is *Ailanthus glandulosa* commonly called the Tree of Heaven. It has an ultimate height of 18m (6oft) approximately, and has beautiful pinnate leaves which turn a lovely yellow color in the autumn. It can be established for the beauty of its foliage alone.

**Alnus** (*Alder*)   The Alders are very attractive specimens which have catkins hanging

*Above: the Betulas or birches make graceful specimens for a large garden. They cast only light shade, so it is possible to grow a wide range of other plants and shrubs around them as shown here.*

# Permanent planting

*Below: these are the unusual flowers of the hardy deciduous tree Davidia involucrata. Davidia vilmoriniana is an improved form with shiny leaves. Bottom: Catalpa bignonioides is an unusual choice for a specimen tree. It has large green leaves, white flowers and bean-like fruits. Opposite, top: the fruits of the Malus or Crab Apple. Opposite, bottom: Liriodendron tulipifera.*

from their branches in the spring. The appearance of these catkins is around March and April. Alders grow quickly, are easy to establish and are particularly useful for screening purposes. Of the several varieties *A. Pendula* is a particularly lovely specimen which has a handsome weeping habit and grows to a height of about 12m (40ft). The variety *A. cordata*, also called the Italian Alder, grows quite well even in limy soils. It grows to a height of 20m (60ft) or more, so it is a selection for the larger garden only. For variety, *A. incana Aurea* should be selected which has beautiful yellow leaves right through until midsummer. It is best established in a sheltered part of the garden, and can grow to a height of up to 12m (40ft).

**Amelanchier** The Snowy Mespilus or *Amelanchier canadensis* has white flowers in April, and when these are partly open they are attractively tinged pink. It bears crimson fruits in June and in the autumn the foliage turns a rich color. Obviously this is a most useful tree to have in the garden for a fascinating year-round display. It is a round headed type of tree and grows to a height of about 8m (25ft).

**Betula** (*Birch*) The Birches are excellent trees where there is a problem of a light or poor soil. In fact they will grow in a very wide range of soils and are excellent for light shading. They have a whitish bark and a golden colored foliage in the autumn. One of the best kinds to purchase is *B. costata* which has striped peeling bark and produces rich yellow leaves in the autumn. Height is about 16m (50ft). Another beauty is *B. pendula Purpurea* which has a pleasant purple bark and upright habit. Height is about 16m (50ft) or more.

**Catalpa** *Catalpa bignonioides* is a tree which has large ovate green leaves and white flowers flecked yellow and purple in July and August. It should be planted in a well prepared soil and likes a sunny position. It has an attractive rounded wide head and grows about 16m (50ft) high.

**Davidia** A fascinating tree is the Handkerchief or Dove tree, *Davidia involucrata vilmoriniana*. It has long pendulous white bracts, and the bright green leaves are gray on their bare undersides. Unfortunately this tree has to be established for many years before it comes into flower and approximately ten to twelve years may have to elapse. It is a tree which does not do well on poorer soils.

**Fagus** (*Beech*) The Beech trees are extremely handsome specimens but for the smaller garden it is important that the dwarf or smaller types are selected. The Beech is a useful tree if one is gardening on limestone soil. There are several beautiful species such as *F. sylvatica Asplenifolia*, the Cut-leaved Beech, which is round headed, and has long deeply serrated leaves. It grows to a height of at least 18m (60ft). For a weeping specimen the type *F.s. Pendula* is a gem. It has a very irregular large head. The Copper Beech *F. s. Purpurea* grows to an approximate height of some 18m (60ft) and is excellent as a specimen tree.

**Fraxinus** (*Ash*) The Ash is another stately tree which is excellent as a specimen. The common Ash, *F. excelsior*, is oval headed and its branch framework is nice and open. It is a graceful tree but is rather large, attaining a height of at least 36m (120ft) or more. For the smaller garden, where there is room for a tree that will attain a height of 18m (60ft) or more, the variety *F. ornus*, the Flowering Ash, is a very attractive specimen, with a dense rounded head and numerous panicles of fragrant white flowers which are produced in May. Another plus is the fact that the foliage turns or is tinted purple in the autumn months.

**Ginkgo** If you have an extremely large garden then you might well be tempted to have a tree which can attain a height of about 36m (120ft) in time. This is the

Maidenhair tree or Ginkgo, *G. biloba*. It is a very attractive conifer and has very pretty fan shaped deciduous leaves of soft green which turn yellow in the fall.

**Laburnum**   A very popular tree for smaller gardens is the Laburnum. It is particularly welcome for its May and June display of beautiful, long trailing yellow flowers. The only drawback is the fact that this tree can produce brown pods which contain black seeds, and these are unfortunately poisonous, so where there are children or pets its introduction to the garden has to be considered rather carefully. There are several pretty sorts, especially *L. x vossii* which is perhaps the best garden form with lovely long racemes of flowers. Fortunately this particular specimen does not produce many seeds. It will eventually grow to something in the region of 8m (25ft).

**Liquidambar**   There is a lot to be said for having intriguing trees in one's garden, and a tree which has a corky bark and exudes a fragrant resin is the Sweet Gum or *Liquidambar styraciflua*. This has a pyramidal habit and its leaves are needle-like with beautiful crimson and gold tints in the autumn. It is not a tree to be planted on limy soils. It attains a height of about 8m (25ft).

**Liriodendron** (*Tulip Tree*)   The Tulip tree, *Liriodendron tulipifera*, is quite a tall tree growing to a height of at least 54m (180ft). It has wide foliage: the leaves are almost square and they turn yellow in the autumn. It bears in June or July a greenish-yellow tulip-like flower.

**Magnolia**   Most limy gardens cannot grow the beautiful magnolia, but the variety *Magnolia kobus* is one which is fairly lime tolerant. It has creamy white cup-shaped flowers in April and attains a height of about 18m (60ft).

**Malus** (*Crab Apple*)   No tree planting scheme could be complete without the inclusion of the beautiful Crabs or Malus. They are available in a very comprehensive range of varieties and they are conveniently divided into four main sections. There are the *floribunda* types with pink flowers; the purple-leaved varieties; the *pumila* group which produce those lovely fruits which are ideal for jelly-making; and the Canadian crabs which have vivid pink or rose colored flowers followed by the lovely ornamental fruits. Most of the kinds grow to a height of about 8m (25ft) but for the rather small garden there is one particular beauty which attains a height of only some 2m (6ft), *M. sargentii*. This forms more of a bush growth than a tree formation. Here are a few particularly beautiful types in the Malus group: 'Neville Copeman' is an improved seedling which grows fairly upright and has large soft pink flowers; 'Golden Hornet' has bright yellow tapering fruit, which is rather unusual; *Lemoinei* has lovely deep purple foliage and dark crimson flowers; 'Red Glow' is a lovely broad-headed tree and has broad purple leaves when they are young and very large attractive pink flowers.

**Populus** (*Poplar*)   For an exposed situation where a fairly rapid screen is desired then the Poplar should be considered. They are useful trees to have where the soil is particularly heavy and wet. Growing to a height of some 24m (80ft) is the White Poplar, *P. alba*. It is a tree which can resist high winds and is a useful subject for the seaside. The Lombardy Poplar, *P. nigra Italica*, is another excellent windbreak but it should be sited well away from property as its roots can cause damage to foundations or drains. It, too, sometimes attains heights up to 24m (80ft), but it is narrow so does not need a lot of room, whereas the White Poplar is broad, and is therefore a tree which requires a fairly large garden.

**Prunus**   Now we come to the very large Prunus family which embraces the almonds, peaches, plums, sloes and cherries. In the almonds section a particularly lovely

# Permanent planting

*Below: Prunus x sargentii, with deep pink flowers.*

species is *P. amygdalus*, the Common Almond. This is a useful medium-sized tree attaining a height of about 10m (30ft), but a bush form can be obtained which grows only some 3–4m (10–12ft) in height. The Common Almond has pale pink flowers produced in March and its nuts can be used for cooking. The flowering Peach is another section and *P. persica* 'Pink Charming' is a very pretty semi-double flowering type with pink rosette-like flowers which are produced in April.

The Flowering Plums have the attraction of very eye-catching purple foliage and the tree types can attain a height of about 6–7m (20–24ft), whereas the bush types, which are ideal for smaller gardens, will grow to an approximate height of up to 4–5m (15ft). *P. Atropurpurea* is the Purple-leaved Plum, and this bears single white flowers in March. The variety *Nigra* is very similar but it has rather deeper colored foliage.

Among the Flowering Cherries there are some beautiful types such as 'Pandora' which has single flowers of a delicate pale color produced in March and very pretty bronze foliage. The trees attain a height of about 8–16m (25–50ft) according to type, but bush types can be purchased and these attain a height of only some 3–5m (10–15ft). The variety *P. subhirtella Autumnalis* flowers late in the autumn and has single or semi-double white flowers. For a pink type the variety *Rosea* should be selected. Exceedingly attractive are the hybrid Japanese Cherries or *Prunus serrulata*. An ideal variety for the small garden is called 'Pink Perfection'. It has a semi-erect habit, is very free flowering and bears delightful double rosy pink flowers. Another lovely variety is 'Shiro-fugen', known as 'White God'. This is a variety which flowers late in the spring season. It has bronze young foliage and pendulous double pink buds which open into lovely lush white and pink flowers. It has a delightful spreading habit. Most of these cherries attain an approximate height of around 8m (25ft). The Weeping Cherry is a beautiful specimen plant which makes an ideal focal point in a garden. It is also a suitable tree to have in the front garden where its splendid display of beautiful pink flowers in April or May is delightful. An excellent variety is *P. subhirtella Pendula*. Its long branches weep or trail down to the ground and it is a wonderful sight when in full flower.

**Pyrus**   The Ornamental Pear or Pyrus is a small to medium-sized tree which has attractive silvery gray-green leaves in April, and the white flowers are quite attractive too. The species *P. communis* 'Beech Hill' has a spire-like habit and it has lovely pear-like blossoms in the spring. It grows to a height of 8m (25ft). Another beautiful weeping form is *P. salicifolia Pendula*. A particular attraction of this variety is its leaves which are clothed in a silky white down until the early summer. It produces lots of beautiful white flowers in April and its height is about 8m (25ft).

**Robinia** (*False Acacia*)   The Robinia is another lovely tree, which should be considered for its foliage effect. It is also a tree which can do quite well in poorer soils. It is not a good choice, however, for exposed sites, as the branches can be damaged by winds. Flowers are fragrant, white, and born in June. A good variety is *R. pseudoacacia Bessoniana* which has a close, rounded head and grows to a height of about 12–16m (40–50ft). Another variety *Frisia* is excellent; it has bright yellow foliage in the spring and it is quite fast growing to an ultimate height of about 6m (20ft).

**Salix** (*Willow*)   Weeping Willows or Salix are very good trees to include in a garden when there is a water feature or rockery, as the tree provides an excellent background for this feature, especially where the branches weep or trail down. It should not be sited too close to water, however, as the autumn fall of leaves can pollute the water, but if kept reasonably well clear it is excellent. It is a tree which can be used as a focal point in a garden and is ideal for planting on a bend in a pathway or drive where it adds interest to the layout. For the small garden the variety *S. purpurea Pendula* can be thoroughly recommended. It attains a height of about 2–2.5m (5–8ft). If a non-trailing or weeping type of willow is desired then the variety *S. sericea* is ideal as it

MOIST GROUND
Waterlogged ground can be improved with proper drainage, but for low-lying ground, and particularly for planting near water, the following are recommended. See General Lists for further details.

*Carpinus betulus* (Hornbeam) T
Cornus (Dogwood), *alba* and
  *stolonifera* varieties S
Cortaderia (Pampas Grass) S
Philadelphus (Mock Orange) S
Salix (Willow) T
Sambucus (Elder) S
*Spiraea bumalda* S
*Viburnum opulus* varieties

T: Tree   S: Shrub   C: Climber

*Left : willows, naturally waterside trees, are successful in wet soils, and look particularly good when positioned near a water feature.*

*Below : the rowans are highly decorative trees with pretty foliage which colors well in the fall and freely produced orange berries.*

has a medium-sized round head and very attractive silvery gray-white leaves. Its height is approximately 4.5m (15ft) maximum.

**Sorbus** (*Rowan*)  The Sorbus is an excellent tree for most gardens because it starts off with a display of flowers in the spring. It has autumn foliage colors and also berries in the winter. The Mountain Ash, *S. aucuparia*, is a good tree for the garden where there is plenty of room because it can attain a height of about 12–18m (40–60ft). It is a round headed tree with smooth silver-gray bark and produces orange-red berries too. Another kind for the small garden is *S. sargentiana* which has leaves at least 30cm (12in) in length. These are a brilliant vermilion color in the autumn, and attractive orange-scarlet berries are also produced. The eventual height is about 14m (30ft). The Whitebeam, *S. aria*, is another tree worthy of consideration, especially the variety 'Leonard Sprenger'. This makes a nice upright tree with large flower heads and large clusters of orange-red berries. It grows to a height of up to about 12m (40ft).

**Tilia** (*Lime*)  Most lime trees or lindens grow to great heights, but the lovely *T. fastigiata*, with fragrant yellow flowers, is ideal for smaller gardens.

Now we take a look at the beautiful shrubs which can be considered for all sorts of planting situations in a garden. The following shrubs have been selected for their particular beauty or special features which will appeal to a wide range of gardeners and will suit a wide range of requirements.

**Acer** (*Maple*)   There are some Maples which can be selected as shrubs and these are quite low-growing compared with the tree forms. The variety *Acer palmatum Atropurpureum*, as a tree, grows to a height of approximately 6m (20ft), but a much smaller-growing shrub form is sometimes obtainable.

**Artemisia**   Artemisia is the most beautiful shrub with filigree foliage and silvery leaves. The species *A. arborescens* is particularly delightful and is incidentally very useful for floral decoration. Height is about 90cm (3ft). Another particularly lovely shrub which is evergreen is *A. abrotanum* or Southernwood. It has feathery gray-green fragrant foliage. It grows to a height of approximately 60cm (2ft).

**Atriplex**   A semi-evergreen shrub with graceful arching branches and silvery leaves is *Atriplex halimus*. It is a very useful plant to have in seaside gardens and it can also be used as a hedge. It grows better in well-drained soils and likes full sun. Height is about 3m (9ft).

**Aucuba**   If there is a dense or deep shaded area, or the garden is situated in a town or near an industrial area, the shrub Aucuba is evergreen and should be planted. The species *A. picturata* is evergreen with large foliage. Height is about 1.2m (4ft). *A. japonica*, the familiar Spotted Laurel, makes a bigger shrub with variegated foliage.

**Berberis** (*Barberry*)   A lovely section in the shrub world is the Berberis. They are available in evergreen and deciduous forms, they have beautiful berries in the deciduous range, and also the foliage can be beautifully colored in the winter. Of the deciduous varieties the following types can be recommended: 'Buccaneer' with yellow flowers in June and red berries in the winter, height about 1.5m (4ft); 'Pirate King'

*Above : one of the huge and diverse Berberis family is this hybrid, Berberis x rubrostilla, with pendulous coral-red berries.*

*Right : Acer palmatum dissectum turns the most brilliant fiery orange in the fall.*

grows to the same height, with yellow flowers in May or June and beautiful foliage coloring in the autumn. For a bushy spreading type, *B. thunbergii Atropurpurea* is a really lovely plant with beautiful rich bronzy red foliage in the spring which turns to a deep red in the late summer and winter. Height is about 1.5m (5ft).

Of the evergreen varieties the following are excellent: *B. darwinii*, which has rich orange-yellow flowers in May and delightful purplish berries in the winter. It has holly-like leaves and is useful for coastal planting as it will tolerate salt-laden winds. *B. stenophylla* is another lovely subject, with arching branches and yellow flowers produced in April. It is excellent as a hedge where its spiny foliage deters animals and children. Height is about a maximum of 3m (9ft).

**Buddleia**   The Buddleia is a shrub which is extremely strong growing and, when cut down in the autumn, will quickly throw up young sturdy growth the following season. A beautiful sort is *B. davidii* which flowers in July and August. Its lovely purplish colored blooms attract masses of butterflies. It likes full sun and grows to a height of about 2m (6ft). In this group there are some particularly lovely varieties such as 'Black Knight', which must be the darkest purple variety. 'Fascination' has lilac pink flowers as a contrast, and the variety 'Peace' has beautiful large heads of white flowers. For a complete change of flower shape the species *B. globosa* should be planted. Like the others it is a very vigorous plant and produces delightful round or ball-shaped tangerine-colored flowers earlier which are quite fragrant. Height is about 2–2.5m (6–8ft). It is semi-evergreen in California.

*There are numerous improved forms of the common Camellia, Camellia japonica. This is 'Tricolor'.*

**Buxus** (*Box*)   The Box is ideal for lovely closely-trimmed hedging and the variety *B. sempervirens* (Common Box) is the best type to select. It grows to a height of about 2–6m (6–20ft).

**Camellia**   This is a big group of shrubs. They do not tolerate lime or chalky soils, and plenty of peat or composted vegetable waste should be worked into the site. Some of them are ideal for growing in containers or tubs. There are four flower formations, which are the anemone form, formal double, semi-double and singles. In the *C. japonica* group there are white, pink and red colors as well as multicolors. Of the whites, the variety 'Mathotiana Alba' has double flowers; in the pinks 'Elegans' and 'Guest of Honour' are particularly lovely. Of the reds the variety 'Mercury' has semi-double flowers and 'Laura Walker' has bright red semi-double blooms. Of the multi-colors, which are particularly fascinating, a good example is 'Lady Vansittart' which has a whitish pink semi-double bloom, which is striped rose pink. 'Tricolor' is another pretty variegated form with attractive pink-flushed petals. Heights are very approximately up to about 1–2m (4–7ft).

**Caryopteris**   *Caryopteris clandonensis* known as the Blue Spirea has gorgeous violet-blue flower spikes which are produced between August and October. The foliage is an attractive grayish green and the plant will grow in a wide range of soils. The height is about 1m (3–4ft).

**Ceanothus** (*Californian Lilac*)   is a deciduous shrub flowering from about July to October, which appreciates a nice sunny border and a well-drained soil. 'Gloire de Versailles' has sky-blue flowers and a lovely arching habit. Height is about 2m (6–7ft). There is a delightful evergreen Ceanothus, *C. thyrsiflorus repens*, a creeping type of plant forming a close mound of dense foliage which is attractively covered in blue flowers in May. Maximum height is about 75cm (30in).

**Ceratostigma**   Plumbago or *Ceratostigma willmottianum* flowers in July to October with beautiful blue flowers. It is ideal for planting against a low wall and grows to a height of about 90cm (3ft).

**Chaenomeles** (*Quince*)  Chaenomeles, the Flowering Quinces, are very useful shrubs to consider because they are very versatile. They will grow in a wide range of soils and they are also very hardy. *C. japonica* produces scarlet flowers in April to June and lots of useful fruits which can be made into jelly later. Height is about 1m (3–4ft). Other named varieties are 'Crimson and Gold', 'Knap Hill Scarlet', and 'Nivalis'.

**Chimonanthus** (*Wintersweet*)  The Wintersweet (*Chimonanthus praecox*) has very delightful fragrance. It grows to a height of about 2–2.5m (6–8ft). It will grow well in any well-drained soil and is an ideal subject for planting as far north as Long Island.

**Choisya** (*Mexican Orange Blossom*)  The Mexican Orange Blossom is an evergreen shrub. *Choisya ternata* is an excellent choice for most gardens and will grow well in semi-shade. It is also a fragrant plant, producing beautiful little white flowers in May. It grows into a rounded bush and has attractive glossy foliage. Eventual height is about 3m (10ft) in warm areas.

**Cistus** (*Rock Rose*)  For very confined planting areas, and especially where a very low growing subject is required, the Rock Rose is a very useful evergreen plant. It produces most of its flowers in May or June. The variety *C. crispus* 'Sunset' has deep rose flowers and attains a height of about 1m (3ft). For even smaller growth the variety 'Silver Pink' is a slow growing plant with pretty pink flowers and silver gray foliage and attains a height of about 60cm (2ft).

**Colutea**  A good problem solver is *Colutea arborescens* because this is a shrub which grows quickly, likes a hot, dry site and will even grow well on a poorish soil. The flowers themselves are particularly fascinating as they are pea-shaped and bright yellow in color, and during the late summer the flowers are followed by bladder-like pods. The eventual height is about 5m (15–16ft).

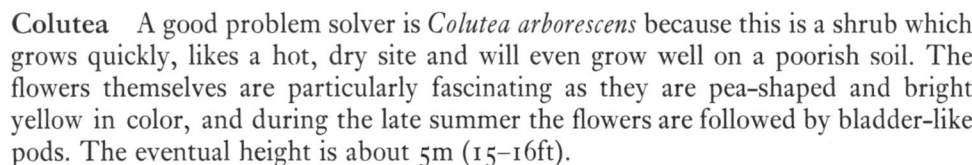

**Cortaderia** (*Pampas Grass*)  Cortaderia is a most fascinating shrub to include in any shrub planting scheme. It produces lovely elegant white plumes and is an ideal subject for winter flower arrangements. It thrives well in shade or partial shade and is very handy because it will grow in drier, lighter soils. The species *C. argentea* has lovely silvery plumes in August to September and can reach a height of about 3m (9–10ft). For silky white plumes the variety 'Sunningdale Silver' must be considered, which also grows to about the same height.

**Cotinus** (*Smoke Tree*)  The Smoke Trees or shrubs are particularly fascinating— these are the Cotinus. One of the most outstanding varieties is 'Notcutt's' which has dark green foliage. It grows to a height of approximately 3m (9–10ft). *C. coggygria*, sometimes classified as *Rhus cotinus*, has striking plume-like flower panicles which turn smoke-gray, hence the common name of Smoke Tree or Wig Tree. It grows to 5m (15–16ft).

**Cotoneaster**  The Cotoneasters are particularly versatile shrubs because they can be had in various forms: those which will cover the ground and virtually creep over the soil, the slightly taller growing varieties, and the quite tall ones. They are one of the few shrubs which will establish well in difficult situations such as full shade, but they can of course be grown in partial shade also. They have masses of white or pink flowers produced in the spring and in the autumn the brilliant red berries are particularly eye-catching. Among the ground cover varieties 'Skogholm Coral Beauty' is a lovely evergreen subject, producing masses of tiny leaves and bright orange fruits. The height is about 60cm (2ft). The slightly taller growing Cotoneasters

*Opposite, top: Cotoneaster horizontalis has flat, fan-like growth and masses of bright red berries. Opposite, bottom: Colutea arborescens produces inflated, bladder-like fruit pods.*

*Left: Cytisus or Brooms are not long-lasting plants, but they are ideal for a seaside garden.*

*Below: the brooms are sometimes confused with gorse. This is Ulex europaeus, the common gorse.*

include the variety *C. horizontalis*. This produces flat horizontal branches and is ideal for situating against or on top of walls. It could also be planted near such difficult features as manhole covers, where eventually the plant will creep over the area and hide it most effectively. For taller growths there are other Cotoneasters in evergreen or semi-evergreen forms. For a semi-evergreen type choose *C. x cornobius*, which has arching branches and grows to a height of about 3m (9ft). An evergreen is *C. lacteus* which has beautiful deep green oval leaves and white flowers in June. The lovely red fruits or berries are borne throughout the winter, making it a very attractive plant during the duller months in the garden. Height is a maximum of about 3–4m (12ft).

**Cytisus** (*Broom*) The Brooms are very lovely shrubs which flower very easily. They will grow well in a light soil, but do best where they can have a very sunny situation. There are many hybrid types which produce their flowers in approximately June and they grow about 1m (3–4ft) high. For good crimson color the variety *C. scoparius* Andreanus should be selected, and for cream color 'Cornish Cream' is a real beauty. For an orange shade 'Killiney Salmon' is excellent.

**Daphne** For welcome fragrance in the early part of the year from February to March, the Daphne is a lovely shrub. It likes a lime-free soil, and one of the out-standing species is *Daphne mezereum*. This has purple red flowers and scarlet

*Above, left: the Ericas are excellent plants for ground cover. This is Erica tetralix, the cross-leaved heath. Above, right: Deutzias are hardy, free-flowering shrubs available in white and many shades of pink according to variety.*

berries later on in the summer. It grows to a height of about 90cm (3ft). An evergreen form is *D. odora* Variegata. This too is delightfully fragrant, grows to the same height, and has reddish purple flowers which are produced early. It is not hardy in the North.

**Deutzia**   The Deutzia produces a lovely flowering display in June. It will grow in full sun or in semi-shade. The variety 'Magician' is a lovely plant, with deep lilac pink flowers in June. The height is approximately 1.5–2m (4–7ft). Another lovely variety is 'Mont Rose' with mauve pink flowers. It grows to the same height.

**Elaeagnus**   For pure foliage effect *Elaeagnus pungens* Maculata is an evergreen variety with golden variegated foliage. It grows to a height of about 1.2m (4ft).

**Erica** (*Heath, heather*)   For labor saving the Heathers or Lings are excellent subjects to introduce into the garden. Once established they cover the ground densely and will effectively smother the weeds. Most are lime-haters and should be planted chiefly in full sun. All are evergreen, and moreover the winter and spring flowering groups (which are more tolerant of lime) will provide color from about November to April. There are some lovely varieties such as 'December Red', 'Ruby Glow', 'Springwood Pink' and 'Springwood White'. The summer and autumn flowering types include such lovely varieties as *E. cinerea* Atropurpurea, a good purple color; 'Mrs. D. F. Maxwell', deep cerise, flowering from July to October; 'Gold Haze', with golden foliage and white flowers; and 'Peter Sparkes', a lovely deep pink. *Erica tetralix* has pretty rose-pink flowers in summer.

**Escallonia**   The Escallonias are mostly semi-evergreens, and many are particularly suitable for coastal areas. Most of the flowers are produced in June, and the small deep foliage is very attractive. Many can be used for hedging purposes. There are several lovely varieties, which include 'Donard Star' with rose pink flowers, and *E. edinensis*, which has rosy pink flowers and is especially good as a hedge. 'Peach Blossom' is a lovely plant, and most grow to a height of about 1–2m (3–6ft). For an arching type of growth the variety 'Slieve Donard' should be used. This is an evergreen plant and has deep pink flowers. It makes a really beautiful hedge and grows to a height of about 2m (6ft).

**Euonymus**   Euonymus is a shrub which is very easy to cultivate and has lovely autumn foliage and attractive fruit. In the deciduous range the species *E. alata* has very attractive corky bark and rosy scarlet foliage. It grows about 2m (6–7ft) high. *E. sachalinensis* has fascinating five-sided fruit which is produced in the autumn. The foliage turns a very attractive deep red in the autumn and the eventual height of this particular variety is about 8m (12–13ft).

In the evergreen sections, which can be planted in semi-shade or full shade, the species *E. japonica* has a bushy habit with leathery foliage. It is a very handy variety for planting on the coast. It can be used for hedging and grows to a height of about 1.2m (4ft). For a golden variegated foliage *Aureopictus* should be considered. This grows to a height of just over 2.5m (10ft). 'Silver Pillar' has white variegation and *E. fortunei Vegeta* has very glossy foliage and orange berries in autumn. This is quite a small plant, very handy therefore, and grows to an approximate height of about 60cm (2ft).

**Fatsia**   For a touch of the tropical atmosphere the shrub *Fatsia japonica*, which is evergreen, is worthy of consideration for its very attractive large palmate leaves. It has clusters of white flowers in the fall and grows to a height of about 6m (20ft) in warm climates. It is an ideal choice for a rather shady area and especially useful for town gardens.

**Forsythia**   A breath of spring is introduced to the garden if Forsythia is planted. It is a very handy shrub for early spring decoration, because if a few branches are cut while still tightly in bud, after Christmas it will flower very early indoors before the outdoor bush produces its floral display. The species *F. Spectabilis* has very bright yellow flowers and grows to a height of about 3m (10ft). 'Spring Glory' is a very lovely plant slightly smaller in growth, attaining a height of about 2.5m (8ft).

**Fuchsia**   Fuchsias bear fascinating ballerina-like flowers in the height of the summer and well into the autumn. The plants can be used in seaside gardens and can also be encouraged to form a very pretty hedge in coastal areas. There are many beautiful varieties such as 'Mrs. Popple', which has carmen sepals and a violet corolla. It is a very tough plant and will grow well in quite cold areas. The height is about 1.5–2m (5–6ft). Another hardy specimen is *F. Riccartonii*, and for quite a dwarf plant 'Tom Thumb' should be considered, as this grows only to a height of about 45cm (18in). This has violet and carmine colored flowers. There are very many named varieties. Fuchsia specialists' nursery catalogs should be obtained for a really comprehensive selection.

**Garrya**   For particular fascination in the very early part of spring, the evergreen shrub *Garrya elliptica* should be selected for its beautiful long silky catkins. It is a very useful shrub for planting against a wall and grows to a height of about 6m (20ft). It likes a semi-shady situation, and needs a warm climate.

**Griselinia**   For the really tough coastal site exposed to salt-laden air, or for any

*Below: for pure foliage effect, the various types of Elaeagnus are hard to beat. Elaeagnus pungens Maculata (top) has golden variegated foliage, and the type E. pungens (bottom) is also a useful shrub though not so attractive as its variegated leaf forms.*

reasonably exposed situation, the shrub *Griselinia littoralis* should be planted. It is an evergreen of upright habit and will grow well on limestone, but will not thrive on a heavy soil. Eventual height is about 16m (50ft) in California.

**Hamamelis** (*Witch Hazel*)   The Witch Hazel is a very useful shrub to have for winter flowering purposes. It produces peculiar twisted petals and these are reasonably fragrant. The variety *Hamamelis mollis* is excellent and has sweetly scented yellow flowers which are produced from December until about February. Height is about 3–8m (10–25ft).

**Hebe**   A useful evergreen range of shrubs is the Hebe, sometimes classified as Veronica. They will do well in sheltered areas but prefer a very well drained soil. They like semi-shade. There are lots of interesting varieties such as 'Autumn Glory', which has violet blue flowers in June to October. It is a useful front of the border shrub as it grows quite low, about 40cm (16in) high in fact. 'Carl Teschner' is hardy and has violet flowers in June. This is even smaller. *H. speciosa* is a very useful sort for planting in seaside gardens. It flowers in August to October with lilac colored blooms.

*Below : Hebes are good shrubs for seaside conditions, preferring a mild climate and well-drained soil.*

**Hibiscus**   A very attractive tall shrub producing flowers similar to the Hollyhock in August and well into the autumn. It requires a moderately sunny situation, and a well prepared site is essential. It grows about 2.5m (8ft) high. There are single and double flowered varieties. In the former the varieties such as 'Bluebird' and 'W. R. Smith' are particularly good: the former has blue flowers, the latter white flowers. Of the double flowering varieties, 'Jeanne d'Arc' is white and 'Ardens' has rose flowers.

**Hydrangea**   The Hydrangeas are useful shrubs for summer and autumn flowering. They like a semi-shaded situation and the variety *H. macrophylla* is the popular type used in most gardens. On acid soils blue flowers are produced but in limy situations pretty red or pinkish flowers are borne. The shrubs grow to a height of about 1m (3–4ft). There are two distinct flowering types. The mop heads include such types as 'Hamburgh' with deep pink flowers and 'Madam E. Mouilliere' with white flowers. Then there are the lace caps, where the flower heads are flat and very lacy. The variety *Mariesii* has pink flowers, *Veitchii* has very delightful white flowers. Heights are up to about 1.2m (4ft).

**Hypericum** (*St. John's Wort*)   A low growing shrub which is very useful as a weed suppressor and therefore a great time and labor saving plant. The variety *H. calycinum* is evergreen and has cup-shaped flowers produced from June to early autumn. It grows to a height of approximately 60cm (2ft). A semi-evergreen is 'Hidcote' which has quite large flowers which are golden in color and produces a bush shaped plant some 1m (3–4ft) in height.

**Ilex** (*Holly*)   For a Christmassy effect in a garden the Holly should be planted. These are evergreen and do well in shade or semi-shade. The variety 'Gold King' has golden variegated foliage and the variety 'Golden Queen' is another beautiful plant. Heights are up to about 5m (15–16ft).

**Kalmia**   *Kalmia latifolia* is an evergreen shrub for lime-free soils. The shrub has glossy leaves and pretty rose flowers which are produced in June. A semi-shaded site is ideal for this plant, and its eventual height is 5m (15–16ft).

**Kerria**   *Kerria japonica* is a shrub which produces single yellow flowers in April and May. The shrubs have slender branches and grow to a height of about 2m

*Left : Ilex 'Gold King'. Below, top : on acid soils hydrangeas produce blue flowers. Below, bottom : Lavendula spica, the common lavender, likes a dry location.*

(6ft). For a pretty double flowered variety with orange colored blooms *K. Pleniflora* should be considered. It is also an ideal plant for growing against a wall where its blossoms are displayed to advantage.

**Laurus** (*Laurel, Bay*)  A shrub for coastal areas is the Sweet Bay or *Laurus nobilis*. This is evergreen with aromatic foliage which is delightful to smell when the leaves are crushed in the fingers. It likes a semi-shaded position and grows to a height of at least 6m (20ft).

**Lavandula** (*Lavender*)  Another fragrant subject is the Lavender, which has attractive evergreen foliage. It is a shrub which grows better in the lighter well drained soils. The Old English Lavender is the variety *L. spica* growing to a height of about 60cm (2ft). 'Hidcote' is well known also, with beautiful silvery foliage. This is slightly dwarfer than *L. spica*. 'Twickel Purple' produces very eye-catching long purple flower spikes and has nice gray foliage. This grows to a height of about 60cm (2ft). Lavender is a particularly useful shrub for planting along edges of a border and especially down pathways and drives.

**Leycesteria** (*Nutmeg*)  The flowering Nutmeg, *Leycesteria formosa*, is a shrub which is useful for shady or semi-shady situations. It grows to a height of about 2m (6–7ft) and is particularly attractive with its very deep sea-green stems. It also has peculiar pendulous claret colored bracts which are produced in June.

**Ligustrum** (*Privet*)   A very common and popular hedging shrub is the Privet. This is a plant which will grow in a wide range of conditions, and the evergreen species include *L. japonicum* and 'Golden Wax' which is the golden version. The shrub grows to a height of about 3m (10ft). The Common Privet, *L. vulgare*, is another good hedging variety and it is tall growing, reaching over 5m (15–16ft).

**Lippia** (*Lemon Verbena*)   If the leaves of the frost-tender shrub *Lippia citriodora* are crushed a delightful lemon scent is produced. This shrub is popularly known as the Lemon Verbena. It produces tubular mauve colored flowers in August and grows to a height of about 1.2m (4ft), taller in warm climates.

*Below : Pittosporum is a pretty evergreen for mild areas, with flowers fragrant of orange blossom.*

**Magnolia**   Most gardeners want to have a magnolia in their garden and there are some beautiful varieties to select from. The first only grows well in a sheltered warm site however and the soil needs enriching with peat or composted vegetable waste. The evergreen *M. grandiflora*, 'Exmouth' has beautiful evergreen foliage which is glossy. Underneath the leaves a brown down is produced. Flowers are creamy white and beautifully fragrant, appearing from July into fall. Height is about 25–30m (80–100ft). *M. soulangiana* has white flowers produced in early spring and grows to at least 8m (25ft). The variety *Lennei* is one of the best types to plant, growing to the same height or more. This is a particularly good shrub to have in the smaller garden. Another beauty for the small garden is *M. stellata*, the Star Magnolia. This produces its fragrant flowers still earlier in the season. Height is about 6–8m (20–25ft).

**Mahonia**   For dealing with a shady situation the Mahonias are excellent. They are not too fussy either about their soil although they must have fairly well-drained sites. For a low growing plant growing some 1m (3–4ft) in height the variety *aquifolium* should be selected. The leaves are bronzy in color in the spring and eventually turn reddish in the winter. Flowers are fragrant yellow and it is an excellent plant for the smaller garden. The variety *Atropurpurea* has purple foliage throughout the year. The species *M. japonica* has very fragrant flowers which can be out at Christmas time. It is a much taller growing plant reaching a height of about 2m (6–7ft).

**Olearia** (*Daisy Bush*)   Olearia is an evergreen, and a very good shrub to plant at the seaside. It will grow well in a wide range of soils. The evergreen hybrid *O. haastii* is a rounded shaped shrub with small oval leaves, which produces white fragrant flowers in the summer. It likes semi-shade and grows about 3m (10ft) high, and is good for a windy seaside site in California.

**Osmanthus**   For fragrance, the evergreen shrub *Osmanthus delavayi* should be planted in every garden in mild climates, with care as far north as Long Island. It produces sweet-scented flowers in early spring. The height is about 60cm (2ft) plus. The species *O. illicifolius* has fragrant white flowers in the fall and is taller, growing to a height of about 6m (20ft).

**Osmarea**   For a specimen shrub or for use as a hedge *Osmarea burkwoodii* is evergreen and quite compact. It has pointed leaves and fragrant white flowers in April. It grows to 2.5m (8ft), or more in mild climates.

**Pernettya**   An evergreen which carries masses of very attractive berries is the Pernettya. It is a particularly useful shrub because the berries are borne throughout the winter. It is very important to appreciate the fact that in order to produce good berrying one male and *three* female plants should be planted together. Another point too is that this shrub requires a soil which is lime free. The male version is *P. mucronata*. Other beautiful varieties are 'Bell's Seedling' where the berries are big

and of a deep red color, 'Davies' Hybrids' which are pink, and for a white variety the name is simply 'White'. It is a fairly low-growing shrub attaining an approximate height of only 60–75cm (2–2½ft) and is reliable about to Long Island.

**Philadelphus** (*Mock Orange*)   The Mock Oranges have lovely arched branches covered with fragrant white flowers in June and July. They will grow quite well in a poor soil and will establish themselves in semi-shade. Some kinds are reasonably tall-growing, attaining an approximate height of about 2.5m (8ft). The following varieties can be especially recommended: 'Belle Etoile', which has single white flowers; *coronarius*, which is very fragrant and has yellowish white flowers; its variety *Variegatus*, which has a creamy white margin to its foliage; and *P. grandiflorus* which bears single white flowers, unfortunately without fragrance. This is a tall plant attaining a height of over 3m (10ft). Coming back to the smaller growing plants 'Sybille' grows to a height of up to 2m (6–7ft), and has white, very fragrant flowers. If you are looking for a Mock Orange which is quite low growing (some 1m (3–4ft) high) then the variety 'Manteau D'Hermine' flowers very freely, and has fragrant blooms which are creamy in color.

**Pieris**   Pieris is an attractive evergreen which has shiny narrow oval leaves. Its urn-shaped flowers are produced in March to May, and there are several attractive varieties to choose from. *P. floribunda* has creamy white flowers and produces a bushy and thick shrub. Height is about 2m (6–7ft). There are two varieties of the species *P. forrestii*. 'Fire Crest' has long racemes of large white flowers and the foliage is a brilliant red. This color is retained for several weeks. The height is about 2m (6–7ft). 'Forest Flame' has white flowers and red foliage in its young stage and flowers are produced in spring. This variety grows to a height of slightly less.

**Pittosporum**   Rather tender evergreen shrubs for a mild area. They are grown for their attractive foliage and small fragrant flowers.

**Potentilla**   There is much to be said for selecting a shrub which by itself will give as long a period of flowering as possible. Such a shrub is Potentilla. The flower display extends from about June to September. It is a shrub which does well in quite a wide range of soils. It can be planted in full sun or semi-shade. There are several interesting kinds such as *P. fruticosa* 'Abbotswood', which has white flowers

*Top left: Pernettya mucronata. Top right: Pernettya varieties may have pink, white or red berries. Above: even the humble privet, Ligustrum vulgare, can produce quite a striking show of jet black berries when it is allowed to grow unclipped.*

and grayish-green foliage. Height is about 60–120cm (2–4ft). 'Farreri' or 'Gold Drop' has fern-like foliage with buttercup yellow flowers. Height is a little taller. For a primrose yellow flower 'Katherine Dykes' is excellent, growing to a height of about 1–1.5m (2–5ft). 'Knaphill Seedling' has deep yellow flowers but only grows to a height of 60–120cm (2–4ft).

*Below : two unusual Rhododendrons are Rhododendron cinnibarinum roylei (top) with bell-shaped flowers, and Rhododendron keyseii (bottom) with tubular flowers.*

**Prunus** There are bush forms of the Prunus, and their maximum height after several years is only some 3–4m (10–13ft) or so. Particularly lovely varieties are *P. amygdalus tenella* 'Fire Hill' which has rosy crimson flowers produced in early spring. *P. glandulosa Albiplena* has double white flowers which are borne early. *P. triloba Multiplex* has attractive upright branches which can be covered with double pink flowers in rosette fashion. These are also produced in early spring.

**Rhododendron** We now come to a very important section amongst the shrubs, and these are the Rhododendrons, which include the beautiful Azaleas. Many of these are evergreen. These shrubs like a semi-shaded position and produce wonderful displays of flowers from about May to June. Many are the wonderful varieties available, but here are a few grouped according to colors. In the whites and yellows there is 'Cunningham's White' which grows about 2.5m (8ft) high, 'Loder's White' which grows a little taller and 'Sappho' which is white with a dark marking. In the pinks there is 'Betty Wormald' which is coral pink and grows about 2.5m (8ft) high, 'Mrs. R. S. Holford' which is deep salmon growing to about the same height, 'Pink Pearl' which is one of the finest pink flowers growing to a height of just a little more and 'Souvenir of Dr. Endtz', even deeper than 'Pink Pearl', which grows a bit shorter. Of the purples there is 'Purple Splendor' which is a rich deep color and is about the same in height and 'Blue Peter' which has beautiful pale lavender blue flowers and grows to a slightly greater height than most varieties.

There are some glorious red shades such as 'John Walter' with rich crimson flowers. Another beautiful glowing scarlet crimson is 'Britannia', and a lovely new introduction is 'Francesca'. This is semi-dwarf in habit, attaining a height of only about 1.5m (5ft) and is a very useful subject to have in the smaller garden. For a dark red color with attractive black spotting or blotching, the variety 'Lord Roberts' is excellent. This grows somewhat taller.

Where there is not a great deal of room in the garden for Rhododendrons it is a good idea to look at the low-growing varieties such as 'Blue Tit', which grows to a height of only some 60–75cm (2–2½ft). This particular variety has lavender blue flowers which are produced somewhat earlier. Another pretty little plant is 'Elizabeth', with orange-red flowers, growing to the same height. Slightly larger in growth is 'Praecox'. This has mauve flowers produced very early and grows to a height of about 90cm (3ft). This particular variety is semi-evergreen. There are some beautiful Azaleas which are deciduous, and these like either a sunny situation or partial shade. There are the Ghent hybrids which have fragrant flowers in late May or June in the North. The Knaphill and Exbury hybrids have trumpet-shaped flowers. Then there are the Mollis hybrids which have large flowers produced in trusses. These are among the earliest of the types, producing their flowering display ahead of the others. The Ghent and Knaphill hybrids attain a height of some 2–2.5m (6–8ft), whereas the Mollis hybrids grow only about 1–1.5m (3–4ft) in height. In the Ghent hybrids there is the lovely variety 'Bouquet de Flore' with double flowers in salmon pink striped white. Other lovely varieties are *Coccinea Speciosa* which is orange, and *Narcissiflorum* which has double yellow flowers, very fragrant indeed. Of the Knaphill and Exbury hybrids, 'Hotspur Red' has brilliant scarlet flowers with darker markings on the upper petals, and 'Satan' has geranium-red flowers. 'Cecile' has large salmon pink flowers, and for an orange vermilion color 'Fireglow' is exceptionally good. Of the Mollis azaleas 'Koster's Brilliant Red' is charming, and 'Hortulanus Witte' is another excellent variety.

Then there are the *Rhododendron luteum* types. These are very useful varieties because they thrive in slightly drier and poorer soils. The flowers are orange-yellow, perfumed and appear moderately early. This type is especially useful for the smaller garden because they are low growers and have a very attractive spreading habit. Height can be up to 3m (10ft). There are some other colors in the range such as 'Blue Danube' and among the reds 'Vuyk's Scarlet' is a very pretty plant. For a salmon orange color, 'Orange Beauty' should not be omitted, and for a beautiful bright pink choose 'Esmeralda'. For a startling white color the variety 'Palestrina' is excellent.

**Ribes** (*Flowering currant*)  These are very easy shrubs to grow as they are quite accommodating as far as their soil conditions are concerned. They produce their flowers early, and grow to a height of 1–2m (3–6ft). Especially lovely varieties are the Golden Currant *R. odoratum* and the variety *R. sanguineum* 'Pulborough Scarlet' which has very deep red flowers.

**Romneya**  For fragrance the Californian Poppy or *Romneya hybrida* shrub is worthy of inclusion in any shrub planting scheme. It produces white flowers in summer and grows to a height of about 2.5m (8ft). It is an excellent shrub for a position in full sun in climates like California.

**Rosmarinus** (*Rosemary*)  The evergreen Rosemary has aromatic gray-green leaves, and these can be taken when young for flavoring in cooking. It grows in full sun and will make a very good hedge. The variety 'Miss Jessop's' is an excellent one. *R. officinalis* produces bluish flowers in May and attains a height of approximately 1m (3–4ft).

**Sambucus** (*Elder*)  This shrub has large fragrant clusters of white flowers. The fruit are produced in midsummer, and the shrub is not too particular about its soil conditions. It is a useful mid-height shrub growing to about 2.5m (8ft). *S. canadensis Aurea* has very attractive golden leaves and produces black berries later on. Another beauty is the Golden Cut Leaf Elder or *Plumosa Aurea*. It grows to a height of about 2m (6ft). The fruit is used for jellies, pies and wines.

**Santolina**  Santolina is a very low growing shrub with aromatic leaves. It should have a light soil, however, and will not do well in the heavier types of soil. The Cotton Lavender, *Santolina chamaecyparissus*, has very narrow saw-edged leaves and produces pretty yellow flowers from June to August. It is a good hedging subject, growing to a height of about 75cm (2½ft). Another good variety is *S. c. Nana*, a dwarf form attaining a height of only about 30cm (1ft).

**Senecio**  Gray foliage is restful and very attractive in a planting scheme and in this respect the Senecio shrub is outstanding. A good sort is *S. laxifolius* which grows to a height of only about 1.25m (4ft).

**Skimmia**  A good berrying shrub is Skimmia. It has very pretty glossy leaves and is rather a slow-growing plant. It will not do well in a limy soil, and in order to obtain good berrying both the male and female forms must be planted. The female variety has red berries, and a good variety is *S. japonica rubella*. *S. laureola*, which is nicely fragrant, has white flowers in spring.

**Spartium**  A good shrub for the seaside garden, and especially one which has a light or limy soil, is the Spanish Broom (*Spartium junceum*). It has a nice fragrance and pea-shaped yellow flowers which are carried for most of the summer. The leaves are very thin and rush-like. For the Deep South and California.

---

**SEASIDE PLANTING**
Certain trees and shrubs are better adapted than others to the special conditions found in coastal gardens. The following are particularly recommended: see General Lists for fuller information.

Atriplex S
Buddleia S
Berberis S
Cytisus (Broom) S
Elaeagnus S
Escallonia S & C
Fuchsia S
Hydrangea S
Pittosporum S
Populus (Poplar) T
Sambucus (Elder) S
Senecio S
Spartium S
Ulex (Gorse) S
Yucca S

T: Tree   S: Shrub   C: Climber

**Spiraea** Deciduous shrubs which can be easily grown in most positions, though they flourish best in a loamy soil and in full sun. *S. bumalda.* 'Anthony Waterer' has brilliant carmine flowers in June and July, borne on flat heads in June, 60–90cm (2–3ft). *S. salicifolia* is a vigorous species with willow-like leaves and spikes of pale pink flowers in late spring. It grows to 2m (6ft). Many more species and named varieties are available.

**Symphoricarpus** (*Snowberry*) The Snowberry has fairly insignificant flowers; its chief attraction being the beautiful white berries produced in the winter. It is a shrub which the flower arranger would particularly welcome. *S. albus* has pink flowers and nice white berries, and grows to a height of about 1m (3–4ft). A particularly lovely variety is 'Mother of Pearl', which has exceptionally large white berries.

**Syringa** (*Lilac*) The Lilacs are very important shrubs to consider for the shrub border or even as specimen plants. There are many beautiful shades, and varieties can be obtained with single or double flowers. All are nicely fragrant.

**Tamarix** (*Tamarisk*) This is the ideal shrub for a seaside location, and it has very pretty fine feathery flowers and foliage. The variety 'Pink Cascade' has lovely rose pink flowers, and for a deeper pink *T. parviflora* is very attractive. Flowering time is May to June and approximate height is some 3m (9ft).

**Ulex** (*Gorse, Furze*) For a shrub growing about 1.5m (5ft) high, with beautiful yellow fragrant flowers in early spring, the Common Gorse (*Ulex europaeus*) is excellent. It is a very handy shrub to include where gardens have very dry soil. The height is about 1.5–2m (5–6ft). For a double flower variety *U. e. plenus* is particularly good, flowering a little later. This grows to about 1m (3–4ft).

**Viburnum** The Viburnums should be considered because they can be selected for a long season of flowering and also for the production of berries in the autumn

*Below: the red berries of Viburnum iantana are unusual in that they are first red and then ripen to black. Bottom: the ribbed leaves and deep blue berries of Viburnum davidii. Below, right: Viburnum opulus, the Guelder Rose. This is a yellow-berried form.*

and winter. They grow in most soils and are particularly useful for the small to medium-sized gardens as most of the varieties grow to a height of 1.5m (5ft) or more. The winter flowering varieties are best planted in a sunny position and *Viburnum fragrans* (not fully hardy) has white fragrant flowers in very early spring, a very useful time to have some color in the garden. One of the evergreen species is the tender *V. Tinus* Laurustinus. This flowers in winter–early spring and also has berries. It is quite happy in full sun or in a shaded situation.

The later flowering varieties like a semi-shaded situation. One particularly lovely fragrant white flowered type is *V. burkwoodii*, and another beautiful one is *V. carlesii*, which is also heavily fragrant and flowers in late spring. The Snowball tree (*V. opulus* Sterile) has lovely flowers of snowball shape and has yellowish leaves in the autumn. 'Pink Beauty' is a lovely pale pink flowered variety and bears scarlet berries in the autumn. For autumn berrying the tender *V. davidii* grows only to a height of some 60–75cm (2–2½ft). It is also an evergreen. The Guelder Rose (*V. opulus*) has lovely berries in the autumn and white flowers in June.

**Vinca** (*Periwinkle*) The Periwinkle is a lovely low-growing evergreen and extremely useful for covering banks, especially in shaded areas. It is not too particular about its soil either, and is happy in full shade or partial shade. The species *Vinca major* is evergreen and produces bright blue flowers in early spring. Another is *V. minor*, which is quite small and also flowers in spring.

**Weigela** Weigela is another lovely shrub for the garden which likes partial shade. The variety *W. florida* Foliis Purpureis has purple foliage and pinkish flowers. It grows to a height of about 2.5m (8ft) or more. There are some very pretty hybrid varieties such as 'Abel Carriere' which has carmine flowers and grows to approximately the same height. 'Bristol Ruby' has ruby red flowers and 'Newport Red' bright red flowers.

**Yucca** The Yucca is a lovely feature or focal point shrub to include in a planting scheme. The species *Y. filamentosa* is evergreen and has white pendulous flowers produced in July to August. The plant likes either full shade or partial shade and grows to a height of about 1.2–2m (4–6ft).

*Above, left: Weigela florida, a good shrub for partial shade.*
*Above: also for shade, this is the white-flowered form of Vinca minor with variegated leaves.*

POISONOUS SHRUBS AND TREES
Children are attracted by bright seeds and berries, so if you have young children it may be wise to avoid the following trees and shrubs altogether in your planting scheme.

*Cytisus scoparius* (Broom)—Seeds
*Daphne mezereum* (Mezereon)—All parts, particularly bark and berries
*Laburnum anagyroides* (Laburnum)—All, particularly bark and seeds. This tree causes the most cases of accidental poisoning
*Prunus laurocerasus* (Cherry laurel)—All, particularly leaves and kernels of fruit
Rhododendron species; Azalea and Kalmia species (Rhododendron, Azalea, Kalmia, American laurel, calico bush, sheep laurel, mountain laurel)—Leaves and flowers
*Taxus baccata* (Yew)—Leaves and seeds: the latter are deadly. The aril (red pulpy covering surrounding the seed) is the least harmful

# CONIFERS

*Opposite, top: conifers should be chosen not only for their variety of form but also for their wide color range which embraces all the shades of green. Opposite, bottom: dwarf conifers make excellent container specimens. This is the horizontal form of Juniperus sabina.*

Conifers are particularly beautiful plants, which give character to the garden all the year round with their wonderful variety of size and form. The size, color and texture of their foliage also varies, and many of them have the additional beauty of cones. In fact it is quite amazing how many subtle variations in the color green there are when one considers conifers. The green hues can range from the palest of greens to the blue-greens and blue-grays, and there are delightful golden and silvery colors too. As specimen plants few subjects can surpass the stately conifers. There are fortunately many different types: many are suitable for the fairly small garden, some will make great handsome specimens for the larger garden, and there are also dwarf kinds which are suitable for planting in the rock garden.

The conifers like a deeply cultivated soil and one which is well drained. They should have a good amount of organic matter worked in, such as very well rotted manure, peat or composted vegetable waste. Before planting a slow acting fertilizer such as sterilized bonemeal may be applied at the rate of 90–120g per sq. m (3–4 oz per sq. yd). The planting time for conifers is approximately from early November to about mid March. The conifers have fairly narrow and very small leaves which do not lose moisture rapidly and therefore they can be planted at a different time from other types of evergreen. There are, however, one or two conifers which do not transplant well, and a good example is *Cupressus macrocarpa*. Many conifers are obtainable in containers, and well grown container specimens are ideal as they will transplant extremely well with little or no check to growth.

*Below: well-chosen conifers provide interest all through the year.*

# A GENERAL LIST OF CONIFERS

**Araucaria** (*Monkey Puzzle*)   A fascinating conifer which is seen in many gardens is the Monkey Puzzle, *Araucaria araucana*. This has lovely glossy dark leaves in a tight overlapping spiral fashion, and the tree can grow at least 8–16m (25–50ft) high or more, so it requires a fairly large garden.

**Cedrus** (*Cedar*)   A conifer to be wary of unless you have a very large garden is the Cedrus. These can form very large trees in time, so should be kept well away from boundaries and house walls. A particularly beautiful specimen with silvery blue foliage is *C. atlantica glauca*. Lebanon Cedar (*Cedrus libani*) is slower growing than the previous specimen but when fully mature it is very large and spreading.

**Chamaecyparis**   A very popular conifer is the Chamaecyparis, closely related to the true cypresses (*Cupressus*). The variety *C. lawsoniana alumii* has bluish gray foliage borne in a spiral formation. It can be kept to a height of about 2.5m (8ft), and a row of plants kept to this height make a spectacular hedge quite quickly. For a narrow column of growth the variety *C. l. columnaris glauca* cannot be bettered. For more compact growth *C. l. erecta* is an ideal specimen which has yellow foliage. Under favorable conditions Chaemaecyparis can grow to 30m (100ft).

**Cupressocyparis**   A bigeneric hybrid of Cupressus and Chamaecyparis. A particularly lovely sort is *C. leylandii*, one of the fastest growing hedging subjects. Kept clipped back it fills out extremely well and has beautiful gray green foliage. It is an ideal subject for planting in coastal regions as it is quite resistant to salt-laden air and will quickly form a protective screen in exposed situations.

**Cupressus** (*Cypress*)   The conifer *Cupressus macrocarpa* 'Donard Gold' is a compact specimen which has lovely deep yellow foliage. It grows to about 3–3.5m (10–12ft) or more in height. Another beautiful specimen is *C. pyramidalis*.

**Juniperus** (*Juniper*)   With their aromatic foliage and gray green berries the junipers are ideal plants for any garden, and *Juniperus communis hibernica* is a particularly attractive specimen to acquire. It is a pillar growing type and fortunately can be used even in small gardens as it grows to only about 2m (6–7ft).

**Picea** (*Spruce*)   The spruces should not be omitted as they are attractive specimens with their pyramidal habit and closely packed branches. They are useful because they will grow in a wettish soil. The Norway Spruce, *Picea abies*, is popular as a Christmas tree. It is an attractive specimen for the garden but as it attains a height of a least 45m (150ft) or more when fully grown it needs plenty of room. For a smaller specimen *P. pungens glauca* 'Koster', known as the Blue Spruce, has silvery blue dense foliage and grows to a height of some 30m (100ft).

**Pinus** (*Pine*)   For the large garden the Pines should not be forgotten. Tender *Pinus radiata* (Monterey Pine) has long grassy green needles. It is a quick grower and easily attains a height of 25m (80ft). *Pinus sylvestris* (Scots Pine) has distinctive red bark on its trunk. It grows to a height of about 30m (100ft).

**Taxus** (*Yew*)   Another excellent hedging subject in the conifer range is the Yew, and *Taxus baccata* (Common Yew) can reach a height of 12–16m (40–50ft) eventually. *Taxus b. fastigiata*, has lovely dense green foliage, and with its upright columnar habit makes a particularly striking specimen plant. It grows tall eventually.

**Thuya**   Another beautiful conifer is *Thuya plicata atrovirens*. This has very dark green foliage and a slightly bushy habit. It is also useful for hedging but in the humid Pacific Northwest it can reach 60m (200ft).

# DWARF CONIFERS

One of the exciting things about the conifer family is that there are some delightful small-growing and spreading types of conifer which are particularly suited to the smaller garden. These are, of course, slow-growing, but they are fascinating subjects to include in any planting scheme. Here are some suggestions:

**Chamaecyparis**   *C. obtusa nana gracilis* has very beautiful deep green foliage and grows to a height of about 6ocm (2ft). Another lovely variety is 'Ellwood's Gold', which grows to a height of about 3ocm (12in). Yet another lovely specimen is *Chamaecyparis lawsoniana obtusa pygmaea*. As its pygmy name implies, it is a low spreading type of conifer, with lovely bronzy green foliage when it is well established. It grows to an approximate height of 30–6ocm (1–2ft). For a really lovely yellow variety you must try the variety *C. plumosa aurea nana*.

**Juniperus**   The dwarf Junipers are well worth considering, especially as they are very hardy. There are some lovely prostrate varieties such as *J. communis depressa aurea*, which grows to about 6ocm (2ft) and provides excellent ground cover. It has golden yellow shoots when young which gradually turn to bronze. Another mat-forming type is *J. horizontalis glauca*. It has blue green leaves and grows to a height of 3ocm (12in) or less. For slightly higher growth or upright habit the variety *J. communis compressa* is a lovely specimen growing to a height of about 3ocm (12in). It has dense bluish gray foliage.

**Picea**   For an individual conical conifer the variety *P. glauca albertiana conica* is really beautiful. It has bright green dense foliage and while it can grow very tall, it grows extremely slowly.

**Taxus**   A golden yellow leaved plant which is quite slow-growing is *Taxus baccata standishii*.

**Thuya**   For a dense compact plant with a narrow cone of growth *Thuya occidentalis* 'Holmstrup' is a real beauty. It has rich green foliage and stays rather small. A lovely golden yellow form is *T. orientalis aurea nana*. It has foliage of a lacy texture and forms a round compact bush. It, too, is slow-growing and remains comparatively low.

*Below : Thuya orientalis aurea nana forms a compact dwarf bush. Below, right : Juniperus communis compressa. The blue-gray foliage is shown to good advantage in this group grown on a scree.*

# CLIMBING & WALL SHRUBS

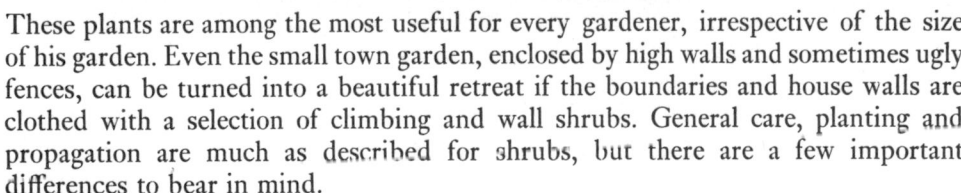

*Above, left: Lonicera periclymenum, the common honeysuckle. Above: honeysuckle grown on a pillar.*

These plants are among the most useful for every gardener, irrespective of the size of his garden. Even the small town garden, enclosed by high walls and sometimes ugly fences, can be turned into a beautiful retreat if the boundaries and house walls are clothed with a selection of climbing and wall shrubs. General care, planting and propagation are much as described for shrubs, but there are a few important differences to bear in mind.

First of all, if you are planting against a wall, the site may be very dry, so extra attention should be paid to the preparation of the site and the incorporation of a good deal of compost and water-retaining material The plant should be placed at least 30–45cm (12–18in) from the foot of the wall as a further precaution against drying out of the roots. Second, the true climbing shrubs, as opposed to wall shrubs, need some form of support unless they are self-clinging. Climbing shrubs which are situated near a wall should have their training material fixed in position, preferably before planting takes place. The success of climbing plants depends to a great extent on the means of support provided, and there are many proprietary designs available ranging from strips of wood fashioned in trellis design to metal and metal and plastic covered systems which look quite smart and are virtually maintenance-free. It must be appreciated that it is very difficult, if not impossible, to provide suitable or adequate training facilities once a climbing or trailing plant has become well established. Several climbing specimens can be planted in unusual situations such as against an old dead tree stump. The plant will cover this natural support quite effectively and what could have been an eyesore is easily transformed into a very attractive feature in the garden. Many of the climbers are also highly effective when trained over supports such as pergolas or pillars, and nothing looks nicer than a covered path or archway clothed with Wisteria, honeysuckle or Clematis.

SOME SCENTED SHRUBS
Many shrubs have perfumed flowers along with their other attributes. These will be especially valuable planted near the house or on a patio or terrace, where their fragrance can be most enjoyed. See General Lists for fuller information on those mentioned here.

Chimonanthus (Wintersweet) S
Clerodendron S
Daphne S
Hamamelis (Witch Hazel) S
Lavandula (Lavender) S
Lonicera (Honeysuckle) C
*Mahonia japonica* S
Osmanthus S
Osmarea S
Philadelphus (Mock Orange) S
Rosmarinus (Rosemary) S
Syringa (Lilac) S

T: Tree    S: Shrub    C: Climber

**Abutilon**  A tender to half-hardy shrub which can be grown in more favored and sheltered gardens. It likes full sun and is ideal for trailing against a warm wall. It is a plant which likes a well-drained soil too. A lovely species is *A. megapotamicum*. This has lantern-shaped flowers from early spring onwards. It grows to a height of about 3m (9ft). Another lovely species is *A. vitifolium*. This has single mauve flowers in late spring. It is a taller growing plant, attaining a height of some 3–8m (10–25ft) or so. It is not a variety for a cold or exposed garden however.

**Acacia** (*Mimosa, Wattle*)  The beautiful Mimosa, *Acacia dealbata*, has beautiful yellow flowers in early spring and also silvery foliage. It grows to a considerable height in California.

*Perhaps one of the best-loved Clematis hybrids is 'Nelly Moser'.*

**Aristolochia**  *Aristolochia durior*, known popularly as Dutchman's Pipe, has very pretty pitcher-formed flowers which have yellowish-green and brown tints. These are produced in summer. The leaves are attractive also, being large and heart-shaped. Height is up to about 6m (18ft) or more. It is a very useful plant for trailing over pergolas or archways.

**Campsis** (*Trumpet Vine*)  This is a beautiful plant for a late summer display. *C. grandiflora* has orange and red trumpet-shaped flowers but it is a plant for the Deep South and California only.

**Clematis**  No garden would be complete without its Clematis. These provide beautiful color from about April to October according to variety. It should be appreciated, however, that to get the best out of these plants the roots should be shaded from the direct rays of the sun, and that the plants like a chalk subsoil.

One section of Clematis is a spring flowering plant which flowers on last season's wood. These are pruned by cutting out flowering growths immediately after they have flowered, so that healthy shoots for next season's display are encouraged to form. There are many lovely varieties in this section including *C. armandii*, an evergreen which produces lots of very fragrant flowers in April. The species *C. montana* has small starry white flowers produced in spring.

Another type of Clematis flowers on short growths of the past season's wood, and flowers are produced mostly in summer and sometimes in October. The latter flowering display is produced at the tips of the new shoots produced that year. The plants are pruned by cutting out weak and dead wood in the spring. New growths form during the flowering season and should be trained in after the dead flowers have been cut away. There are lots of beautiful varieties. Particularly good varieties include 'Barbara Jackman' with deep mauve flowers, 'Lady Northcliffe', deep lavender, producing flowers in June to October, and 'Nelly Moser', which has large white flowers tinted pink with a red bar down the petals from May to September.

A third section flowers later on in the summer on new season's growth. The plant should be cut back in February or March and new growths should be trained as soon as they are produced. Particularly outstanding varieties in this section include 'Ernest Markham', which has petunia-red flowers in July or September, 'Comtesse De Bouchard', which has pale pink flowers in July to October, and *C. jackmanii*, which has violet purple flowers in July to August.

**Cotoneaster**  The Cotoneasters are very useful plants to consider because they can be established in a sunless position. One of the most useful plants is *C. horizontalis* which has scarlet berries. Another, which is evergreen, is *C. lacteus*.

**Escallonia**  The Escallonias are evergreen plants, ideal for clothing walls. Good kinds include 'C. F. Ball' which has deep red flowers, *E. edinensis* with pink flowers, and 'Slieve Donard' with apple-blossom pink flowers.

**Hedera** (*Ivy*)   The ivies are self-clinging evergreen plants and will quickly clothe walls, etc. Although many gardeners fight shy of this plant they are very useful as long as the wall is sound. It is not wise however to plant against an old wall where mortar is crumbling, as the plant can cause damage by loosening the mortar. The variety *H. helix* 'Gold Heart' is a very pretty plant, and so is 'Jubilee', which has small silver and green variegated leaves.

**Hydrangea**   The Climbing Hydrangea, *H. petiolaris*, is a plant which is not appreciated as much as it should be for use in a north aspect. It has attractive flat heads of white flowers in late spring. It is self-clinging and grows to about 6m (20ft).

**Jasminum** (*Jasmine*)   The common or summer jasmine, *J. officinale*, is a very attractive climbing plant with trumpet-shaped flowers, and very easy to grow. A variety which is delightfully scented and which is extremely useful for growing up pergolas is *J. officinale* Grandiflorum. It has white flowers in summer and will reach heights of at least 10m (30ft). The winter jasmine, *J. nudiflorum*, has very bright yellow flowers produced from the autumn until April. It grows to an approximate height of about 5m (15–16ft).

**Lonicera** (*Honeysuckle*)   The honeysuckles are very popular climbing plants. They will grow against a wall and are also very attractive when trained over an archway. It is advisable to appreciate the fact that the varieties *L. japonica* Halliana and *L. j. repens* are very rampant. The following varieties should be seriously considered: *L. fragrantissima*, with scented cream flowers in early spring followed by red berries, about 2.5m (8ft); *L. j.* Halliana, exceptionally useful for training over pergolas, with fragrant white flowers in June to October; and the Dutch Honeysuckle (*L. periclymenum* Belgica), also useful for training over pergolas and archways, with pale rosy-purple fragrant flowers late spring to early summer.

**Passiflora** (*Passion Flower*)   If a warm wall and sunny situation can be provided, and also shelter, the Passiflora should be tried. A beautiful sort is *P. caerulea* which is multicolored. It is very fragrant and produces its display for much of the summer. Another beautiful variety is 'Constance Elliott' which has white flowers.

**Polygonum** (*Russian Vine*)   A very quick growing climber is always useful, and certainly *Polygonum baldschuanicum* is the one to select. It can grow about 6m (20ft) in a season without much trouble at all. It produces its flower panicles from summer to fall.

**Pyracantha** (*Firethorn*)   Pyracantha is an attractive climber which produces berries. It is ideal for training against a wall or a fence. It can attain a height of at least 5m (15–16ft). Beautiful types to select from include *P. angustifolia*, an evergreen which produces pretty orange berries. 'Mojave', another evergreen, has orange-red berries. The variety *P. rogersiana*, evergreen, is useful as a bush type of climber.

**Vitis** (*Vine*)   For delightful autumn leaf display the Vitis is superb. It is a plant which is ideal for training over pergolas or other archways. The variety *V. coignetiae* has large leaves which turn to a lovely crimson shade in the autumn. It produces scented flowers in summer, followed by fascinating grape-like fruits. *V. c.* Purpurea is its more handsome variety with colorful foliage.

**Wisteria**   Another very popular climbing plant, which is a quick grower and can be used to cover many areas such as walls, pergolas and even the old stumps of trees. It flowers in late spring. For an attractive pink colored flower *W. floribunda* Rosea is ideal. *W. sinensis* is very fragrant and has very beautiful lilac flowers.

*Above: two lovely wall shrubs for winter color are Jasminum nudiflorum (top), and Cotoneaster.*

# Roses

# Roses

Since the early days rose breeders, especially in France, have concentrated on improving their stocks of roses, aiming for more vigorous growth, bigger and better blooms, different colors and of course trying to increase the gorgeous fragrance which so many roses provide us with today. Some of the famous rose breeders include Wilhelm Kordes, Charles Mallerin, Francis Meilland, and in Britain great growers such as Sam McGredy, Harry Wheatcroft and many leading rose nurseries such as Cants, Fryers, Gregories, Harkness, Le Grice, and Mattock. In America many have been produced by Jackson and Perkins, Paul Howard and others. It is a fascinating task and perhaps few gardeners realize that thousands or sometimes virtually millions of seedlings are grown out of which only a few will show promise. These are then selected for further cultivation and from these perhaps only one may prove its worth and be brought on to the market as another worthy rose to be included among the great names.

## Preparing the ground for roses

It is often said that roses will grow anywhere or in fact in any soil. This is only partly true. Roses are quite accommodating plants and will tolerate a wide range of soil conditions, but to get the best from your roses you must prepare the site thoroughly beforehand. One important consideration must be that of drainage. This is of prime consideration where the garden is unfortunately situated on heavy or sticky clay soils. Planted without due care, roses in these conditions will produce sorry specimens, and will never grow into really first class plants bearing good displays of blooms. Where the ground is wet and heavy it should be deeply dug, incorporating gritty material and humus to open up the close soil particles. The incorporation of large quantities of organic matter in the form of well-rotted manure, composted vegetable waste or horticultural peat should improve the state of this type of soil. In particularly poor conditions it will pay to place some broken rubble at the bottom of the trenches to allow surplus water to drain away. In any case soils must be dug to the full depth of the spade and on soils which are not terribly wet or heavy but which are certainly not light it is good practice to fork over the bottom of the trench to loosen up the subsoil.

All soils should have plenty of organic matter incorporated as previously described, and the rate of application is approximately one good bucketful to the square meter (square yard). Light soils especially could do with extra amounts of this invaluable organic matter so that soil moisture is retained for as long as possible, and for this purpose horticultural peat is an ideal medium. It should be moistened a little before digging in.

About three or four days before planting takes place a general or balanced fertilizer should be scattered evenly over the beds and then either lightly forked in or thoroughly raked in. A slow-acting fertilizer can also be applied, such as sterilized bonemeal, which is given at the rate of 90–120g per sq. m (3–4oz per sq. yd). The general fertilizer can be applied at the rate of 45–60g per sq. m (1½–2oz per sq. yd).

## Planting the roses

When is the best time to plant? This can be from about mid October into December in the South. Where this is not possible, the plants can be planted in the spring, but no later than leafing out time. It goes without saying of course that no planting should take place when conditions are not suitable, which means that plants should never be put in when the ground is wet or frosty or covered with snow. If plants arrive during a difficult period of weather they can be heeled into the soil. This is done by removing the wrappers and then placing the plants singly along the rows in a shallow trench, watering in and then replacing the soil which must be firmed by the feet. Another system is to leave the plants in their bundles or packing, placing them in a shed or garage where they can be protected from hard frosts. If you buy your plants grown in their own containers from a nursery or a garden center you can plant these virtually at any time of the year except of course when ground is in poor condition or frozen. The quality of roses these days has been greatly improved, but it still pays to shop around and only buy the best and healthiest plants. One can buy good quality plants from nurseries, garden centers and some other stores. Perhaps the best way of buying your plants is to obtain some of the beautifully illustrated catalogs produced by specialist rose growers, and from these you can make your own choice with the help of very well produced color reproductions from the tremendous range of roses which these specialist growers have to offer. It does pay to purchase roses which are a little more expensive than the general run-of-the-mill plants. One is then assured of top quality plants which, if planted in well prepared sites, will give many years of rewarding displays.

**Planting distances**  Standard roses should be planted at least 90cm (3ft) apart, and the hybrid tea and floribunda roses 45cm (18in) apart. Where these plants are of particularly strong growth they may need 60cm (2ft) or even more. The beautiful shrub roses need to be spaced about 1.5m (5ft) apart, and the climbers and ramblers at least 2.5m (8ft) apart. The delightful miniatures are the closest spaced plants, going in at approximately 30cm (12in) apart.

No matter where a rose is planted it is important to give it plenty of root room and the planting hole should always be excavated a foot or so wider than the full extent of the rose roots. The correct depth to plant is at the point where the original soil level shows on the plants. It is also important to remember that the junction of the rootstock must not be buried by more than an inch or two. Where roses such as standards need staking, the stake should be driven into the center of the hole before the rose bush or tree is placed in position. This prevents the damage to the roots which would occur if the stake were inserted after planting had taken place. Before planting, it is an excellent idea to prepare some special soil which can be worked around the roots before the main bulk of the soil from the excavated planting hole is returned. A suitable mixture is a bucketful of soil to half a bucket of peat, plus about 45g (1½oz) of sterilized bonemeal (or, better still, a little superphosphate can be worked in beforehand).

Before you attempt to plant any of your roses you must examine them carefully to see if there are any damaged parts especially on the roots. Any damaged roots should be carefully cut off with a sharp pair of shears. Good quality roses are

*Below: the rose bush is placed in the hole and fine prepared soil worked around the roots. The soil is then firmed with the feet. The procedure is the same for standard roses, except that a strong stake is inserted first.*

*Above : two lovely yellow shrub roses are Rosa primula (top), a fragrant primrose color, and 'Frühlingsgold'.*

generally ready for planting immediately, but if there are signs of some dead or damaged branches or shoots on the actual plants these must be cut off cleanly to a bud using pruning shears. Also examine the root systems and if they are at all dry then it is a good plan to soak the roots in a bucketful of hot water for a few hours before planting takes place. Again, quality roses will arrive nicely packed, with plenty of damp moss or other material around the roots to keep them moist during transit to your address.

Place the plant in the center of the planting hole and then carefully spread out the roots all around the base of the hole. Then add your special planting mixture, trickling it in between the roots and gently firming in place with the fingers. Return the excavated soil carefully, making sure that it is well broken down beforehand and, as the soil is replaced, gently—but only gently—firm the soil with the feet. Finally rake or fork over carefully to bring the soil level with the surrounding ground. Likewise, give the plants a watering to settle them in and keep them moving, and bank up the soil around the plants as high as it will mound to prevent drying out.

Where roses require staking (such as the standard type of rose) the plants should be arranged carefully in the planting hole so that the main stem of the plant is placed comfortably close to its stake. Under no circumstances try to bend or pull the rose stem to the stake otherwise this can cause damage. The stake itself should be quite substantial, and either a metal or wooden stake should be used. If wood, it should be at least 2.5cm (1in) square and suitably treated well beforehand against rot. For this purpose the horticultural or green grade of Cuprinol is ideal. The actual tying material should be carefully considered also. Nowadays there are some excellent plant or tree ties which can be used. These are malleable so that there is no danger of chafing, and many of them can be adjusted. If you prefer to make your own rose tie then first of all bind around the stem carefully but not too tightly with some cushioning material such as old sacking. Then make the tie and tie round this area. This banding will prevent the tie material chafing the actual stem of the rose.

Climbers or ramblers are not difficult to plant either. Where a rose is planted against a wall it is important to increase the amount of organic matter in the planting hole, because the area immediately beneath or around the wall's foundations usually dries out rapidly and this compost material or organic matter is of vital importance to preserve the moisture. The hole for the plant should be dug out about 30cm (12in) away from the wall and prepared as for the ordinary types of roses. Plants planted against training material, such as an archway, should also be planted about 30cm (12in) away from the base of the main support of the feature. It is important with climbing and trailing plants to tie them in carefully initially so that their growth can be controlled effectively. In subsequent months occasional tying in is important to keep the plant in orderly fashion. Roses can be trained most effectively against large wall surfaces but for this purpose they need a framework against which they are fastened or trained. This framework can consist of wooden trellis suitably treated against rot if it is a soft wood. Cedar wood can be used, but this is rather expensive and unfortunately a little weak when used in the small sections required for trellis work. Ideally horizontal galvanized steel wires can be used, or the plastic covered wires attached to hooks or eyes which are rawlplugged into the mortar joints on the wall. Another system is to use the plastic covered steel rod type of prefabricated plant support which looks extremely neat when fixed into position. Where a large area of wall is to be covered with a climbing rose, however, this latter type of training material can be rather expensive to erect.

### General care of roses

The main cultural requirement during the growing season is to keep weeds down, especially around the bedding roses, and this can be done with a Dutch hoe, although it may be necessary in some cases to do a bit of hand weeding. It is also important to keep plants well watered during periods of dry weather, and roses appreciate the occasional feed of either a granular type of rose fertilizer, or a liquid feed which can be watered in or sprayed overhead as a foliar feed.

Roses appreciate a mulch or top dressing round the base of their stems with some well-rotted manure or composted vegetable waste. The depth to which this mulch is applied is approximately 5–8cm (2–3in). The dressing helps to conserve soil moisture and also it helps to suppress young weed seedlings. It is a good plan to apply a dressing of a fertilizer which will harden up the plants before winter sets in. This prevents losses during severe weather, and a suitable fertilizer for this purpose is sulfate of potash, which should be applied at rates not exceeding 15g per sq. m ($\frac{1}{2}$oz per sq. yd). The most suitable time to apply this dressing is in August.

### Types of roses

There are six main groups of roses which are particularly invaluable for the gardener. These are the hybrid tea, floribunda and grandiflora, shrub, old fashioned, climber and finally the miniatures.

**Hybrid tea roses** For the finest and most beautifully shaped flowers the hybrid tea roses cannot be bettered. They are readily identified by the high pointed center to the blooms. The flowers are carried either in small clusters or singly, and the flowering period is approximately from June to October. Usually the plants are moderately high or in bush form ranging from about 60cm (2ft) to about 90cm (3ft).

*Below: 'Super Star', a fine hybrid tea rose.*

# Roses

**Floribunda roses** The floribunda roses produce smaller flowers but in larger clusters or groups. There is a little more variety in form as some are single, others semi-double and there are even some really beautiful fully double blooms. There is variety in the actual shape of the flower; the grandiflora type are like hybrid teas with pointed centers, others are reasonably flat or loosely formed or very similar to rosettes. The plants are bushy and relatively dwarf like the hybrid teas and the flowers are produced at the same period as the hybrid teas.

**Shrub roses** These are hardy, dependable, and their growth is much freer and larger. Many varieties produce flowers reasonably continuously during the period June and July, but most only have one flush of flowers and then finish their display.

**Old fashioned roses** The old fashioned roses are particularly delightful, though most only flower once in the season in approximately June or July. They have the advantage, however, of great versatility in their growth and their flower formation. There are those varieties with large fully double flowers, others are rather flat but still fully double, and there are also the moss roses which have a moss-like outgrowth on the flower stems and the green sepals which surround the flower buds. Most of the shrub roses are very fragrant and so too are the old fashioned roses.

**Climbers and ramblers** Most of the climbers have flowers of the hybrid tea type, while others closely resemble the floribunda or shrub varieties. Most flower successively from about June to late October but some only flower over a very short period. The ramblers are an example of roses which only have a short flower display. Most of the ramblers have pretty small to medium sized flowers which are produced in very attractive large clusters.

**Miniature roses** Finally one has the delightful miniature roses which grow to a height of approximately 30cm (12in) maximum. They have very dainty tiny flowers of a rosette type and these are produced in very eye-catching clusters. There is a succession of flower display from about June to late October.

Of particular interest are the shrub roses. These provide a touch of nostalgia and a group of them can give the atmosphere of the old world cottage garden. There are several different types of shrub rose which can be purchased. The white rose *Rosa X alba* is a very robust shrub growing up to a height of about 1–1.5m (3–5ft). They flower from June to July, have bluish leaves and a glorious scent. They also produce attractive oval hips. For really superb fragrance and for a long continuous display of flower, the Bourbon roses (*Rosa X borboniana*) are delightful plants to have. There are also the very attractive cabbage roses (*Rosa X centifolia*). They have very rich scents as well and flower from about June to July. The moss roses are an offspring from the centifolias and are mostly semi-perpetual flowering types with a rich deep green (or in some cases a wine red) type of moss which makes them particularly attractive. They have delicate colors and a very rich perfume.

The china roses, or *Rosa chinensis*, flower in June. They can then flower well into the autumn and produce masses of beautiful blooms. The Damask roses (*Rosa X damascena*) have beautifully rich perfume and heads of nodding flowers. They flower from about June to July. The French rose (*Rosa gallica*) makes a compact shrub with flowers borne very upright on stems. These roses are semi-perpetual flowering, but the best flowering period is from June to July. They have pointed and finely toothed foliage. The hybrid musk roses have exquisite perfume and quite a long flowering period. They have semi-double flowers and are ideal for hedging. The hybrid perpetual roses have semi-double blooms with large globular shaped flowers. They are very richly scented. There is another group, the modern hybrid shrub roses; these flower from June to July and are richly perfumed. *Rosa moyesii* are

*Below and opposite : pruning roses is largely a matter of cutting out weak growth and pruning back the remaining growths to keep the plant well-shaped and vigorous. A newly-planted climbing rose (below) should be pruned back severely to suitably positioned buds. The four pictures (opposite) show how a typical hybrid tea rose might be pruned. Weak and badly-placed growth is first cut right out to admit light and air. The strongest growths are shortened to two to four dormant buds and medium growths are cut back harder to about two buds. This fairly severe pruning of hybrid teas encourages stronger growth and better flowers.*

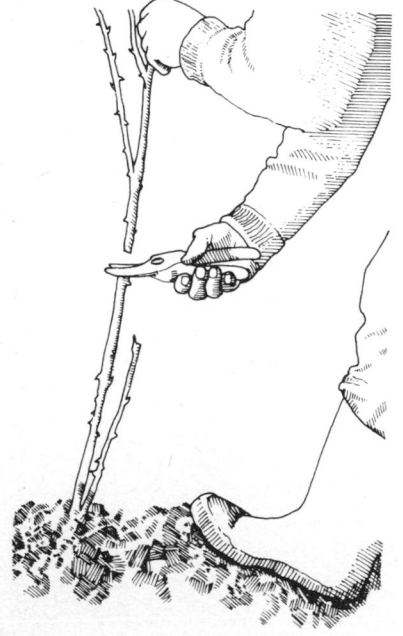

noted for their bottle-shaped fruits which are produced in the autumn. They all have single flowers on strong growth. Most of the roses mentioned in this section have an approximate height of 1–2m (3–6ft).

There are several shrub roses which are particularly useful as hedges. The only drawback is that they lose their leaves during the autumn and are therefore bare during the winter. They are best planted fairly close together to produce a quick dense amount of growth. Some of the best roses for this purpose are the old or *rugosa* types because these produce particularly dense foliage. They also have the attraction of a long flowering period. Some make fairly tall hedges, growing to a height of at least 1.2m (4ft). Where a lower form of growth is required the old *gallica* roses should be selected. One advantage of the rose hedge is the fact that with their thorns they produce a very good barrier to animals and children.

### How to prune roses

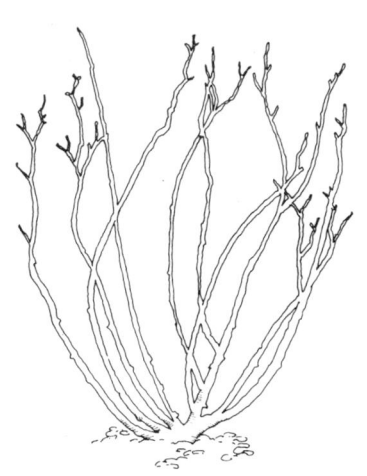

The main aim of pruning is to encourage as much healthy new growth as possible which will bear the best quality flowers. Another reason is to keep the plant in a good shape. The rose bush or climber should never be allowed to become overcrowded, and another aim of pruning is to keep the growths nicely spaced apart and under no circumstances to have a plant with a crowded center, especially in the bush roses.

Good pruning can only be carried out with the use of a suitable pair of pruners and the blades must be extremely sharp. A blunt shear will only make a ragged or jagged cut into which disease spores may enter later on. Most pruning cuts should be made to a suitable bud or eye, which can be either a growth bud or a plump flower bud. The angle at which the cut is made is very important also. The cut should be made not more than 5mm ($\frac{1}{4}$in) above the eye or bud and it should be slightly angled away from the bud. This allows moisture to drain away, but a cut made the other way round with the slope entering the bud or pointing towards the bud will encourage moisture or rainfall to fall around the bud and could cause rotting or disease problems.

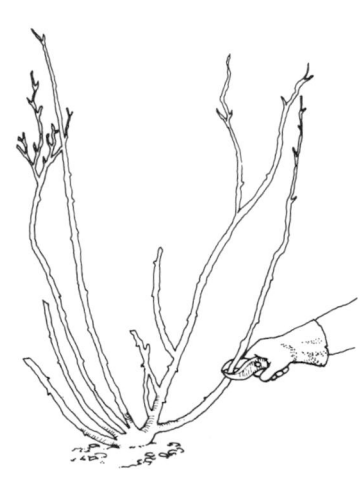

What is the best time to prune roses? There is a certain amount of controversy over this point; gardeners in mild areas may prune in autumn or winter, others like to leave their pruning until the spring. Most experts would agree however that in the colder areas of the country the most suitable time is usually when danger of hard frosts and severe weather has passed. For other areas, in reasonable conditions, the pruning period can be from about January to early March. If pruning is carried out in the winter in cold areas and a mild period follows, early growth can be encouraged which could be damaged by late frosts. Later pruning means that growth will not commence until well into the spring period when the danger of frost damage is relatively over.

**Pruning newly planted roses**  After planting, all the roses with the exception of the climbing sorts must be pruned quite hard. The strong growths on the plant should be cut back to within three to five growth buds of the soil level. The weaker growths can be cut back to one or two buds and thin shoots are best cut out completely. In the case of the climbing sorts which are known as climbers they should have their strong growths cut back by approximately one third of their lengths, medium growths cut back by about two-thirds, and the weak growths removed completely.

**Hybrid teas** benefit from hard pruning once established and a mistake many gardeners make is being too kind-hearted and not cutting growths back hard enough. A good plant growing in well prepared soil will make an amazing amount of growth despite the fact that its original growth has been cut really hard back to near ground level. This hard pruning really does pay off with the hybrid teas because it produces some lovely young growth which produces really large well-formed flowers. The strong growths on newly planted hybrid teas should be shortened to between two and four dormant buds and for the medium growth the shoots should be cut back to about two buds. If there are any old or thin growths these should be cut out completely. If you are keen on showing at your local show then very severe pruning is ideal for the production of quality flowers.

**Floribundas** and **grandifloras** are pruned in a similar way but in this case the strong growths can be cut back to about six buds, the medium growths to about four buds and weak growths can be cut back a little harder to two buds. Very thin wood again is best cut right out. For the **polyantha** roses the main growths should be cut back by about half their length and thin, weak or dead wood, if any, should be cut out completely. The **climbing roses** have their healthy young stems cut back to about one-third to two-thirds of their length, but this will depend on the amount of room available against the wall or fence. Any old or diseased growth and thin stems should be removed completely. **Ramblers** which make a lot of their new growth from the base should be pruned as soon as possible after they have produced their flowering display. Their pruning is very similar to raspberries in the fruit garden when the old stems which have borne the flowers should be cut right out and the new growth trained in their place. Shrub roses are pruned quite lightly and usually they only require thinning and the removal of dead, diseased or worn out growth.

It is important to appreciate the fact that, where standard roses are being grown, any growths which arise from below the main head of the plant will be unwanted, as they are what is known as suckers and will never produce flowers. It is important therefore that these are cut right back to the main stem as soon as they are noticed.

*Below : the old-fashioned roses can have an attractive display of hips as well as flowers. This is Rosa moyesii.*

### Propagating roses

This is a fascinating part of rose cultivation, and a cheap and relatively easy way of increasing favorite varieties. One method is by using **cuttings**: the shrub and rambler roses and some bush varieties can be increased this way. The growth should be selected from well-ripened young shoots which are usually ready in October or November. The selected shoot should be cut to a length of about 30cm (12in) and taken from the stem just above a bud. Afterwards the base of the shoot should be cut cleanly through with a sharp knife or pair of pruners making the cut just below a bud. The cuttings are then inserted in a hormone powder or liquid and then placed about 15cm (6in) deep in a shallow trench, the bottom of which has been lined with some sharp sand. Select a sheltered position outdoors for this purpose, and a light soil is best. The soil should be carefully replaced, and as this is done it should be gently firmed with the feet. Here the cuttings will remain until the following autumn. Keep an eye on watering whenever necessary and by the end of the following year they should have made sufficient roots so that they can be lifted carefully and planted out elsewhere in their permanent flowering quarters.

Most roses however are propagated by **budding**, especially the hybrid teas. The principle is that an eye or growth bud is budded on to a wild rootstock. It is essential to purchase these special rootstocks or produce your own from suckers. One of the best is *Rosa canina*. Another, and the most popular, is *Rosa multiflora*. For standard plants the rootstock *Rosa rugosa* is the best. The selected rootstocks should be planted in November in rows about 30–38cm (12–15in) apart, and the crown or collar of each plant should be well covered. The following year, in July or August, these rootstocks will be ready for budding. The bud for this purpose must be chosen from a really healthy plant and from a good firm stem. A growth which has just produced its flowers will be quite suitable. The stem (or stems if several buds are to be taken) can be cut from the plant to a length of about 30cm (12in) and then the thorns should be carefully pulled off and all the leaves cut off but leaving about 1cm (½in) of the leaf stalk on the stem. The selected bud is then cut out carefully using a very sharp knife. Ideally a special budding knife should be purchased from a good garden shop or garden center. A cut into the stem is started about 1cm (½in) above the selected bud and the knife is guided through the stem behind the bud going a little deeper behind the bud and then coming out about 1cm (½in) or so below the bud. What you should have then is a complete bud with a small piece of leaf stalk attached, with a sliver of stem and flesh 1cm (½in) above and below the bud itself. The next stage is to peel back the bark of the shield or the piece of bud and this sliver of wood is then discarded. What you should be left with then is the outer skin of the stem with all the flesh removed, and you can see the tiny bud inside which appears as a small pimple. Do examine the prepared bud because if there is no little pimple but a hollow it is possible that the bud has been torn out, and this bud will be of no use.

You must now turn your attention to the stock in which this bud or the buds will be grafted. The soil should be very carefully scraped away from near the base of the rootstock and the area just above the exposed roots should be wiped clean with a damp cloth. Then, using the budding knife, make a T-shaped cut about 2.5cm (1in) long into the bark and close to these roots. The cut must not be made deeply but just into the wooded tissue. If you purchase a budding knife the opposite end of the handle to the blade will be wedge-shaped, and this can be inserted carefully into the cut, prying the bark slightly away on either side of the T. The bark is then carefully folded outwards. Taking the prepared bud and holding it by the short leaf stalk the bud is carefully slipped into the T cut. With a little practice you will find that the prepared buds will enter into the T-shaped cut in the stock quite easily. Once in place the top end of the shield of the bud is cut off cleanly and then the flaps of the T cut are carefully closed around the bud or shield. The bud is then finally secured in position by wrapping raffia or rubber budding strips above and below the short leaf stalk and tying neatly in place.

The position of the bud is important, according to the type of rose tree you want. For a low-growing bush rose the prepared bud is inserted in the stock just below soil level. For standards the stock should be much higher, either 1m (3½ft) for full standards or 75cm (2½ft) for half standards, and the buds are inserted around the stem at the required height.

## Popular varieties

There are obviously many hundreds of beautiful rose varieties on sale today and every year there are new ones added to the list. However it is possible to pinpoint some particularly lovely varieties in the different types of roses, most of which can be relied upon to give an extremely good account of themselves during the flowering season.

**Hybrid tea roses**   There are some wonderful colors in these roses. Let us take a look at the **yellow** shades first of all. One of the most outstanding varieties is 'Golden Prince' which is deep yellow. It is fairly disease-resistant and makes an even upright bush. Another lovely variety, perhaps the best-loved rose we have, with light to deep yellow flowers with pink edging on the petals is 'Peace'. This variety produces really large well shaped blooms which are particularly useful for cutting and for local flower shows. 'Oregold' has primrose yellow blooms and the foliage is particularly attractive as it has good substance. An orange-yellow shade is particularly effective in roses, and an outstanding variety is 'Yankee Doodle'. This has a lovely fragrance and the flowers are produced on nice long straight stems which makes it a particularly useful flower for cutting and home decor. 'Eclipse' has a superb fragrance and lovely pointed yellow buds and flowers. Another lovely variety is 'Chicago Peace' which is yellow with delightful pink shadings. It has little perfume but the blooms are particularly well shaped.

How lovely the **pink** roses are, and there are some really beautiful varieties in this

*Roses can be grafted onto a standard rootstock to make a specimen standard plant. The top picture shows the rambler 'Albéric Barbier' grown as a weeping standard, and below is the lovely red rose 'Prestige' grown as a standard.*

# Roses

*Opposite, top: Rose 'Princess Margaret'. Below: a weeping standard rose. Bottom: one of the loveliest of the miniature roses, 'Baby Masquerade'.*

*Below: Rose 'Penelope' makes a lovely fragrant hedge.*

color range. An outstanding rose is 'Helen Traubel', a soft apricot pink color. The flowers are large and very fragrant. Another beautiful one is 'Confidence' which is a mixture of pink with yellow and pastel. It is very free-flowering and has a soft fragrance. Then in a rich rose color there is 'Pink Peace', and another lovely deep rose pink flower is 'Electron'. This is a very useful variety because it is highly floriferous.

A lovely shade in roses is the **red**. The variety 'Crimson Glory' has very deep red flowers, beautifully fragrant and the foliage is disease-resistant. For a really heavenly perfume and delightful red and cream flowers 'Double Delight' takes some beating. Again this is a plant which is resistant to disease. Undoubtedly the most superb deep red color, in fact practically a velvet color, is 'Chrysler Imperial'. It has well-formed flowers and a most delicious fragrance. 'Oklahoma' is also deep red and has beautiful flowers which are ideal for show purposes. The foliage is likewise attractive. 'Gipsy' is bright rosy red and it has fragrant well formed flowers. For a change a luminous orange color can be found in 'Polynesian Sunset'.

Strangely enough there are very few good **white** colors in the hybrid teas but there is no doubt that the variety 'Pascali' is the best. It has a very lovely fragrance and ivory white flowers. It produces its medium-sized blooms quite freely.

A subtle color is a mauve and 'Lady X' is what can be described as a soft lilac color and the flowers are very fragrant and nicely formed. It is a good variety for cutting and floral decoration.

Quite fascinating are the bicolors. An outstanding variety amongst these is 'Colorama'; the flower is yellow suffused with salmon pink.

**Floribunda roses** In the **red and vermilion** shades there is that delightful variety 'Comanche' which is fiery red and is a very vigorous grower. 'Fire King' has very lovely bright orange scarlet blooms and lovely glossy green foliage. 'First Edition' is a bright coral, and its flowers are semi-double and nicely perfumed. 'Cathedral' is medium sized and has semi-double flowers of a coppery peach that turns to a lively scarlet orange as the flowers mature. 'Redgold' has gorgeous yellow and orange flowers and it is a very vigorous grower which produces masses of lovely small but well-shaped blooms.

In the **pink** shades 'Camelot' is coral pink. The plant bears beautifully shaped flowers which have a deep scent, and this is a very good variety for the show bench. For a single variety bearing large clear pink unscented flowers the variety 'Betty Prior' is excellent. It is also weather resistant. There are two other lovely varieties: 'Queen Elizabeth' with clear pink flowers sweetly scented, and 'Bon Bon' with its pink and white bicolored flowers which make it a first-rate landscape plant, suitable for planting en masse for a superb color display.

There are some **yellow** shades including 'Golden Girl' and 'Arizona'. 'Sunspot' has deeper yellow flowers and a slight perfume. In the **orange yellow** shades 'Circus' has rich orange and yellow flowers. 'Fashion' has nicely shaped flowers of a bright apricot with a nice tint of amber. Of the **purple** a variety called 'Angel Face' is a strongly scented soft lavender and is of compact growth. In the **whites** 'Saratoga' cannot be bettered with its glorious snow white flowers which are double and very sweetly scented.

Of the **multicolors** 'Masquerade' is outstanding. This starts with yellow buds which mature to a salmon pink and finally to a nice dark red. It is very free-flowering and all colours may be seen at one time in the cluster. 'Starburst' has orange-red flowers with orange-yellow reverse. The flowers are well scented and the plant grows to medium height with deep glossy green foliage.

**Climbing roses** In the **pink** shades there is 'Pink Pereptue' with lovely china rose flowers which are very fragrant. 'Madame Gregoire Stachelin' is an old long established variety which has gorgeous deep pale pink blooms with splashes of carmine on the outside. It has a lovely deep perfume.

In the **red and vermilion** shades there is 'Danse du Feu' which is a lovely orange and red, and the flowers are large and double. 'Etoile de Hollande' is another old variety with dark red blooms which are very fragrantly scented. It bears masses of flowers. 'Copenhagen' has bright red flowers, very strongly scented. 'Super Star' is a vermilion and has fragrant flowers which last well after they have been cut. In the orange yellow shades 'Compassion' is a particularly lovely variety, very fragrant, with pale salmon orange blooms.

In the **yellows** 'Casino' is delightful with a soft yellow flower. It has a nice perfume, and flowers over a long period. 'Gloire de Dijon' is another very old variety and still keeps going well. It has lovely double blooms with a buff orange center with yellow and apricot tints. It has a very nice perfume too. 'Marigold' is a deep yellow and very deeply scented with semi-double blooms. 'Golden Showers' is a golden yellow and has large blooms borne singly in clusters.

Of the **multicolors** 'Handel' has white petals edged with red. Of the **whites** 'Iceberg' is outstanding, also 'Swan Lake'. Another very old long established variety is 'Madame Alfred Carrière'. This is pure white, fragrant and free flowering.

**Rambling roses**  There are some very old varieties in this range such as 'Albéric Barbier'. This has double creamy white flowers which are nicely perfumed. 'Albertine' has a coppery color which fades eventually to a rich pink. 'American Pillar' has rose colored flowers, while 'Emily Gray' has semi-double golden yellow flowers. A very famous variety of course is 'Blaze' with semi-double ever-blooming flowers of a vivid scarlet. It is a very vigorous grower.

**Miniature roses**  In the orange and scarlet shades an outstanding variety is 'Scarlet Gem' which is brilliant orange scarlet and the flowers are double. Of the pink shades 'Bo Peep' is rosy pink and 'Rosy Gem' is a light pink and fully double. Of the yellows, 'Baby Gold Star' is an excellent color and of the reds 'Red Imp' is a good choice, with very double deep crimson blooms. There are several lovely varieties in the red shades. 'Shooting Star' has flame colored blooms and 'Starina' is a deep orange scarlet. Of the bright colors 'Gold Coin', yellow, is particularly pretty, and so too is 'Cinderella', a good brilliant white.

*A well-planned ornamental garden need never be short of color. Here flowering plants are shown to their best advantage against a background of trees and a broad sweep of lawn.*

Creating a beautiful garden is very much like an artist painting on canvas, because color plays a vital role in the finished product. Where the artist uses subtle and brilliant colors as the mood takes him, so the gardener selects plants which will provide many permutations of color. Care taken in planning and selection can produce a long season of display—even during the duller winter months. Many plants have their own special fascination such as beauty of foliage or fascinating fragrance. As an artist manipulates his colors, so the gardener can mix form, fragrance and color to enhance his garden layout.

Some plants are raised from seed, others propagated or increased by division or cuttings. There is a section of flowering plants which is grown from tubers, corms and bulbs. For convenience, these attractive plants can be arranged in sections or divisions for our consideration, starting with perhaps the easiest and quickest method of providing glorious color in the garden, the sowing of annual flowers.

Technically, an annual is a plant which completes its cycle of life in one year. In that period it germinates, produces its flowering display, forms its seed in seed pods and then dies down. There are two types of annual: the hardy annual which is "tough" enough to be sown outdoors when the ground is unfrozen in all the milder climates; and the half-hardy annuals which are more tender and require the protection of glass during their early stages of growth in the North and must have warm, frost-free weather conditions before they can be planted safely outdoors.

There are two main sowing times for hardy annuals. The most popular period starts in March or April and sowings can continue until June. A few really hardy types of annual can grow through mild winters. Seeds of these are sown in August or September if soil conditions permit. The plants will be small, yet large enough to live through the winter, although they will progress very little and will "stand still" for most of that time. Eventually, they will flower in the late spring and early summer of the following year.

**Soil and site**  Choose a sunny position for these plants and avoid a very shady border or a situation which is exposed to strong, cold winds. Low-lying ground should be avoided as this can be damp and cold, with the result that poor, weak seedlings will be produced which will not provide a good color display. Fortunately, the hardy annuals are not too fussy about their soil, and ordinary garden soil will produce reasonable results. It does pay, however, to go to a little extra trouble in basic preparations.

The selected site should be dug or forked over well, either in the autumn or the very early spring. Incorporate some well decomposed compost material from the compost heap or bin. Failing this, some moist horticultural peat can be added. The compost or the peat can be applied at the approximate rate of two spade or forkfuls per square meter (square yard). Follow this by a dressing of a general or balanced fertilizer at 50g (2oz) per square meter (square yard) about 10–14 days before sowing takes place.

The soil *must* be broken down as fine as possible to facilitate seed sowing. The larger lumps will break down by striking them with the back of the fork, and then a finer and final surface or "tilth" is achieved with the rake. Use it first in one direction across the site, followed by a raking at right angles to the first raking. The preparation of the soil will be easier if the work is carried out when the soil is drying. A bright, sunny day is ideal for this work, particularly when there has been a cool, drying wind blowing which helps to crumble the lumps of soil. It is far better to wait a day or so until the soil is in a suitable state for working.

**Sowing the seed**  A plan of campaign should have been previously worked out. This entails drawing up a rough plan on paper indicating the positions of the various varieties and types so that an attractive color scheme can be achieved. This is very useful when you are sowing a complete border with annuals, as you can arrange them according to ultimate height and flowering time as well as color. It will not be necessary if you are just using annuals to fill in gaps in a mixed border.

The basic idea is to sow in batches or sweeps of color using one area for one particular color. One can arrange to have subtle blends or shades of color close to each other, or a much bolder or startling scheme can be worked out where vivid contrasts of color are arranged. For example, a red area can be partnered by a contrasting yellow color.

The plan can then be transferred to the actual plot or soil border simply by marking out the appropriate areas on the soil, either by trickling some sand or lime to form the boundaries or by using a stick to make grooves in the fine soil surface. The site for the hardy annual border can be narrow or wide as the size of the garden dictates. For a most impressive display a wide and deep border is ideal, but a narrow bed can still look most attractive. A width of less than two feet is not advisable if sweeps of color are desired.

The seed *must* be sown as *thinly* as possible so that the seedlings will have plenty of room in which to become established. There are two methods of sowing the seed. The first is by making shallow drills or rows about 15–20cm (6–8in) apart. The seed is sown thinly along each row and then covered lightly to a depth of 1cm (about ½in) with the rake by pulling the soil over the rows or drills. The second method is to scatter the seed evenly and thinly over the marked out area and then cover with the rake, lightly pulling the soil over the seeds. For small scale sowing, the seeds can be covered by scattering some fine, sifted soil over them. This soil can be prepared in advance and kept in a bucket or box.

The soil may require watering later on if the weather is dry and especially if there are drying winds blowing. It is as well to remember that the seeds have been only lightly covered. This thin layer can dry out quickly and, as a result, germination could be poor or rather erratic. If artificial watering is necessary, use a fine spray or rose on the end of the watering can.

*Below : two methods of sowing hardy annuals. They can be sown in shallow parallel drills, which is probably the best method for a large area. Alternatively, an irregular patch can be marked out with a trickle of sand and the seed broadcast thinly over the marked area.*

# Choosing flowers

*Opposite, bottom : Calendulas or marigolds are among the easiest annuals to grow from seed.*

*Below : tall-growing annuals need to be supported. Twiggy sticks, as used in the top picture, are ideal, or canes can be inserted around a group of plants with string attached to them to hold the group upright.*

*Below, right : this bedding scheme is formed entirely from annual plants. Hardy Alyssums are combined with half-hardy plants such as Lobelia, Salvia and Tagetes.*

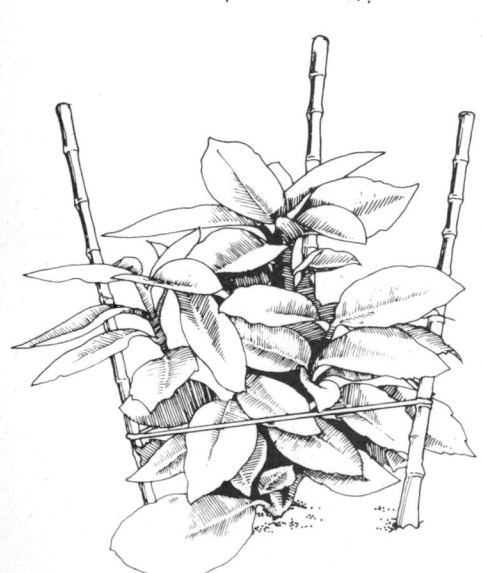

**Thinning out**   This is necessary, even if sowing was carried out as thinly as possible. There will be some seedlings which are too close together for good development and the strongest and sturdiest should be allowed to remain and the weaker ones removed. Remove unwanted seedlings carefully and slowly so that the seedling which remains is disturbed as little as possible.

The space between each seedling can be calculated approximately if the distance between plants is equal to three-quarters of the plant's ultimate height. If it does not rain shortly after the thinning operation has taken place, give the plants a light watering, using a fine rose or fine spray. This will help to firm or consolidate the soil around the plants' roots. You need not waste the seedlings which have been removed if they have a reasonable root system attached. They can be planted out in other borders if you so wish.

**General care**   The taller varieties or types will need some support to keep them neat and to promote good growth. This is very important if the garden is exposed and, despite careful siting, there is a chance that strong winds could disturb these plants occasionally.

The best material to use for training is twiggy sticks—twigs of the common gray birch would be suitable, for example. The branches make ideal supports for the growths and eventually most of the twiggy material will be concealed by the annual plant's own growth. These twiggy sticks are not always easy to come by, so an alternative method may have to be used. Small to medium-sized cane sticks can be purchased and one or two of these can be inserted close by the taller annuals and the foliage loosely tied on to the supports.

When flower buds are noticed, a feed can be given to the plants and this can be applied either in diluted liquid form or dry and scattered carefully around the base of the plants. Water in well afterwards. Any general or balanced type of plant food or fertilizer is suitable. A further feed about three weeks after the first one will promote a good, lengthy flowering display.

If you can spare the time, it is a good idea to go over the flowering plants occasionally to remove the dead flower heads. It is quite surprising how this produces even better flowering. It also promotes a much longer display of flowers.

# A GENERAL LIST OF HARDY ANNUALS

**Alyssum** These are very popular dwarf plants, ideal for edging and formal bedding schemes. Useful too for use in crevices in paving, sunny rock gardens and window boxes. 'Carpet of Snow' is a white, very dwarf variety with a creeping habit, 10cm (4in). *Minimum* is also white and very tiny indeed, making it ideal for crevice planting in paths, 8cm (3in).

**Amaranthus** (*Love-lies-bleeding*) These striking plants (*Amaranthus caudatus*) make ideal border plants, either singly or massed in groups. The variety 'Crimson' has large, downward-falling crimson tassels. 75cm (2½ft).

**Anchusa** (*Bugloss*) The variety 'Blue Angel' makes a neat plant with ultramarine-blue star-like blooms in clusters on long sprays which remain flowering for a long time. 23cm (9in) or more.

**Bartonia** (*Blazing Star*) *B. aurea* has large golden-yellow flowers which last throughout the summer. 45–60cm (1½–2ft).

**Calendula** (*Pot Marigold*) Also known as "English" or "Scotch" marigolds, these plants are available in many colors and forms, and are ideal for cutting and border display. As the plants grow and flower so easily, children would enjoy growing them. 'Golden King', as its name suggests, has very large blooms, golden-yellow in color. It grows to 30–45cm (12–18in). 'Pacific Beauty' has double flowers in orange, apricot, primrose and yellow, occasionally bicolored, 30–45cm (12–18in).

**Campanula** (*Bellflower*) *C. speculum veneris*, commonly known as Venus's Looking Glass, has large flowers with white centers surrounded by violet blue, which are ideal for rock gardens, flower beds or borders. 30–38cm (12–15in).

**Centaurea** (*Cornflower*) The annual cornflower, *Centaurea cyanus*, will do well in a sunny situation and in any sort of soil. Seeds of Tall Double Mixed will produce flowers of differing shades of blue, pink and red which grow to 90cm (3ft). 'Polka Dot' is a dwarf variety. The bushy plants have flowers of blue, maroon-red, rose-pink, lavender and white, and only grow to 38–45cm (15–18in).

**Chrysanthemum** The annual chrysanthemums make beautiful edging plants, ideal for cutting. Rainbow Mixture produces large tricolored flowers, 6cm (2½in) across, in many color combinations—yellow, scarlet, red, orange, bronze, rosy lavender, buff, white, etc., 60cm (2ft). Double Mixed will produce double and semi-double flowers in a variety of attractive colors, 60cm (2ft). The *Spectabile* Varieties were developed from crosses between *C. carinatum* and *C. coronarium*. They are tall, and ideal for large borders and for cutting. 'Cecilia' has white, daisy-like flowers, striped with yellow, 75–90cm (2½–3ft). *C. coronarium* 'Golden Gem' has lemon-yellow, button-like flowers blooming on bushy plants throughout the summer, 45–60cm (1½–2ft).

**Clarkia** Clarkias are deservedly popular annuals. *C. elegans* Double Mixed has double flowers, which are shown to their best advantage when grown in small groups or clusters. They can be grown in shades of salmon-pink, purple, mauve, carmine, red or white, 60cm (2ft). *C. pulchella* Mixed: double or semi-double flowers in white, light violet and carmine-rose, 45–60cm (1½–2ft).

**Convolvulus** These are easy annuals to grow in a sunny position, even on poor or dry soil. *C. major* Mixed: quick-growing climbers with trumpet-shaped flowers in many colors. *C. minor* Mixed: attractive flowers with contrasting centers, 30cm (12in). 'Royal Ensign' has trumpet-shaped, deep blue flowers with white and yellow middles, 38cm (15in).

HARDY ANNUALS TO SOW IN AUTUMN
The following hardy annuals can be sown in a sheltered position in autumn to stand over the winter. They will make little top growth during the colder months but they will form sturdy plants with a strong root system, and will generally flower earlier than spring-sown annuals. Refer to the General List of Hardy Annuals for more details on those listed here.

*Calendula officinalis* (Pot Marigold)
*Centaurea cyanus* (Cornflower)
*Clarkia elegans* (Clarkia)
*Delphinium ajacis* (Larkspur)
Eschscholtzia (Californian Poppy)
Godetia
*Gypsophila elegans* (Annual Gypsophila)
Iberis (Candytuft)
*Lathyrus odoratus* (Sweet Pea)
*Limnanthes douglasii* (Butter and Eggs)
*Lobularia maritima* (Sweet Alison)
*Malcolmia maritima* (Virginian Stock)
*Nigella damascena* (Love-in-a-mist)
*Papaver rhoeas* (Shirley Poppy)
*Saponaria vaccaria* (Annual Soapwort)
*Scabiosa atropurpurea* (Sweet Scabious)
Viscaria (Catchfly)

**Cosmos**  Pretty plants, available in a variety of colors and suitable for borders or for cutting. 'Goldilocks' is a good variety with golden-yellow flowers in a star shape above fern-like foliage. 60–120cm (2–4ft).

**Delphinium** (*Larkspur*)  The annual delphinium, *D. ajacis*, is more commonly known as Larkspur. Among the best are the Giant Imperial Varieties. Seed sown in September will gratify the gardener with beautiful flowers early the following summer, growing to a height of 1–1.25m (3–4ft). Named cultivars include 'Blue Spire', dark violet blue; 'Salmon Rose', a lovely salmon color as its name suggests; 'White Spire', pure white. The Dwarf Hyacinth-flowered Mixed would be more suitable for a small garden. They come in shades of pink, lavender, violet and white and grow to 45cm (18in).

**Dianthus barbatus** (*Annual Sweet William*)  The Dianthus family gives us the Annual Sweet William, *D. barbatus*, which can be sown directly into the open ground in spring for flowering in summer.

**Dimorphotheca** (*Star of the Veldt*)  Daisy-like flowers requiring plenty of sunshine. They are quick to flower from seed. 'Orange Glory' has large bright orange flowers with a black central disc, 30cm (12in).

**Dracocephalum**  *D. moldavicam* is much sought after by bees and has pretty lavender-blue flowers. The plants grow to 30cm (12in).

**Echium**  A plant suitable for any sunny position. 'Blue Bedder' has deep blue flowers and grows to only 30cm (12in).

**Eschscholtzia** (*Californian Poppy*)  These annuals must be grown in a sunny position, though poor soil will not be a disadvantage. 'Ballerina' has double and semi-double flowers of red, pink, orange and yellow with white, 30cm (12in). 'Miniature Primrose' is a dwarf variety suitable for rock gardens or borders, with small primrose-yellow flowers, 15cm (6in).

**Euphorbia**  *E. marginata* is the annual known popularly as Snow-on-the-Mountain. It is a foliage plant, and its light green leaves are shown to their best advantage among flowering border plants. 60cm (2ft).

**Godetia**  The Dwarf Varieties are most suitable for the small garden. These colorful plants grow easily in sunny situations. Azalea-flowered Mixed: double and semi-double flowers of many different colors, 38–45cm (15–18in). Dwarf Bedding Mixed: single flowers, perhaps patterned or striped, in pink, salmon, crimson and carmine, 23–30cm (9–12in).

**Gilia**  *G. capitata* is a very easy-to-grow plant, with lavender-blue flower heads, 45cm (18in).

**Gypsophila**  The white annual gypsophila is well-known and very popular with flower arrangers. Try also *G. elegans Rosea*, a pretty little plant with rose-pink heads which grows to 60cm (2ft).

**Grasses, ornamental**  Sow directly into the growing position from March onwards. These grasses can be used either on their own or among other flowers. They are also very suitable for use in dried flower arrangements. Varieties available include *Agrostis nebulosa* (Cloud Grass), with spikelets carried on spreading heads, 45cm (18in); *Lagurus ovatus* (Hare's-Tail Grass), with long stems topped with fluffy plumes up to 5cm (2in) long, 45cm (18in) tall; *Panicum violaceum*, with green tassels eventually changing to purplish-brown, 60–90cm (2–3ft); *Tricholaena rosea* (Wine Grass), with long stems carrying brown, fluffy spikelets, 45–60cm (1½–2ft).

**Helianthus annuus** (*Sunflower*) Beautiful and striking flowers, lasting many weeks. The common sunflower is rather coarse-growing and can reach 2m (8ft) and above, but there are many alternative varieties to choose from. 'Autumn Sunshine' bears flowers of different colors including yellow and red, and grows to only 1.2m (4ft).

**Iberis** (*Candytuft*) Virtually any soil or position is suitable for these quick-flowering annuals. The Giant Hyacinth-flowered White makes an erect plant with long sprays of fragrant white flowers, reminiscent of the hyacinth, 38cm (15in) tall. 'Red Flash' is a distinctive crimson-carmine plant, 30cm (12in). 'Rose Cardinal' is often seen as a bedding plant; its flowers are rosy-carmine and it grows to 30cm (12in).

**Lathyrus** (*Sweet Pea*) The annual Sweet Pea, *Lathyrus odoratus*, is probably too well-known to need description. Sweet Peas are available in many forms and named varieties, including dwarf forms. They are fragrant, and the fully climbing forms

*Left: Iberis, commonly known as
Candytuft.*

*Opposite, top to bottom: Cosmos,
and orange and yellow color forms
of Eschscholtzia, the Californian
Poppy.*

can be trained up netting or trellis or supported with twiggy sticks. They appreciate a rich soil and a sunny position.

**Leptosiphon**   Rainbow Mixture will produce many small plants with star-shaped flowers in beautiful colors, ideal for the front of borders. 10–15cm (4–6in).

**Limnanthes**   *L. douglasii* is sometimes known as the Meadow Foam. It has bright yellow flowers edged white and is suitable for rockeries and borders.

**Linaria** (*Toadflax*)   Similar to small antirrhinums and very easy to grow. *L. maroccana* 'Fairy Bouquet' is dwarf and compact, but with large flowers in many brilliant colors, 23cm (9in) tall.

**Linum** (*Annual Flax*)   This plant will thrive almost anywhere, whatever the soil or position. *L. grandiflorum album* has white flowers with a crimson center, 45–60cm (1½–2ft). *L. grandiflorum Rubrum* (Scarlet Flax) has silky petals of a crimson-scarlet shade and is best grown in large clusters. 30–45cm (12–18in).

**Malcolmia** (*Virginian Stock*)   *M. maritima* Mixed has flowers of red, yellow, lilac and white, and will grow in almost any position. 23cm (9in).

**Matthiola** (*Stock*)   A valuable genus for the gardener, most of them tender and therefore listed as half-hardy annuals. *M. bicornis* is the night-scented stock, well worth planting close to a house window or on a patio for the sake of its superb fragrance, which is particularly noticeable in the evening. 30cm (12in) or more.

**Nemophila**   *N. insignis* (Baby Blue Eyes) has a mass of sky-blue flowers, and is most suited to cool and moist conditions. 15cm (6in).

**Nigella** (*Love-in-a-mist*)   Ideal for borders or cutting and very easy to grow. 'Miss Jekyll' has deep sky-blue flowers and is 38cm (15in) tall. 'Persian Jewels' is a good mixture including pretty colors of light and dark blue as well as pink and white.

**Papaver** (*Poppy*)   The poppy family provides many distinctive colors to brighten up the garden. Shirley Poppy, Double Mixed: large double flowers in many colors, 75cm (2½ft). Shirley Poppy, Single Mixed: single flowers color range, 75cm (2½ft).

**Reseda** (*Mignonette*)   The mignonette, *R. odorata*, is very sweetly scented. 'Machet' has tall spikes, sweetly fragrant, and grows to 30cm (12in).

**Salvia horminum** (*Clary*)   Ideal for flower arrangements as the leaves (or bracts) keep their color for many weeks. 45cm (18in). 'Color Blend' includes pink, blue and white varieties.

**Schizanthus** (*Butterfly Flower*)   Butterfly Mixture: pretty little flowers in pink, crimson, purple and white, growing best in a sunny situation, 30–45cm (12–18in).

**Silene** (*Annual Catchfly*)   *S. armeria* 'Electra' is very easy to grow and bears clusters of bright pink flowers. 30cm (12in). Dwarf Double Mixed: excellent for bedding out or a rock garden, with double flowers in pink, scarlet and white.

**Tropaeolum** (*Nasturtium*)   The common nasturtium, *T. majus*, will grow quite easily even in poor soil and produces brilliantly colored flowers. Nasturtiums are also useful for climbing up trellis, over walls, etc. The semi-double sweet-scented Varieties make bushy plants which are colorful, and useful for hanging baskets.

# HALF-HARDY ANNUALS

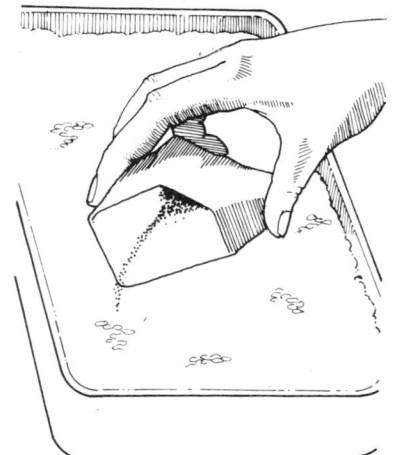

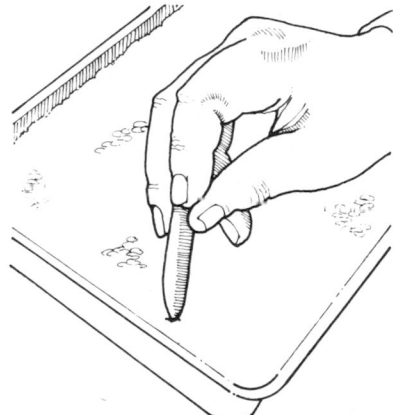

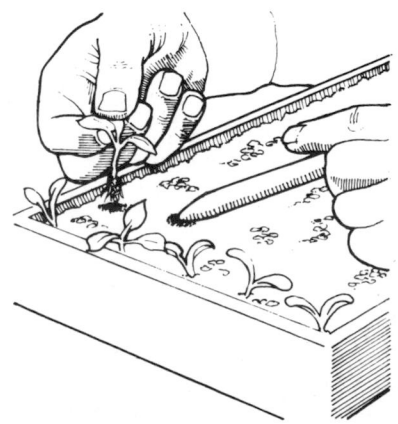

Half-hardy annuals will produce a glorious display of flowers in the garden throughout the summer and well into the autumn months. As their name implies, they are not as tough as the hardy annuals mentioned earlier on in this section and therefore require a slightly different form of treatment or cultivation. Included in the half-hardy annuals are familiar and popular names such as *Salvia splendens*, stocks, Ageratum, and African and French Marigolds. In this group of plants will be found some different types such as Begonias which are correctly half-hardy perennials. However, these are treated and grown as half-hardy annuals.

Because half-hardy annuals cannot withstand cold conditions it is impossible to start them off successfully outdoors in the open garden. It is necessary to provide them with some glass protection in the form of frames or a greenhouse. It is also better if some heating can be provided so that a minimum germination or growing temperature of 10°C (50°F) is maintained. If the economics allow it, a slightly higher temperature than this will ensure even quicker germination and a temperature of 15°C (60°F) is ideal. Heating is necessary where a really early start is required and we are talking of February or March sowings (depending upon climate). Later sowings can be made in a garden frame without heating and this can be carried out in late April or May in the open. Obviously these sowings will produce plants which will flower much later than those raised in warmth.

**Sowing**  The seed should be sown in a good quality seed mixture, or a soilless mixture can be used. These are in fact based on peat with special additives; alternatively use any good proprietary brand of seed mixture. Specially formulated soil based mixtures are readily available from garden shops or garden centers, conveniently packaged in plastic bags. These mixtures also have special ingredients or additives in the way of plant foods.

Seed trays or large pots can be used filled with the seed mixture, and then the seed must be sown very thinly and evenly over the surface of the soil. After a very light covering with some fine soil the mixture should be watered with a fine rose attached to the end of the watering can. Cover with glass and sheets of newspaper. Frequent examination is necessary to ensure that these covers are removed as soon as the seed has germinated. Failure to do so will encourage very straggly or weak growth. A careful eye must also be kept on watering as such media can dry out rapidly, especially the soilless types. Water again using a fine rose on the watering can.

When the young seedlings are large enough to handle easily they must be pricked out. This is a term which refers to the transplanting or moving on of the plants into deeper receptacles and with more generous spacing so that they have more room in which to develop. Carefully loosen the seedlings by inserting a label or special dibber under the soil, and lift out the seedlings individually, handling them only by the seed leaves and never by the tender stems. Make a hole large enough to accommodate the root system and place each seedling in the deeper receptacle, spacing them about 5cm (2in) apart each way. Gently firm the mixture around each seedling as it is placed in position. When each seed tray is filled in this way it should be given a light watering.

The pricked out seedlings must be kept in the greenhouse in warmth until about April or May when they are transferred to a frame so that they can be hardened off. This means allowing the plants to receive more air and cooler outdoor conditions by gradually removing or opening up the frame light tops. Those half-hardy annuals which were sown without heat in a garden frame later in the season should also be carefully hardened off in the same manner.

*Above : the seedlings are gradually hardened off and then planted out in their final flowering positions when all danger of frost is past. The seedlings should be lifted gently from their boxes or individual pots and carefully transplanted so that minimum root disturbance is caused.*

It is possible to sow many of the half-hardy annuals outdoors without protection but this cannot be done until May in the North. This is when weather conditions are better, the soil is warmer and there is less or no chance of those dangerous late frosts. They are sown in exactly the same way as for the hardy annuals.

**Planting out**   The site selected should be as open and sunny as possible and the ground prepared in exactly the same way as for the hardy annuals. It may not be necessary to prepare quite so fine a surface or finish to the soil where plants are being planted out after being hardened off, but of course if seed is being sown a fine surface is essential. Plants must have a generous planting hole, and a hand trowel is the best tool to use during planting operations. Take out a hole which is larger than the root ball or spread of each plant, place the plant carefully in the hole, return the soil, and very gently firm with the knuckles of the hand around the plant. Avoid planting during very dry weather and if dry conditions prevail at planting time it is a good plan to water the site thoroughly a day or two beforehand. After planting it will be wise to keep a careful eye on watering, and artificial applications may well be necessary if dry conditions prevail.

**Bought plants**   If you do not wish to raise your own half-hardy annuals you will find that a reasonable range of varieties and types will be on sale at your local shop or garden center. A word of caution however. Unfortunately many nurseries raise and sell bedding plants such as the half-hardies a little too early on in the season, and there is a danger that one will be tempted to buy and plant out these plants too early in the year, when there is still danger of cold weather, and even frosts which will harm and even kill many of the plants. Why the raisers do this is difficult to appreciate, but it is wise wherever possible to delay purchasing, especially if your garden is situated in a cold, exposed area. Wait until late May or even early June, when the danger of frosts is gone

# A GENERAL LIST OF HALF-HARDY ANNUALS

**Ageratum**   These plants are ideal for borders and flower beds. 'Blue Chip Hybrid' has lavender-blue flowers and grows to 20–25cm (8–10in). 'Blue Mink' is about the same height with bright azure-blue flower trusses. 'White Cushion' is a smaller variety with fluffy white flowers to 15cm (6in). The plants form little clumps.

**Antirrhinum** (*Snapdragon*)   These plants can be treated as hardy annuals in many areas, but sow under glass for early bloom. Hybrid bedding varieties include Bedding Mixture, with beautiful colors in shades of pink, crimson, yellow and white. No support is required, and each plant will produce many colorful spikes, 45–60cm (1½–2ft). Pixie Mixed are dwarf antirrhinums in crimsons, oranges, pinks and whites, 20–30cm (8–12in). 'Orange Pixie' has the same dwarf habit. Flowers are of the open-petalled butterfly type in a lovely shade of orange-cerise, 20–30cm (8–12in).

Double Hybrid Types include 'Madame Butterfly', with double flowers in many colors, 60cm (2ft); Supreme Double Mixed, with large semi-double flowers, about half a dozen spikes on a single plant and a color range which includes pink, yellow, orange and cream, 75cm (2½ft); 'Sweetheart', with large heads of double flowers in red, bronze, pink, yellow or white, 30cm (12in).

The Hybrid Coronettes have many flower spikes on each plant and grow to 55–65cm (22–26in). They include 'Crimson', deep red; 'Bronze', bronze salmon; 'Rose', deep pink; 'Scarlet', brilliant scarlet; 'Yellow', brilliant yellow.

Ordinary Tall Varieties include Tetraploid Mixed, with large flowers in shades of orange, yellow, pink and white, 60–75cm (2½–3ft).

Intermediate or Semi-dwarf Varieties are very popular for flower beds and also extremely colorful, 38–45cm (15–18in). Giant-flowered Mixed will produce large flowers in many brilliant colors, and there is also a Rust-resistant Mix available.

Tom Thumb and Dwarf Bedding Varieties are ideal for window boxes or for the front of the border, and are very free-flowering. Floral Carpet Improved Hybrid has large flowers that form one mass of color, 30–38cm (12–15in). A sowing of Tom Thumb Mixed will give you a dazzling display of neat plants only 15cm (6in) high.

**Asters**   The ideal plant to brighten up the garden from August onward. Dwarf Bedding Asters may produce up to thirty double flowers on a single plant. They grow to 15cm (6in) only, and are available in a wide range of colors.

Dwarf varieties include 'Pepite' Mixed, each plant bearing such a profusion of blooms that the leaves are quite hidden, 30cm (12in); 'Pinnochio', with small double flowers in shades of pink, blue, red, yellow and white, 15–20cm (6–8in); and 'Waldersee', pretty little plants covered in white, pink and blue flowers, 23cm (9in).

Other varieties to consider when making your selection are Unicum Mixed, with large double flowers in many different colors including red, yellow and white, 45cm (18in), and the Ostrich Plume types, which have feathery flowers with curly petals. Ostrich Plume Mixed have very large flowers, suitable for cutting, 60cm (2ft). 'Super Princess' types thrive in bad weather conditions; colors available include 'Deep Blue', bright blue with a yellow center, 60cm (2ft), and 'Goldstrike', deep yellow, 50cm (20in). The Bouquet Type Asters are tall plants with large double blooms and grow to 45–60cm (1½–2ft).

For an early-flowering variety grow 'Earliest of All', with pink, blue and white flowers on tall stems, 45cm (18in). 'Cut-and-come-again' is an ideal variety for cut flowers, each plant having between twelve and fifteen blooms. Pompon Mixed have button-shaped, long-lasting flowers in blends of pink, red and blue, 38–45cm (15–18in). Victoria Mixed bear large flowers with attractive curving petals.

**Begonia**   The fibrous-rooted begonias bloom throughout the summer and well into the autumn. Hybrid Compact Varieties include 'Cocktail' with brightly colored

HALF HARDY ANNUALS TO GROW FOR FRAGRANCE
**Carnation**: Sow 'Chabaud Special Mixture'. In many areas these large, fragrant, double flowers will survive the winter. In shades of crimson, scarlet, pink, salmon, rose, yellow and white, they grow to 45cm (18in). Hybrid Dwarf Mixed have strong stems and bear double flowers in shades of pink, scarlet and purple with some striped blooms. Early flowering, 30cm (12in).

**African Marigolds** (see Tagetes): All of these plants have a pleasant pungent smell. 'Hawaii' is a particularly good variety with orange, globe-shaped flowers, which grow to 60cm (2ft).

**Stocks** (see Matthiola): Sow mixed stocks, which are available in a wide variety of colours, 30cm (12in).

*Below: begonias are fibrous-rooted plants, usually raised as half-hardy annuals.*

flowers which contrast superbly with the dark foliage, 20cm (8in). Hybrid Tall Varieties include 'Pink Charm', very free-flowering with rose-pink blooms, 25–30cm (10–12in). Ordinary Intermediate and Dwarf Varieties include the popular 'Scarlet Bedder', an ideal bedding plant with flowers of bright scarlet, 20cm (8in).

**Brachycome** (*Swan River Daisy*)    Small, daisy-like flowers in white, lavender and blue, 15–23cm (6–9in) or more.

**Calceolaria**  'Hybrid Sunshine' is a pretty plant, best displayed in window-boxes and tubs, 20–25cm (8–10in). Best grown in a sheltered position.

**Carnation**    Members of the large and diverse Dianthus family. Sow under glass in February and March for flowers during the following summer.

**Cosmos** (*Cosmea*)    Frequently grown as hardy annuals, but for early bloom they really need half-hardy treatment. Early-flowering Mixed will produce a delightful array of crimson, pink or white flowers among ferny leaves, 90cm (3ft). The Dwarf Klondyke Types include 'Bright Lights', with a mass of brightly colored flowers in yellow, red and orange, 45–60cm (1½–2ft).

**Dahlia**    Dahlias are often purchased as tubers, but they can also be grown very successfully from seed; the plants will flower during their first year, throughout the summer and right into the autumn. The tubers can then be replanted. The Cactus-flowered Hybrids have attractively shaped petals and semi-double and double flowers in many colors. The Coltness Hybrids bear very large single flowers, again in many different color blends, 45cm (18in).

**Delphinium**    Sow under glass in March, to be planted out in May. Tom Thumb is a compact variety, with very large flowers in an outstanding shade of deep blue. 23cm (9in).

**Dianthus** (*Annual Pinks*)    Sow under glass to be planted out in May, or directly where they are to flower from mid May onwards. The Magic Charms Hybrids will

produce a dazzling array of color in shades of pink, red and white, 15–20cm (6–8in). 'Persian Carpet' is a dwarf strain, suitable for rockeries and the front of the border, with small flowers in pink, salmon, scarlet and white. 10cm (4in).

**Gaillardia**   These are colorful hardy bedding plants, but treat as half-hardy for earlier blooms. 'Blood Red Giants' are in shades of red, perhaps tipped with yellow in some flowers. They reach 38–45cm (15–18in).

**Gazania**   The flowers will last until early autumn. *G. longiscapa* 'Treasure Chest' bears yellow, orange, bronze and red flowers on tall stems, 30–38cm (12–15in). 'Sunshine' is another lovely cultivar, with very large, late-flowering blooms in scarlet, bronze, orange and pink, 30–38cm (12–15in).

**Heliotrope** (*Cherry Pie*)   Very easy to grow plants with fragrant flowers, usually in shades of blue or purple.

**Helichrysum** (*Strawflower*)   Easy to grow, attractive plants with everlasting flower heads which are popular with floral arrangers. *H. monstrosum* 'Dwarf Art Shades' bears long-lasting flowers in colors of rose, crimson, yellow, white and orange. These plants are ideal for edgings or flower beds, growing to about 45cm (18in).

**Impatiens** (*Balsam, Busy Lizzie*)   Suitable as either a bedding plant or a pot plant. Camellia-flowered Double Mixed should be tried: they have flowers in many pretty shades of pink, scarlet and white, 45cm (18in).

**Ipomoea** (*Morning Glory*)   A beautiful free-flowering climbing plant for a sunny position outdoors. *I. rubro-caerulea* 'Heavenly Blue' has trumpet-shaped flowers in deep blue with white centers.

**Lobelia**   A very popular edging plant, available not only in the traditional blue but in many other colors. 'Aubrieta Shades' is a good mixture, with pretty little flowers in blends of blue, purple, red and white, 15cm (6in). 'Mrs Clibran', Improved, is a penetrating blue with a white center. There are also trailing varieties available, which are ideal for hanging baskets and window boxes. 'Sapphire' is a good trailing type, with deep blue flowers. The Petite Double Types are compact and tidy plants, only 15cm (6in) tall. Petite Mixed is a good mixture comprising many different shades. Lobelias are often planted with Alyssum in formal bedding schemes.

**Matthiola** (*Stocks*)   The old types which had fragrant single flowers have largely been superseded by Hansen's 100% Double Stocks. '100% Double Bedding Beauty' is suitable for flower beds, borders or cutting. The flowers are in many different colors, and the plants grow to 38–45cm (15–18in). The 100% Double Ten Week Stock is a dwarf plant, free-flowering and scented, 30cm (12in). Of the ordinary-type stocks, 'Beauty of Nice' Mixed will produce many flowers on tall stems fairly late in the season, 45cm (18in).

**Mesembryanthemum**   *M. criniflorum* is the Livingstone Daisy, a plant which is cold-tender but likes a dry, sunny position. It has flowers, which only open in full sun, in shades of pink, carmine, salmon, apricot and orange. 8cm (3in).

**Mimulus** (*Monkey Flower*)   Sow early under glass for planting in a moist, shady situation, perhaps alongside a pool. The strain 'Queen's Prize' has large flowers in a variety of colors, many of the petals being attractively speckled or mottled. 30cm (12in).

*Opposite, top: Heliotrope is commonly known as Cherry Pie, and makes a lovely fragrant container plant.*

*Opposite, bottom: two color forms of the beautiful Gazania.*

*Below: Mesembryanthemums are eye-catching summer bedding plants. They should be massed together in a position which receives full sunlight.*

**Nemesia**   Easy to grow and quick to flower. 'Carnival' has large flowers in many different colors, including bronze, scarlet, cerise, pink, orange, primrose and white 23–30cm (9–12in).

**Nicotiana** (*Flowering Tobacco*)   Grow Sensation Mixed for fragrant flowers in shades of mauve, pink, crimson, lemon and white, 60–75cm (2–2½ft) or more.

**Ornamental Corn**   This is an excellent plant to grow for dried floral arrangements. 'Rainbow' bears large multicolored cobs in red, yellow, orange and blue, 1.2–1.5m (4–5ft).

**Penstemon**   Sow in warmth in February or March and plant out from May onward. The plants will thrive throughout the summer and even into the winter in mild areas. The Giant Hybrids have large blooms which are trumpet-shaped, in contrasting colors of white, pink and crimson, 45cm (18in).

**Petunia**   These strong plants make a lovely display in window boxes, hanging baskets and tubs. Multiflora Varieties include 'Resisto' Mixed, resistant to all weathers and with flowers in shades of blue, purple, pink, scarlet and white. The Double Multifloras will succeed in a sheltered position or in window boxes and tubs. They include 'Delight', with carnation-like, double flowers in colors of red, pink, blue, purple, cerise and white, together with some bicolored blooms.

Among the ordinary types of Petunia the free-flowering Bedding Varieties should be tried, or Dwarf Bedding Mixed for compact plants in a wide range of colors, growing to only 38cm (15in). The Giant Flowered Varieties need to be grown in a sheltered, sunny situation, but are worth a little attention for their very large flowers. The Giant All-double Strain has really enormous flowers, up to 13cm (5in) across, which make a really brilliant splash of color in the garden. The flowers are scented in shades of pink, salmon, mauve, violet, purple and white.

**Phlox**   *Phlox drummondii* are small bedding plants with brightly colored clusters of flowers. Dwarf Beauty Mixed will yield a wide color range including blue, violet, pink, salmon, scarlet and white, 30cm (12in) or more.

**Portulaca**   Easy-to-grow plants which will thrive in any sunny position. Double Mixed is ideal for flower beds, borders and rockeries. The flowers are in brilliant shades of rose, orange, purple, yellow and white, and the plants grow to only 15cm (6in).

**Rudbeckia**   Beautifully colored, late summer blooms. After cutting, dip the last inch of stem into water for half a minute to make the flowers last longer. The Giant Tetraploid Hybrids, sometimes known as Gloriosa Daisies, bear single flowers in shades of yellow and red on tall stems. The flowers, some of which are bicolored, can be as large as 18cm (7in) across. 75–90cm (2½–3ft).

**Salpiglossis**   'Bolero' has beautiful flowers in many different colors including gold, scarlet, rose, crimson and blue, as well as some bicolored blooms, all with the attractive veining and flushing which makes these plants so distinctive.

**Salvia**   Varieties of *S. splendens* include 'Blaze of Fire', bearing spikes of flowers in a dazzling shade of red. It is early and free-flowering, about 45cm (18in).

**Scabiosa** (*Pincushion Flower*)   Should be sown directly outdoors when danger of frost is past to flower during the autumn. Dwarf Double Mixed are neat plants with flowers in shades of pink, scarlet, mauve, blue and maroon, 45cm (18in).

*Opposite, top: the fragrant Tobacco Plant, Nicotiana, can be grown under a window where its perfume will be particularly noticeable in the evenings. Opposite, bottom: Nicotiana 'Lime Green' is a modern cultivar, very popular with flower arrangers because of its unusual and striking coloring.*

## FOLIAGE PLANTS

These plants in differing forms and colors complement the brightly colored flowers among which they are situated. They are also useful for flower arrangements. All the plants in this list are best raised from seed in the way described for Half Hardy Annuals.

### Colored foliage

Amaranthus 'Illumination': tricolored rosettes of foliage—a yellow center, bright red middle and bronze outside, 60cm (2ft).
Ornamental cabbage: Popular in Japan for 'floral' decorations. Sow Mixed Colors in the flower border —the plants are also edible. The middle leaves are generally rose-pink or white with outer leaves veined with rose or white, 30cm (12in).

### Silver and gray foliage

*Centaurea candidissima:* Delicate, silvery-white leaves, 30–38cm (12–15in).
*Cineraria maritima:* 'Dwarf Silver': Attractive plants with fringed, silver foliage, 23–30cm (9–12in).
*Pyrethrum ptarmicaeflorum:* A delicate silver-leaved plant, ideal in borders or flower arrangements, 38cm (15in).

### Foliage dot plants

Use these singly in flower beds both to provide variation in height and to contrast with dwarf flowering plants.
Kochia (Burning Bush): *K. tricophylla* has light green foliage which changes to scarlet and bronze as the summer progresses, 60cm (2ft).
Ricinus (Castor Oil Plant): These plants have large, shapely leaves in bronze, purple or green. They are suitable for potting up to brighten a veranda or patio, but take care—the seeds are poisonous.

**Statice** A popular everlasting flower, ideal for dried flower arrangements. Cut when the flowers are at their richest and hang in bunches in a cool place. 45cm (18in). 'Art Shades' is a good variety with pretty flowers in shades of pink, red and purple.

**Tagetes** Very useful and popular plants for flower beds and borders. The genus includes French and African Marigolds.
DWARF FRENCH MARIGOLDS Dwarf singles include 'Dainty Marietta', with bright yellow flowers tinged with red, 15cm (6in). Giant Crested French Marigolds are early-flowering and will thrive even in bad weather. Their large, double flowers give a dazzling display of reds and golds, 20cm (8in). A good Dwarf Double French Marigold is 'Golden Boy', which bears large double golden-yellow blooms. The Giant-flowered Varieties are very early-flowering with double flowers up to 5cm (2in) across.

Hybrids have been made between the African and French Marigolds. The 'Red and Gold Hybrids' are early, free-flowering plants giving a delightful show of color for many weeks. The double flowers are at least 6 cm ($2\frac{1}{2}$in) across.
AFRICAN MARIGOLDS Hybrid African Marigolds give a beautiful display of flowers during July or August. The double flowers are very large, neat and long lasting. Compact types are ideal for flower beds or edgings. These include 'First Lady', an early flowering plant with double blooms up to 8cm (3in) across of a bright yellow color, 38–45cm (15–18in). 'Golden Jubilee' is a lovely hybrid; one plant can bear up to sixteen or more flowers over 10cm (4in) across. As the name implies, the flowers are a deep gold. It grows to about 45cm (18in). For a tall variety try 'Doubloon', a very free-flowering type with double blooms in primrose-yellow, 60–75cm (2–$2\frac{1}{2}$ft).

Ordinary African Marigolds include 'Cream Puff' with pretty double pale primrose flowers, 60cm (2ft); 'Sierra' Mixed, giving a brilliant display of large flowers in blends of primrose, orange and gold, 60cm (2ft); Dwarf Double African, an ideal type to plant among petunias; and 'Spun Gold', with large flowers of brilliant gold, 30cm (12in).

*T. signata* Pumila is the plant sold as Tagetes, a neat plant suitable for beds and borders. 'Paprika' has dark green leaves which contrast well with the bright red petals tipped with gold. It grows to 15–25cm (6–10in).

**Ursinia** Plants with vividly-colored flowers which glow in the sun. 'Sunshine Blend' is a mixture of African Daisies made up of lemon, yellow and orange flowers, with some of the blooms being edged with a darker, contrasting color.

**Venidium** (*Monarch of the Veldt*) *V. fastuosum* must be planted in a sunny, well-drained position. The flowers are shaped rather like a daisy, up to 13cm (5in) across. They are bright orange spotted with maroon and with a black center. The leaves are woolly. 60–90cm (2–3ft).

**Verbena** Suitable for flower beds, borders and window boxes. Verbenas bloom for many weeks, even in wet conditions. Rainbow Mixed will produce early-flowering plants in a fine color range which includes apricot, lavender, mauve, pink, salmon and crimson. 23–30cm (9–12in).

**Zinnia** As zinnias do not like to be transplanted it is better to sow them directly outdoors, under Hotkaps if necessary. 'Super Giants' have very large flowers up to 15cm (6in) across with quilled petals. They make a beautiful show of color in shades of scarlet, orange, salmon, yellow, pink and purple. 30–45cm (12–18in). Lilliput or Pompon Varieties are also lovely plants. The double pompons are suitable for flower beds and borders, and will withstand wet conditions fairly well. They are available in many bright colors and are about 60cm (24in) tall.

# BIENNIALS

*Opposite, top: Sweet Williams in mixed colors give a good summer display and are sweetly scented.*
*Opposite, bottom: Lunaria or Honesty is an easily-grown biennial. The flowers, usually purple, are followed by pretty silvery seed pods.*

First of all it is important to appreciate what a biennial plant is. The true biennial is a plant which takes about two years to germinate, grow, flower and produce seed. After this cycle the plant dies, and new plants will have to be raised from seed.

New gardeners are often confused by the terms annual, biennial and perennial. After all, there are, as we have already seen, some hardy annuals which can be sown in the autumn of the previous year to stand over winter in much the same way as biennials. The classifications are perhaps better understood when one bears in mind the fact that many of our garden plants are developed from species which are accustomed to a very different climate. Thus some of the plants that we grow in our temperate climate as annuals would be perennials in their natural habitat; similarly some of the plants we treat as biennials are in fact short-lived perennials. Examples of these are hollyhocks, wallflowers and forget-me-nots. Some wallflower plants will indeed live on for a further year or so after flowering, if given the chance, but they tend to become leggy and unattractive, and as new plants are so easy to raise from seed the wallflowers are generally rooted up after flowering in spring to make way for summer-flowering plants.

Biennials should be sown in May and June in a prepared seed bed outdoors. They can be sown in drills or broadcast. The young plants should be severely thinned and can be given an occasional liquid feed. They should be ready for planting out in their final quarters by October.

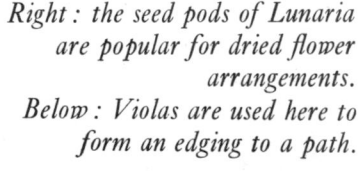

*Right: the seed pods of Lunaria are popular for dried flower arrangements.*
*Below: Violas are used here to form an edging to a path.*

94

# A SELECTION OF HARDY BIENNIALS

**Althaea** (*Hollyhock*)  The most popular type of Hollyhock (*Althaea rosea*) is an example of a plant which is really perennial but usually treated as a biennial. Plants for a striking show at the back of the border, they may grow 2m (7ft) tall or more. They prefer heavy soil enriched with organic manure, and except in the most sheltered garden they will require staking.

**Dianthus** (*Pinks*)  The dwarf Dianthus are really beautiful plants. They are low growing, attaining a height of some 15cm (6in), and are therefore ideal for either the rock garden or for edging borders. There are several lovely varieties, and new varieties are being added from year to year (this applies also of course to many other of the biennials). *Dianthus allwoodii alpinus* is a delightful variety for the rockery, and another lovely plant for the front of the border is called 'Delight'. Where taller plants are required, growing some 38cm (15in) in height, then there are two beautiful varieties to grow: one is called 'Loveliness' and the other 'Sweet Wivelsfield'. The flowering period for both types is from about June to July.

**Dianthus barbatus** (*Sweet William*)  Another popular plant is the Sweet William. The varieties flower from about June to July giving a nice midsummer color display and many are sweetly scented into the bargain. Heights are about 45–60cm (1½–2ft) and there are lots of pretty varieties such as 'Auricula Eyed', 'Indian Carpet', 'Pink Beauty', 'Scarlet Beauty' and some nice mixed varieties too.

**Cheiranthus** (*Wallflower*)  Wallflowers are indispensable plants, producing an early display of color from about March to May. Most are beautifully fragrant and are splendid for planting beneath windows. There are lots of good varieties including some dwarf ones called the 'Tom Thumb' variety which grow only some 23cm (9in) in height. These are especially handy for smaller gardens and for those gardens which are exposed to strong winds. There are also the dwarf bedding varieties growing to a height of 30cm (12in) or so. There are taller varieties in the ordinary strains growing to a height of some 45cm (18in), and these can be bought in particular colors such as 'Blood Red', 'Carmine King', 'Cloth of Gold' etc. It is a good plan to go for the mixed varieties so that you obtain a nice spectrum of color.

**Dictamnus** (*Burning Bush*)  Another lovely biennial is the Dictamnus which grows about 90cm (3ft) high and produces nice spikes of rose or white colored flowers from June to August.

**Digitalis** (*Foxglove*)  The Foxglove is another lovely plant which is sown about May or June like most of the other biennials. Heights are from about 90cm (3ft) to 1.5m (5ft) according to variety, and a very good type is the 'Excelsior' strain.

**Doronicum** (*Leopard's Bane*)  Doronicum is a very pretty perennial which can be given biennial treatment, particularly in colder areas. Its bright yellow flowers are produced in the early spring, and it grows to a height of about 45–60cm (1½–2ft).

**Lunaria** (*Honesty*)  This is a very pretty true biennial plant and is ideal for the flower arranger as it produces very attractive silvery seed pods. Height is about 60cm (2ft) and the plant flowers in June or July. The purple variety is the most popular, but seeds of mixed colors are also available.

**Matthiola** (*Stocks*)  No planting scheme could possibly be complete without the stocks. The 100% double Brompton stocks are spring flowering types producing a lovely display from March to about May. A mixed variety can be purchased giving a wide range of attractive colors. The East Lothian stock flowers from late spring and during the summer, and again a mixed variety is ideal for a splendid display of scarlet, crimson, purple, pink, rose, lavender and white colors. Heights are from about 30–38cm (12–15in) or more over the range of biennial stock varieties.

**Myosotis** (*Forget-me-Not*)   This is a particularly good plant for bedding purposes, flowering over a fairly long period from about March to early June. 'Blue Bouquet' has very large blue flowers and is a very good plant for cutting. 'Rose Pink' bears very attractive pink flowers and 'Royal Blue' is a nice contrasting color to use with it. Left to their own devices, Forget-me-nots will seed themselves year after year without any assistance from the gardener, and in the old-fashioned garden they can be allowed to propagate themselves, the young seedlings being lifted and transplanted to their final flowering positions in the autumn.

**Penstemon**   The dwarf hybrid types can be sown as biennials to produce compact dwarf plants some 23cm (9in) high, flowering from about May to July. There are lots of pretty colors, including pink, lavender, mauve and rose.

**Viola** (*Pansy*)   The violas and pansies belong to the same family, and both are strictly perennials which are often raised as biennials for summer bedding. Pansies thrive in well-drained, deeply-dug soil and appreciate plenty of well-rotted manure or compost. The seed is sown in seed trays during July or August and placed in a shady frame. Overwinter in the frame in the North, otherwise plant out in September, spacing about 25–30cm (10–12in) apart. As well as the wide range of summer-flowering pansies and violas in many colors and color combinations there are winter-flowering pansies which flower from February onwards indoors and in the South. Particularly attractive specimens can be propagated by cuttings.

*Below, top: these are winter-flowering pansies, ideal for an early display in the garden. Below, bottom: this colorful display of pansies can be prolonged if dead blooms are removed. Below, right: red is quite an uncommon shade in pansies.*

# BULBS CORMS & TUBERS

These can be the real labor savers in the garden. Once they have been planted they will grow on happily for many seasons, and with careful selection it is possible to have a beautiful and fascinating display of color right through the year.

They are extremely versatile and accommodating subjects because they can be used for many different features in the garden. They can be used for naturalizing in grass, the most natural effects being obtained when they are simply scattered unevenly and planted where they fall. They can be used in herbaceous borders, and they can be planted in beds on their own. The miniature varieties are ideal for planting in a rockery, and of course bulbs can be grown in containers such as tubs or window boxes.

It is as well at this stage to appreciate the subtle differences between bulbs, corms and tubers. The **bulb** is constructed, as it were, of a large number of scales which form layers packed tight together one on top of the other. A popular example is the onion. A **corm**, however, has no scales, and is a solid tissue right throughout its form. It is in fact a form of thickened stem, and is usually covered by membraneous sheaths. A **tuber** is also a plant which has solid flesh but does not have this sheath.

**Where to plant bulbs and corms**  Being such versatile plants, these flowers can be used in many parts of the garden but the main consideration must be that they must not be sited where they could be subject to strong winds which could damage the flowers and even break the fairly brittle stems of many. Many of the plants can be naturalized as previously described, but most subjects appreciate a sunny situation. There are a few which will grow happily in a shaded site, and these plants include the snowdrops especially.

Where bulbs are to be planted in turf there are special bulb planting tools available which take out a rounded plug of soil, and the bulb or corm is then placed at the bottom of the hole and the plug replaced and gently firmed. It is quite a novel idea to use some of the small or low-growing bulbs for planting in pathways where, for example, gaps between crazy paving stones can be opened up, filled with good soil and the tiny bulbs established in these prepared sites.

**Soil preparation**  Fortunately most of these plants will grow in a wide range of soils, but it is as well to go to a little extra trouble to ensure that they have a really good start. This is done by digging or forking over the site to a depth of about 20–25cm (8–10in) and as the work proceeds some moist horticultural peat or well rotted compost should be worked in. About four or five good handfuls of either of the materials should be scattered over each square meter (square yard) of ground. If the soil is in a poor or impoverished condition, work in a general or balanced fertilizer at the rate of 45–60g per sq. m ($1\frac{1}{2}$–2oz per sq. yd). If the soil is on the light side and tends to dry out badly the amount of peat or composted vegetable waste should be increased so that the material holds moisture as much as possible, and this will prevent a great deal of drying out.

**Aftercare**  Fortunately bulbs and corms require the minimum of care and attention once they have been planted out. It is important, however, especially in new gardens or where a neglected site has been reclaimed, that special attention is paid to weeding. Otherwise, where smaller bulbs are established, these could get smothered by strong and persistent weeds. Where bulbs, such as daffodils for example, are left in the ground for several years it is a wise policy to give them an occasional feed. A balanced or general fertilizer is ideal, and this should be applied at the rate of about 60g per sq. m (2oz per sq. yd). Preferably the application should be given during wet weather but you can apply the dressing when weather conditions are dry as long as the fertilizer is well watered in afterwards.

It is a good plan in many cases to remove the dead flower heads from the plants. This is carried out particularly on bulbs such as daffodils, tulips and hyacinths.

*Below: a bulb (top diagram) is constructed of layers. Examples are the onion, narcissus and tulip. A corm (center) is solid and usually flattened in shape, with a sheath-like outer covering. Examples are the gladiolus and crocus. Tubers (bottom) are really enlarged underground stems. Typical tubers are the potato and the dahlia.*

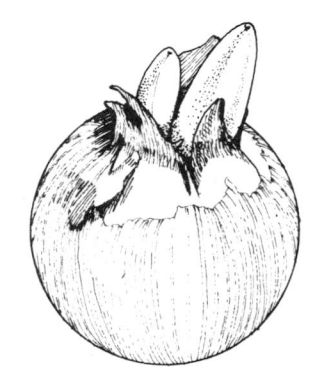

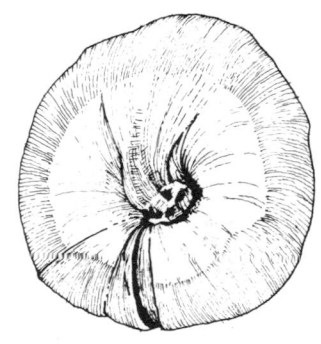

# Choosing flowers

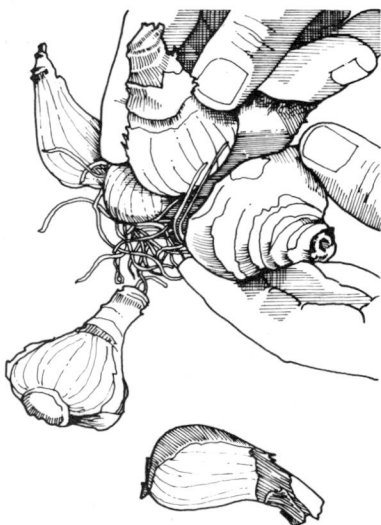

*Above : increasing bulbs by division. The bulblets are carefully detached from the parent bulb and planted up separately. Each will form a new plant, which will flower after one or two seasons.*

Flowering plants such as gladioli should be treated in the same way. It is very important also that as much of the top growth or foliage as possible is allowed to die down naturally after the flowering display has been completed. If foliage is allowed to die back in this way, the valuable nutrients or plant foods in the leaves are slowly returned to the bulb or corm beneath the soil and the plant builds up its strength for the following season. Sometimes bulbs or corms have to be removed to make way for other flowering displays, in which case the lifted plants should be heeled in carefully in a convenient part of the garden where their foliage can complete its natural dying down.

Some attention to staking may be necessary especially if the garden is exposed to strong winds. It is a simple matter to provide a suitable length of cane stick to which the flowering stem or even the complete plant with its leaves can be carefully tied. Many bulbs are hardy and require very little if any frost protection, but where conditions can be severe or if exceptionally hard weather is forecast then some protective material should be handy to place over the area where the plants are growing. Materials such as straw, peat, leaf mould or even thick plastic sheeting can be used for this purpose.

**Lifting and storing bulbs** It has been previously explained why some bulbs have to be lifted to make way for another flower display, but there is another good reason also. This particularly applies in a case of the naturalized plants, where after several seasons (and especially where the soil is good and growth has been vigorous) it is necessary to lift clumps occasionally as they become overgrown or overcrowded. If the bulbs or corms are left too close together the flowering display gradually becomes poorer. They should be lifted and then replanted to allow more space between the corms or bulbs. Care must be taken during this operation to insert the fork well away from clumps to minimize the possibility of the corms or bulbs being pierced by the fork prongs. If bulbs *are* damaged badly they are best thrown away, otherwise they can be subjected to pest and disease attack.

Bulbs or corms should only be lifted when the foliage is dying down well, and if necessary they should be heeled in to complete the process in a convenient part of the garden. Keep an eye on the plants and eventually, when the foliage has died down completely, the bulbs can be lifted and dried off ready for storage. There are several ways in which the plants can be dried off. If the weather is dry at the time the bulbs or corms can be carefully arranged on wire netting and suspended above the ground so that a good circulation of air moves between them, which will encourage rapid and satisfactory drying off. If the weather is poor at the time of lifting they can be placed in the greenhouse on the benches, or on trays or other suitable receptacles. Even a frame or a row of Hotkaps would provide a very adequate means of protection. Afterwards carefully remove any shrivelled outer skin (only the loose skin should be dealt with) and then place them in a cool, airy and preferably frost-free shed where they can be stored until they are planted again. It is a good plan also to dust the corms or tubers with BHC or flowers of sulfur to give protection against pest attacks such as thrips and also to prevent attack by fungus disease. Any bulbs or corms which are doubtful as far as damage is concerned should be thrown away, otherwise they could contaminate the other healthy plants in storage.

**Increasing bulbs or corms** During the lifting process several tiny bulblets or cormlets will be noticed around the base of the mature or parent bulbs or corms. It is from these that new plants can be raised and in this way the original stock can be readily increased.

The best way to deal with them is to carefully break them away from the parent plant and then to sow them thinly down shallow drills, pulling the soil back afterwards. The depth to which the sowing drill is taken out will depend on the size of the bulblets or cormlets. As an approximate guide, however, they should be covered with about their own depth of soil. Usually planting is carried out immediately after the parent bulbs or corms have been lifted. The little bulblets or cormlets will take a year or two before they flower and during that time they will gradually increase in size. Keeping them in a special bed enables the gardener to keep an eye on them and at the end of each season, when their small top growth dies down, they can be lifted, dried and then replanted the following year to grow on again and increase their size still further. As far as the amateur gardener is concerned this is the best way to increase most bulbs and corms. Plants can be raised from seed but this is not general practice for the gardener and it takes quite a long time before a plant of flowering size is achieved.

Special methods of propagating certain bulbs are described under that particular plant in the General List: for example, lilies are commonly propagated from scales or by planting the tiny bulbils which grow in the leaf axils. Dahlia tubers are propagated by dividing the tubers into sections or from cuttings.

*Below : bulbs will provide a superb display year after year with very little attention. Fritillaria meleagris, the Checkered Lily or Snake's Head Fritillary, combines well here with Muscari.*

# A SELECTION OF BULBS CORMS & TUBERS

**Acidanthera**   This is a pretty plant which produces its flowers from about August to September. Colors are white with usually a purplish center and the flowers are also nicely fragrant. It grows to a height of about 1m (3–4ft) and is planted out in April and May. It prefers a sunny situation and must have a well–drained soil.

**Allium**   There are many species of this plant with heights ranging from about 23cm (9in) to as much as 1.2m (4ft). Flowering time is from May to June or July and the colors are very attractive, ranging from a delicate rose pink to a deep rose color. Most of them are quite easily grown and are especially attractive when grown in clumps. The smaller types are particularly useful for the rock garden. Planting time is September to October in the North, later in the South.

**Anemone**   The most popular species of this bulb is *A. blanda*. This grows only 15cm (6in) high and is ideal therefore for the rock garden or on the very front edge of the herbaceous border. It flowers late February to May, depending upon climate with flowers of white, pink and mauve. The St. Brigid anemones fall in this group too, and these grow a little higher, up to about 30cm (12in), and flower from early spring to fall depending on the time when the corms are planted out. They are particularly easy plants to cultivate and have delightful colors ranging from white through to a lovely crimson hue. The de Caen anemones are also very popular, with large single flowers mainly in red and blue shades.

**Chionodoxa luciliae** (*Glory of the Snow*)   A very welcome flower in February or March. It grows only to a height of about 15cm (6in) and is a very handy flower for the rock garden or small containers such as window boxes. It is planted in the early autumn and the color range is pink, white and light blue.

**Colchicum**   The pretty late-flowering Colchicum is a plant attaining a height of about 15–25cm (6–10in) according to type. Planted in July the corms flower from September to November. Colors are rose, purple or white and they are particularly delightful if they are naturalized in grass.

**Crocosmia**   Also known as Montbretia. This is a much taller subject attaining a height of 60cm (2ft) or more. It is planted in March and flowers in July to September. It is very easily grown and is especially useful because it provides good cut flowers for indoor decoration. Colors are orange, yellow and red. In more exposed gardens a little staking may be necessary.

**Crocus**   Another very popular corm which gives excellent results in containers such as window boxes. It can also be naturalized in wooded areas or grass, and it provides color if planted in large groups in the front of the herbaceous border. It is a delightful plant also for the tops of cavity walls or even little pockets in pathways constructed from crazy paving. It is planted from August to December (in the South) and flowers early in the year. A wide range of colors is available including yellow, blue and mauve. The spring flowering variety flowers in March and the autumn ones in October. A selection of the crocus family will therefore give color at very useful and sometimes difficult periods of the gardening season. The spring flowering crocus is planted in September to December and the autumn flowering type in August and September.

**Cyclamen**   *C. europaeum* and *C. neapolitanum* are the most delightful miniature cyclamen which are especially useful for the rock garden or the window box or in the tops of the cavity walls. They are dwarf in habit ranging from 8cm (3in) to about 15cm (6in) in height. They are planted in the fall, and colors are usually white or varying shades of pink.

**Dahlias** The dahlia is a really splendid plant for most gardens. It is quite easy to grow and with care the tubers or root systems can be saved to provide plants for next season's planting. There are some beautiful shades in the flowers and the fascination extends to the various forms of bloom which can be had.

Some fascinating types of dahlia can be grown from tubers including the most delightful small decorative or cactus ball and pompon, and there are others such as the single flowered and the anemone flowered. Of course the larger ones can attain huge dimensions. Of particular interest are the fascinating cactus dahlias which have narrow pointed or quilled petals. Then there are the collerettes which have centers made up of stamens with a single row of petals around the outside, very attractive plants indeed. There are also the anemone flowered dahlias, and the peony flowered dahlias, all with fascinating forms of bloom, especially around their centers. The tuberous dahlias are regularly propagated by division of the tubers so that the large clump is carefully cut into sections with a bud or eye attached to each portion. Perhaps the easiest and most popular system, however, is by cuttings, where the tubers are placed in deep boxes of peat and soil in late February or early March, the soil being kept nicely moist and in a constant temperature of about 16°C (60°F). In three or four weeks, or even less, shoots will be produced, and when these are about 10cm (4in) long they are cut off with a sharp knife. The bottom pair of leaves should be removed and a cut made cleanly through the stem just below the leaf joints. The ends are then dipped in a hormone rooting powder or liquid and inserted around the edge of a large 13cm (5in) pot or in deep seed trays using a proprietary rooting mixture. They should be kept moist at all times and in a temperature of about 16°C (60°F). During bright sunny weather some shading is advised until they have rooted well.

When rooted, the cuttings are carefully tapped out of their pot or tray and potted up singly in 9cm (3½in) pots, using a light potting mixture. They are then carefully hardened off by placing them in the garden frame and eventually they will be ready for planting out in their flowering quarters when danger of frost has passed. This point is very important as dahlias are very tender, and in some districts planting is not safe until well into June.

When the flowering displays are over at the end of the season the plants must be lifted and this is usually done when the foliage begins to yellow and die down. In many cases the first frosts will blacken the foliage and the plants must be lifted before the very severe weather sets in. The tubers are lifted very carefully by inserting the garden fork well away from their position so that there is no danger of spiking the tubers with the tines of the fork. Carefully shake out as much of the soil as possible and try to dry the tubers out naturally by leaving them on the surface of the ground during good weather; in inclement weather the tubers can be dried off in a frame or in a greenhouse. It helps to cut the foliage down to within 15cm (6in) or so of ground level before the tubers are lifted.

Dahlia stems are hollow and a lot of moisture or water can collect in the centers, so it is a good policy to turn the tubers upside down if possible when drying out to allow this water to drain away. When thoroughly dry the tubers can be dusted with flowers of sulfur to prevent disease or fungus attacks and then they can be stored away in a cool frost free place. They can be placed in deep boxes filled with dry peat, or they can be stored in boxes of dry sand and kept beneath the greenhouse benches where they cannot be affected by moisture or drips of water. It is important to inspect the tubers occasionally to remove any which may have started to rot. A rotting tuber can quickly affect other sound ones.

**Endymion** (*Bluebell*) This is a most helpful plant where some naturalizing is required. It can be grown in clumps and in borders, but looks at its best in a natural setting of grass. It is planted in the autumn and flowers in the following April to late May.

*Opposite, top : the Autumn Crocus deserves to be as widely grown as its spring-flowering counterparts. Opposite, bottom : Crocosmia or Montbretia bears vividly colored flowers, but where suited the plants can become invasive.*

*Below : dahlia tubers must be lifted and stored in dry peat when the foliage begins to die down. Remember to label each tuber individually if different varieties are stored together.*

**Eranthis** (*Winter aconite*) The beautiful yellow flowers of this winter flower are borne on 10–13cm (4–5in) high stems and flowering time is very early spring.

**Erythronium** (*Dog's Tooth Violet*) An ideal subject for a rock garden, flowering in May and bearing purple, white or pink flowers. The Dog's Tooth Violet grows only some 15cm (6in) high and is planted out in the fall.

**Fritillaria** There are several pretty species of this bulb including the well known Crown Imperial. Flowering time is welcome around April and most of these plants are versatile enough to be used in herbaceous borders, in a rock garden or in small containers. Planting is carried out in late October. The flower range is dominantly yellow though there are some whites and orange and red colors too.

**Galanthus** (*Snowdrop*) What garden planting scheme would be complete without the dainty snowdrop? Here is another ideal subject for naturalizing in grass, especially near or under shrubs or trees planted in the grass area. Planting is done in the early autumn and flowers are produced as early as January where the climate is very mild. The height of the plant is about 15–20cm (6–8in) and flowers are white and green.

**Galtonia** If this plant is established in small groups in the herbaceous border it brings a bright splash of white to the garden in the late summer period of July to late August. It also gives some useful height to a planting scheme as the stems are some 1m (3½ft) long. It is an easy plant to grow, though in the North it may be necessary to dry and store over winter.

**Gladiolus** Again a most popular corm to include in a planting scheme. Heights are from about 45cm (18in) to well over 1.2m (4ft) according to type. The flowering period starts about June and can be as late as October in a late warm summer year. Planting is from April through June in the North or October for the type 'Colvillii' in the South. The color scheme is very varied and some of the newer types have some beautiful deep shades such as reds.

**Hyacinthus** (*Hyacinth*) Here is a bulb which can provide color not only in the open garden but also indoors in the home where specially prepared bulbs can be forced into flower at Christmas time. Height is about 23cm (9in) and the flowering time outdoors is around April in the North. Planting time for outdoor types is in the autumn or in the case of specially prepared bulbs in August or September. Many of the hyacinths are exquisitely fragrant and the color range includes the normal whites, pinks and blues, plus some lovely yellow and orange shades.

**Irises** The iris is another glorious flowering plant which deserves a place in every gardener's layout. There are two types of iris: those which grow from bulbs and those which grow from rhizomes, which are thick underground stems or roots. The irises which are grown from bulbs are those which grow well in pots indoors whereas the iris which grows from a rhizome is not suitable for this type of propagation. There are three classifications of the bulbous iris: these are the reticulatas, xiphiums, and junos.

Where plants are required for dainty habit and only dwarf form of growth, the reticulatas are ideal. They attain an approximate height of 10–20cm (4–8in) and flower from about December until late March in the South, April onward in the North. They have foliage which is of nearly square formation.

For taller growth of some 45–60cm (1½–2ft) the xiphium iris is very useful. There are English, Spanish and Dutch sections in this group, and flowering is from June until about July.

The last group, the juno irises, have a height of 30–60cm (1–2ft) and flower in

spring. They are very pleasant plants but are not as popular as the other two sections, the reticulatas and xiphiums.

Perhaps the most widely grown of the iris are those grown from rhizomes, and there is no doubt that bearded irises are extremely popular. The name refers to the fleshy hairs on the outer petals which are also known as falls. These hairs form a beard-like growth. Another popular name for the bearded iris is the German or Flag iris. They are very versatile plants, particularly as they are available in a range of heights, from under 23cm (9in) to well over 1m (3ft). Taller growing irises of the bearded section are excellent plants to use in the herbaceous or hardy border and planted in small groups of three or four they produce a fine display with their stately spikes of flowers. They flower from late May in the North, whereas the middle section (intermediate) iris flower a little earlier. They are best situated toward the front of the border. For mid to late April flowering, the dwarf irises are excellent and are best accommodated in special features such as the rock garden. They can however be used quite effectively if they are kept toward the front of the herbaceous border layout.

There are some other fascinating types of iris as well as the bearded ones and the bulbous ones. There are, for example, those which do not produce a beard, and these are usually the Siberian irises, with a very handy tall rate of growth up to about 1.2m (4ft) in height. Flowers are generally produced in mid-June. For smaller growth there are the Pacific Coast hybrids flowering in May which grow to 30–45cm (12–18in) or more. For a late June display from quite tall plants (as much as 1.2m (4ft) in height) the Spurias are another useful group of beardless irises. They flower often in late June. If you want a winter display in areas warm enough, then *Iris unguicularis*, also called *Iris stylosa*, is a real beauty. The flowering period is from approximately October to March and the height of the plant is 30cm (12in). Then we have the Japanese or Kaempferi irises and Louisiana types which are ideal for a water feature where they are planted at the edge of the feature in boggy ground. These flower in June and July. Some rather unusual irises which have flowers very similar to orchids are the crested types or Evansias.

Irises which are grown from the rhizomes or thick root systems like a soil which is quite rich, and plenty of organic matter such as peat or composted vegetable waste should be worked in. A few days before planting takes place a proprietary general fertilizer should be applied and raked in using the quantity recommended by the manufacturer. One has to be a little careful about the type of soil in which these plants are grown because if it is limy it will be difficult to grow the crested or Pacific Coast hybrids successfully. The only way to overcome this situation is to try and dig in large quantities of horticultural peat. Many of the other types of irises like a soil which is slightly acid, but if the soil is very high in acidity then some ground limestone should be applied and worked in a week or two before planting is carried out.

The planting period for irises grown from rhizomes is from the end of June until about the second week in July. The plants are planted near the surface of the soil and in order to accommodate the peculiar root system a sloping slit or hole should be taken out to a depth of about 10cm (4in) at its deepest point. The top of the rhizome or the area from which the foliage arises should finish at the top of the plant-ing hole and should be slightly exposed. Make sure that most of the root area is placed towards the deepest part of the hole. As the soil is replaced it must be firmed well with the fingers, and if the weather is dry water should be given.

The planting of the beardless types is slightly easier because they have fibrous root systems and can be planted simply by excavating a large enough hole with the hand trowel. Many of these plants are planted in the autumn, around October in mild climates, but in spring in the North. Those irises which are planted in the bog section of a water feature are usually set out in May when the weather and therefore the water is warmer. The crested irises are planted in late May or early June.

**Ixia** This is a bulb which is best for more favored or sheltered gardens, but it can be nurtured along if frames are used for protection during the winter. It grows to a height of about 45cm (18in) and is planted in fall. Flowers are produced in May, in a range of very pretty shades of yellow, pink, white and red.

**Lilium** One of the most beautiful bulbous plants is the lily. Few plants in fact can be quite so accommodating as this wonderful flowering plant. There is variety in its height as lilies grow from about 45cm (15in) to over 3m (10ft) according to type and variety. The many different types available today also makes it possible to grow this glorious plant in a very wide range of soils and situations. Many of the plants will grow happily in full hot sunlight, while others are at their best in more shaded situations.

The lily in fact is one of the oldest flowers in cultivation, having been known to the Egyptians, for example. There are two main classifications of its flower: the trumpet shape and the Turk's cap. The trumpet-shaped flowers can vary from a narrow formation to an open delightful bowl shape, and two examples of this group are *Lilium longiflorum* and *Lilium candidum*. The Turk's cap type have a pendant type of flower about 5cm (2in) in length, and the flower heads themselves are quite distinctive as the petals are curved or rolled back toward the tips. An example of the Turk's cap lily is *Lilium superbum*.

It is rather odd that, although lilies are available in a multitude of shades such as pink, yellow, purple, orange and even a dark crimson—and of course the beautiful whites—there are no blue lilies up to now. Many of the lilies are exquisitely scented, and the flowering season for those in the open garden is from about May to late September. One of the easiest and most accommodating of the great lily family is *Lilium regale*. Commonly known as the Regal lily, it will grow extremely well in a surprising range of soil conditions. There is in fact a lily type for practically any planting purpose in and around the garden from the tiny plants for a rockery to the tall and stately spires of plants for the back of a border.

The planting time for many of the lilies is from late summer to early spring according to soil conditions, though obviously more care in planting is necessary in the early spring to make sure that the ground is not frosted or too wet. There is one exception to the planting period and that is for the Madonna lily (*Lilium candidum*) which should be planted or replanted as soon as possible when the stem dies down, which is usually in the month of August. There are some lily species which have roots arising from the base, and these should be planted in the early autumn. The planting depth should be according to the size of the bulb and this depth is usually around two and a half times the depth of the bulb. This is a useful average guide. There are a few lilies, however, which must be planted rather shallowly—in fact just below the surface of the soil. Three examples are *L. candidum*, *L. testaceum* and *L. giganteum*. Whatever type of lily bulb is planted it helps to add some peat and sharp sand mixed together. This should be arranged along the bottom of each planting hole. The bulbs should be pressed firmly into the base of the hole, adding some more peat sand mixture around the roots, and then the remainder of the soil is replaced, firming gently at the same time.

**Lily propagation** Lilies can be increased or propagated in several ways. The most popular system is by what is known as scales. The plants will flower in about three to five years by this method. A surprising number of new lilies can be produced in this way because healthy bulbs will provide at least fourteen of these scales. The time to propagate from scales is shortly after the plants have finished flowering. The bulb should be lifted carefully and only the plumpest and healthiest scales should be pulled away very carefully from the bulb. Fill a seed tray with a fairly light potting mixture and carefully insert each scale to about half its depth in the mixture. Very gently firm the soil back around each scale as it is placed in position. The scales

*Opposite, top: lilies, reputed to be difficult to grow, are in fact quite accommodating subjects. This is Lilium speciosum from Japan. Opposite, bottom: Lilium regale, one of the easiest species to establish.*

*Below: Narcissus x cyclamineus, one of the prettiest species. Below right: Narcissus triandrus albus, also known as Angel's Tears.*

should be spaced about 5cm (2in) apart each way in each tray. Place in a propagator; or place in a cold frame, remembering to keep the frame lights closed during colder weather.

In about five to six weeks of planting in this way some tiny bulbs should have formed, and shortly afterwards some small shoots will appear. This is the time when the scales should be removed from the propagating tray and each scale potted up singly in an 8–10cm (3–4in) pot using the same light potting mixture. Place each pot outside in a sheltered warm part of the garden and plunge them up to their rims. They can then be covered with some sand or peat. If this cannot be done then simply place the pots in the soil up to their rims in a frame or under some Hotkaps. The little plants should be ready for planting out in their final quarters in the garden the following autumn.

Many other bulbs such as *Lilium regale* can be lifted at the end of their flowering time and replanted, spacing the new bulbs further apart to provide them with better growing area or room. This may well need doing every three years. Another fascinating method of increasing some types of lilies such as the Tiger Lily is to keep a watchful eye on the joints between the leaves and the stems, in other words the leaf axils. You should notice some tiny bulbils. They can either be blackish-purple in color, or green. These will be ready for careful detachment with the fingers when the parent plant is in full flower, and the tiny bulbils are simply inserted in a suitable seed mixture in a seed tray. They are placed about 1cm ($\frac{1}{2}$in) deep and 6cm ($2\frac{1}{2}$in) apart. The completed tray is kept in a cold frame and eventually the bulbils will root, produce young shoots and be ready for planting out in their permanent growing quarters the following autumn. Many lilies of course can be grown traditionally by seed sowing in seed trays or pots using a suitable seed mixture, and potting the seedlings later on when they can be handled, placing them individually in 8cm (3in) pots using a well-drained potting mixture. The seed is best raised in a temperature of about 13–15°C (55–60°F) in a greenhouse or heated frame. The spring is the best time for seed propagation.

**Leucojum** (*Snowflake*)  This is a bulb which is best planted in masses or drifts and will provide some nice color in the late spring, around April or May. Flowers are white with green tips and the height is about 20–60cm (8–24in) according to type.

**Muscari** (*Grape hyacinth*)  Another versatile plant which is happy in a rock garden, or in the front of the border. Its display of bluish flowers is in April or May.

**Narcissus**  This embraces a very large range of extremely pretty bulbs including

the daffodil, the narcissus and the jonquils etc. Most of the bulbs are very easy to grow and the smaller types such as the jonquils are particularly useful for the rock garden or the window box or other suitable containers. They are a delight to use for brightening up the patio or terrace when planted in suitable containers or even along the tops of cavity walls. Flowering time is from March to May and heights vary from as little as 15–18cm (6–7in) to as much as 45cm (18in). The color range is usually yellow or white.

*Below: this is one of the types of Tazetta narcissus, which bear more than one flower per stem. Below, bottom and bottom left: two pretty varieties of the low-growing kaufmanniana tulips. On the left is 'Kafka', and on the right 'Johann Strauss'.*

**Ornithogalum** (*Star of Bethlehem*)  *Ornithogalum umbellatum* is a front of the border plant, and the smaller low-growing species which attain a height of about 10–15cm (4–6in) are ideal for the rockery. Planting is usually done in October. For the tender *O. thyrsoides* or Chincherinchee planting should take place in April. Flowers are of a white cream color and are produced in May or June and the plant is best grown in well prepared soil and in a sheltered garden.

**Scilla**  The types such as *S. sibirica*, *S. tubergeniana* and *S. bifolia* are delightful tiny plants about 13–15cm (5–6in) high flowering in February to April. They are planted in the early autumn and are quite easy to grow. They have beautiful blue colors and are especially helpful plants when establishing a rock garden.

**Sternbergia**  Planted in August the plant flowers in late September bearing very attractive yellow blooms. It does resent disturbance and is best left to its own devices. It grows to a height of about 10cm (4in) and is best situated in a sunny position.

**Tulipa** (*Tulip*)  The tulips cover a tremendous range of types, from the singles and doubles to those with attractive lily-shaped flower heads, and the very eye-catching parrot tulips with their fringed petals. Planting time is usually in October to December. The color range is quite fantastic including the basic colors of whites, reds, yellows and pinks, plus some with multicolored flower heads which are well worth trying. Flowering time is from about March to June according to type and climate, and the heights vary from 15cm (6in) to 75cm (1½ft). Many of the tulips can be planted in beds or borders on their own, either massed in groups to produce brilliant contrasting splashes of color, or more formally in beds of a single color. Some of the smaller varieties can be used in herbaceous borders in clumps of contrasting colors, and the smallest ones such as the kaufmanniana hybrids and species are especially delightful in the rock garden or the window box.

# THE HERBACEOUS BORDER

*Hostas are among the most useful herbaceous plants. Here different varieties are planted together for pure foliage effect.*

Here we are dealing with a very important feature in the garden which is in complete contrast to the hardy and half-hardy annual border. Hardy perennial or herbaceous plants are those plants which come up year after year and die down each autumn or winter to reappear again the following spring. They are in fact, in the majority of cases, pretty permanent plants. Although many of these wonderful plants will produce glorious displays for very many seasons there are a few which are relatively short-lived, and examples include hollyhocks and delphiniums.

The herbaceous border is a British innovation dating from the 1870s, and today there are many fine examples of these borders in several of the stately homes. Because the herbaceous border is a fairly permanent feature in the garden, the groundwork for it must be undertaken with considerable care and in some detail. Not only is it very important to prepare the site thoroughly in the first place, but it is equally important to make a careful selection of plants which will give pleasure in many ways over a long period.

Herbaceous plants have many and varied delightful forms. There is tremendous variation in heights, there is a wide range of beautiful colors and shades, and by careful planning a fascinating display can be obtained for many months of the gardening year. Herbaceous plants are considered as hardy or tough specimens. There are several which are half-hardy and even some which are relatively tender. For the purpose of this chapter we will consider those which present few cultural problems and which can literally take care of themselves.

## Basic Planning
Although without doubt the most dramatic results are obtained from lavish displays or plantings where long wide beds are established, there is no reason why, with

POISONOUS FLOWERS
Special care should be taken when young children are likely to be using the garden a great deal. The following plants are particularly dangerous if eaten.

*Aconitum napellus* (Monkshood)—All parts poisonous, said by some authorities to be the most dangerous of all British plants
*Colchicum autumnale* (Autumn crocus)—All parts poisonous, particularly corms and seeds
*Convallaria majalis* (Lily-of-the-valley)—All parts poisonous
*Delphinium ajacis* (Larkspur)—Seeds and foliage
*Digitalis* (Foxglove)—All
*Helleborus niger* (Christmas rose)—All
*Iris versicolor* (Iris, Blue Flag) and other species—Possibly all
*Lupinus* species (Lupin)—All, particularly seeds
*Narcissus* species (Narcissus, daffodil)—Bulb
*Podophyllum peltatum* (American mandrake)—All, especially green, unripe berries

# Choosing flowers

**HERBACEOUS PLANTS FOR EXPOSED SITES**
If your garden is situated in open country, perhaps on an exposed hillside, perennial plants need to be chosen carefully. Coastal gardens are particularly vulnerable to strong gales and salt-laden winds. Bear in mind, however, that there is a limit to the tolerance of even the toughest plants, and those listed below are only those which have the best chance of survival in such a situation:

Agapanthus (African Lily)
Armeria (Thrift)
Artemisia (Wormwood)
Bergenia
Centaurea
Echinops (Globe Thistle)
Euphorbia (Spurge)
Hemerocallis (Day Lily)
Kniphofia (Red Hot Poker)
Potentilla
Sedum
Tradescantia

careful thought, beautiful herbaceous border displays cannot be established in the relatively small garden. One must appreciate, however, that herbaceous plants increase in size each season and most will ultimately occupy quite a large area of ground per plant. This means that much wider beds will be required compared to those used for annual displays of flowering plants. Some purists will say that ideally an herbaceous border should be at least 3m (9ft) in width and no less than 6.5–7.5m (20–25ft) in length. Where one has a reasonably large garden this grandiose scale presents few problems. However, as new gardens are becoming smaller some re-thinking is necessary. The following are a few ideas for using herbaceous plants in the smaller garden.

**Mixed borders**    An alternative solution is to have what is known as a mixed border. Here the perennial plants are interplanted or mixed with other garden plants such as roses, bulbs and shrubs, and even our old friends the hardy and half-hardy annual flowers. If it is necessary to keep the border display within strict bounds the gardener will have to consider very carefully his selection of plants, paying particular attention to important points such as the height, spread and vigor of the plants.

**Island borders**    An alternative system is to have what are known as island borders. Here smaller borders can be established in the lawn setting and the beautiful green color of the grass provides a perfect, natural background for the colorful border.

**Other ideas**    There are lots of other exciting ways in which a border can be planned. One can arrange for many of the subjects to produce flowers for cutting. There are many permutations for color displays too. Then there is the fascination of juggling the various heights of the herbaceous plants, not to mention the excitement of color contrasts or subtle blending of colors to form a restful feature in one's garden. There is even the possibility of growing plants for the beauty of their foliage or even for the fascination of their seed heads which, when dried, are so useful for indoor flower arrangements.

**Preparing the site**    As the border will be established for many seasons it is vital that the initial preparations are carried out thoroughly. The ideal time to establish a border is in the autumn, from mid September through October, later farther South. This means that the preparation or cultivation of the site must be undertaken in good time for this important period. Ideally the soil should be prepared in late August and/or during September. If the site is virgin land, the top growth of weeds and perhaps coarse grass must be removed and the soil dug as deeply as possible. At least the full depth of the spade or fork will be necessary, that is to say at least 25cm (10in).

In very neglected sites it may even be necessary to double dig the area. This is carried out by excavating a 60cm (2ft) wide trench. The soil from the trench to the depth of the spade is taken out and this soil is placed at the end of the site where digging will finish. The base of each trench is broken up with the fork, inserting this to its full depth each time. The soil from the next trench is then thrown forward and on top of this forked over base, and then this trench in turn has its base forked over too. Digging proceeds in this manner until the whole of the site has been cultivated. As work proceeds manure, peat or composted vegetable waste should be thoroughly worked into the top trench. On heavy, wet soils it is a good idea to mix some sharp sand or well weathered cinders or ashes into the base of each trench as it is forked over.

On cultivated soils or reasonably clean areas single digging can be carried out to the full depth of the spade or fork. Again the plant food should be worked in as digging proceeds. Leave the surface of the soil as rough as possible and, a few days before planting takes place, the surface should be broken down and raked finer.

During this operation more plant food should be applied, this time in the form of fertilizer which should be a well balanced general fertilizer. The approximate rate of application should be 60g per sq. m (2oz per sq. yd). At the same time a slow release or slow acting fertilizer should be applied in the form of sterilized bonemeal at 60–90g per sq. m (2–3oz per sq. yd).

In the preparation of an herbaceous border its outline should be seriously considered. This advice applies especially to the long border which is usually situated at one side of a garden. Although straight edges to a border are easy to cut out, it is surprising how much the appearance of a border is enhanced if a more natural, irregular outline is cut out. Be careful, though, and make sure these irregular outlines take the form of gentle sweeps or curves so that it is a reasonably easy matter to push the lawn mower along them during the busy grass-cutting months. If an island border is to be established in the lawn its outline can take various forms. It can, for example, be square or rectangular, it can be circular or oval, it can be quite long and reasonably thin or it can have a pleasing irregular curved outline.

How can one mark out these irregular outlines? It is quite easy using either a trickle of sand, or even land lime, or one can pay out the garden hose, curving it like a snake to form the desired outline, and then cut out the edges. The advantage of using a garden hose is that one can keep rearranging the outlines until the most pleasing appearance is achieved. Where there is room it is a good plan to have the border as wide as possible and ideally a width of 2.5–3.5m (8–10ft) is suitable. One advantage of an irregular outline is the fact that here and there the depth of the border can be increased to generous proportions.

**The layout of the border**   This is really an armchair job with pencil and paper. The outline of the border should be marked out to scale and, after careful perusal of catalogs, or preferably using the advice given in the list of plants later in this chapter, one can create a really personalized border.

KEY

1 Achillea 'Coronation Gold'
2 Helenium 'Moerheim Beauty'
3 Anthemis tinctoria
4 Aster 'Marie Ballard'
5 Polygonum amplexicaule atrosanguineum
6 Campanula lactiflora
7 Salvia turkestanica
8 Sidalcea 'Rose Queen'
9 Scabiosa 'Clive Greaves'
10 Solidago 'Lemore'
11 Aster 'Crimson Brocade'
12 Phlox 'Eventide'
13 Hemerocallis 'Golden Orchid'
14 Anaphalis triplinervis
15 & 22 Erigeron 'Darkest of All'
16 Phlox 'Brigadier'
17 Aconitum 'Bressingham Spire'
18 Incarvillea delavayi
19 Geranium 'Johnson's Blue'
20 Sedum 'Ruby Glow'
21 Potentilla 'William Rollison'
23 Aster 'Lady in Blue'
24 Eryngium varifolium
25 Dianthus 'White Ladies'
26 Heuchera 'Shere Variety'
27 Coreopsis verticillata

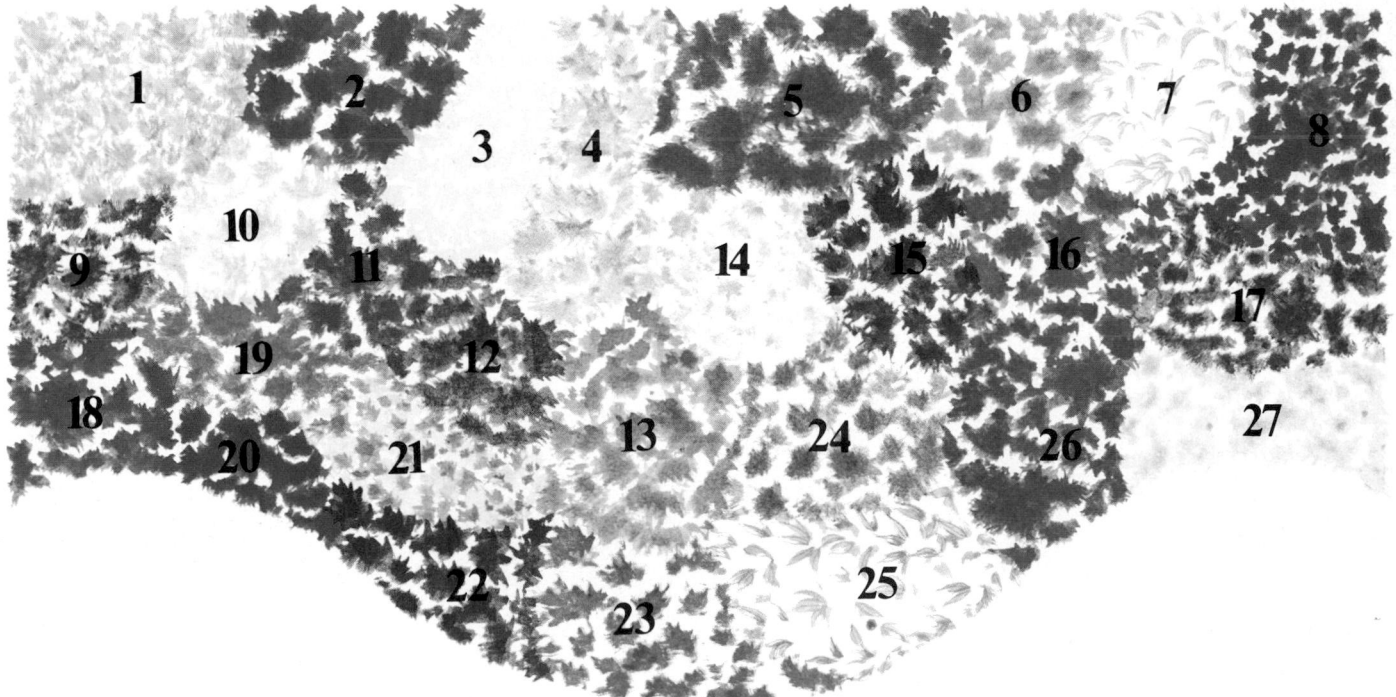

*A ready-planned herbaceous border, using plants arranged according to their ultimate height, flower color and flowering time.*

In the planning stage it is important to make sure that, where some plants finish their display earlier, another suitably placed plant nearby will take over its own display thus filling in the gaps. This can be easily ascertained if attention is paid to the flowering times of various subjects.

Of course, there is also the fascination of planning to create various permutations of color, very similar in fact to the way in which the annual borders are planned. Color planning is a rather personal affair, and no two gardeners think alike when it comes to choosing colors. There are some basic facts to appreciate, however. Colors can be arranged in pastel shades, or groupings of one color can be arranged most effectively: for example, in the red spectrum, plants can be selected with deep, strong red colors shading down to the paler shades such as pink, etc. In contrast to this idea there could be planting schemes where vivid color clashes are arranged. A red color will stand out most effectively against a background of yellow flowers.

Then there is the effect of foliage and forms to appreciate. There are many plants with delicate, wispy or ferny foliage such as the astilbes and the gypsophilas. Others have thick or fleshy leaves; an example of these is the bergenia. Much use can be made of the plants' heights. The stately spires of lupins and the much taller plants such as hollyhocks and delphiniums can create areas or spots of height and character which add relief to borders which could otherwise be a little uninteresting if too many plants of the same height were used.

In the planning of a border due consideration should be paid to the inclusion of plants for special purposes. It would be convenient for example to have some plants which could be harvested and dried for flower arranging and many others which can be cut and used fresh for the same purpose. Planning a border is quite an exciting and fascinating business, and well worth the effort involved, as the plan you eventually evolve will be tailored to your needs, your personal tastes, and the space available.

In the selection of herbaceous plants for the border another important factor must be taken into consideration. This is the vigor and the spread of individual types or varieties. There are plants such as Michaelmas daisies or hardy asters which cover ground quite quickly, so allowance must be made in the positioning of plants for the rapid or moderate spread of varieties. Although the planting scheme can allow for one type or variety per station or planting area, a much better and more natural effect can be achieved if groups of the same plant are planted together. The grouping can include two or perhaps three of a kind. Obviously much will depend on the area the border occupies, and naturally the number of plants in groupings will depend on the total space available.

*Dividing herbaceous plants is the simplest method of propagation. The clump can be gently eased apart using two garden forks placed back to back. Old, dead growth in the center of the clump can be discarded, if necessary.*

There is some confusion amongst gardeners as to the arrangement of plants according to their heights. The simplest procedure is to have the tallest at the back of the border with the remaining plants graduating in size or height towards the front, while at the very edges of the border are the dwarf plants. With a little care and ingenuity, however, plants can be to a certain extent mixed up. Some of the taller plants can be brought forward towards the front of the border, and this dotting of heights will certainly create more interest and produce a more natural border. Care must be taken, however, to see that smaller plants are not overshadowed too much so that their display is concealed by their taller neighbors. In all fairness one should say at this stage that this clever juggling with plant types comes easier with experience, but if the habit of plants is studied carefully this type of natural planning can be easily undertaken by the novice.

### Planting the herbaceous border

There are two main planting seasons. The first is around early spring and the second is September and October in the North, somewhat later in the South. These times are dependent of course on weather and soil conditions, and in favorable areas it could well be that planting could take place earlier or could even be extended later into the season.

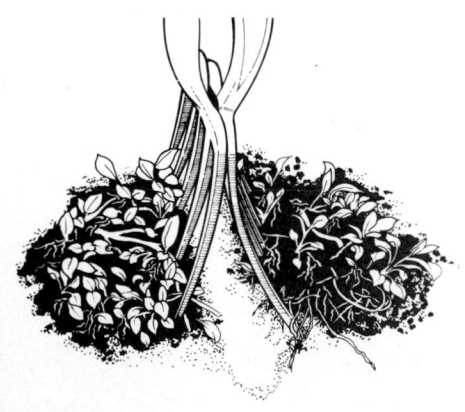

Plants can be obtained in two main ways, either from a nursery or from a garden center. In many cases the plants are sold in small containers or fiber pots. These are probably the best plants to purchase as they should have formed a good root system and will grow away quickly after planting with minimum check. Sometimes plants are sold lifted from the soil in the propagating or growing quarters in a nursery and wrapped in damp material to be sent by mail. If these plants have a good root system they should grow away quite well but will receive a small check to growth initially. The advantage of container grown plants is that most of them can be planted at virtually any time of the year except in the winter months, provided of course that their roots are kept moist, especially during warm dry weather. Even so, it is preferable with these plants to plant out during the dates previously advised.

If you do obtain plants by mail you will have the advantage of a wider selection than that usually carried by the local nursery or garden center. But it often happens that plants arrive from the nursery at a time when they cannot be planted out straight away. In this case a shallow trench should be taken out in a sheltered part of the garden, and the packing material round the plants should be carefully removed and the plants placed along the bottom of the trench practically touching. They should be given a good watering and if necessary some damp peat should be worked around them before the excavated soil from the shallow trench is replaced around their roots and firmed gently with the feet. Here the plants can remain for several days quite safely—provided of course they are not allowed to dry out. When the plants can be planted in their final quarters only a few at a time should be used, taking care to cover the others' roots with some plastic to prevent them drying out while they are waiting. Plant a few at a time, checking their positions from your planting plan, placing them in position first on the soil surface, then planting them. Do make sure that all plants are carefully labelled so that there is no danger of mix-ups.

A good size hole should be taken out for each plant, a little deeper and wider than the extent of the soil ball or root system. Usually a hand trowel is adequate, but for larger plants a bigger hole will be necessary, and this should be taken out with a spade. Place the plant to the correct depth (which is gauged by the old soil mark which will show on the stems). This is the depth to which they were planted in the nursery. Ideally this soil mark should be covered by about 1cm ($\frac{1}{2}$in) of soil at the completion of the planting. The spacing of each plant will depend on its vigor. Very approximately, the spacing will be about 15–25cm (6–10in) for plants at the edge of the border, 30–45cm (12–18in) for the plants towards the center of the border, and 60–90cm (2–3ft) for plants towards the back and at the back of the border. It is a good plan to give the area a good watering from time to time. The best way to do this is to use a sprinkler on the hose or one of the oscillating types which throw their water from side to side giving very even and thorough coverage.

**Aftercare** A careful eye must be kept on the growth of weeds, and regular weeding by hand or with the use of a hoe will be essential. Later on, when the herbaceous plants are well established, much of the weed growth will be smothered each year by the plants themselves. Occasionally, however, some perennial weeds may be discovered, and these must be dealt with individually by carefully pulling or digging them out as soon as they can be handled. Another method of suppressing weeds is to give the beds a good mulching. For this well rotted manure, horticultural peat or composted vegetable waste can be scattered in between the plants to a depth of at least 5cm (2in). This mulching will also serve another purpose and that is to conserve valuable soil moisture during hot, dry weather.

Before a mulching is given in the spring, a light scattering of a general or balanced fertilizer should be given at approximately 45g per sq. m (1$\frac{1}{2}$oz per sq. yd). A dressing of sterilized bonemeal may be applied at the rate of 90–120g per sq. m (3–4oz per sq. yd). One-third this amount of superphosphate may be used instead. A liquid feed is useful from late May until July.

---

**HERBACEOUS PLANTS FOR SHADE**
Sometimes the only site available for the perennial border is a rather shady position where, perhaps, nearby trees not only cast shadow but steal valuable moisture from the plants. Fortunately there are a number of plants which will stand up quite well to such conditions, and the following should be given a trial:

*Iris foetidissima* (Gladwyn Iris)
*Helleborus foetidus* (Stinking Hellebore)
*Polygonum affine* 'Darjeeling Red'
*Ajuga reptans atropurpurea*
*Saxifraga umbrosa*
*Anaphalis triplinervis*

---

**HERBACEOUS PLANTS FOR CUTTING AND DRYING**
Incorporate some of the following plants in your general planting scheme and you will be assured of a constant supply of flowers for cutting in summer and also some to dry for winter floral decoration.
Achillea (Yarrow)
Agapanthus (African Lily)
Aster (Michaelmas Daisy)
Astilbe
Campanula (Bellflower)
Coreopsis
Doronicum (Leopard's Bane)
Eryngium (Sea Holly)
Euphorbia (Spurge)
Gaillardia
Geum
Helenium
Helianthus (Sunflower)
Helleborus (Christmas Rose and Lenten Rose)
Heuchera
Liatris
Limonium
Lychnis (Campion)
Oenothera (Evening Primrose)
Paeonia (Peony)
Phlox
Physalis (Bladder Cherry, Chinese Lanterns)
Polygonatum (Solomon's Seal)
Primula
Pyrethrum
Scabiosa
Thalictrum

# Choosing flowers

*Above: three popular herbaceous plants are, from left to right, delphiniums, peonies and Doronicum.*

## HERBACEOUS PLANTS FOR HEAVY SOIL
Much can be done to improve the condition of a heavy soil such as clay. Particular attention should be paid to drainage, and borders should be double dug as described and plenty of organic material incorporated. The following plants are particularly suitable for inclusion in the planting scheme, as they will stand the best chance of success on this type of soil:

Aconitum (Monk's Hood)
Astilbe
Campanula (Bellflower)
Doronicum (Leopard's Bane)
Echinops (Globe Thistle)
Erigeron (Fleabane)
Helenium
Hosta (Plantain Lily)
Iris—most varieties
Polygonum
Rudbeckia (Coneflower)
Sidalcea
Solidago (Goldenrod)

**Staking and training** This is a particularly important part of the cultivation of herbaceous plants. Many plants grow quite tall and even in the most sheltered garden some support is necessary in order to prevent them flopping over or, in an exposed windy site, to prevent them becoming severely damaged. In any case, good training enables the gardener to arrange the plants so that they give their best display.

The important thing to remember is that all forms of training must be carried out at an early stage of growth so that the training material can be placed around the plants without causing damage. One of the other aims of training is to try and supply support which will eventually be concealed as much as possible by the plants themselves. Nothing looks uglier, for example, than a forest of bamboo canes protruding from the border.

There are several ways in which the plants can be supported. One method is to use bamboo canes of different sizes according to the eventual height of the plant. Some plants may only require one cane stick and the plant is fastened to this by encircling its growth as the plant gets bigger with twine or raffia, tying securely each time to the cane stick. For bushier plants and for more vigorous ones it may be necessary to insert several cane sticks around the plant. These can be inserted so that they point slightly outward to enable the center of the plant to remain reasonably open as it grows. Again the growths are encircled by the tying material which is secured to the cane sticks. It is advisable to know the approximate eventual heights of the plants so that ideally the top of the supporting material is a few inches below the flower heads.

Another system of training makes use of pea sticks or twiggy branches or boughs. Unfortunately, these are not always easy to come by except perhaps in country areas. This material, however, is especially useful because it is concealed quickly by the plants themselves, and the twiggy nature of the material provides ideal support for all growths. Unfortunately the life span of this material is short. It quickly rots and becomes brittle and one must expect to renew virtually every year.

A more modern method of training and support is by special galvanized metal frames or supports which take many forms such as circles, squares, and rectangles. They are manufactured in a mesh form, and are placed over the plants at an early stage of growth, the supports being held by special metal legs or by tying to several cane sticks or stakes. Some sophisticated designs can be adjusted as the plant grows. These supports are easy to use and will last many seasons.

For very tall plants such as delphiniums and hollyhocks very strong supports may be necessary, and one-inch square stakes are ideal. These should be inserted carefully and the plants' stems tied to them. For specimen flowers a stake for each individual stem is a good idea. When inserting any training material make sure that the root systems are not damaged as the supports are pushed into the soil.

*Right: a well-planned herbaceous border. The dark green of the hedge sets off the flower colors to perfection.*
*Below: Aconitum carmichaelii is called Monk's Hood because of the cowl-like form of the flowers.*

Now let us take a look at an alphabetical list of other beautiful plants which can be used for herbaceous border planning. The types and varieties selected are the best modern ones, varieties which have proved their worth. They are plants selected from the lists of many leading perennial specialists and sufficient details, although brief, are given so that the reader can prepare a planting scheme with a knowledge of the flowering period, the approximate height of the plant and what kind of position it needs; whether in full sun, sun, partial shade or full shade.

**Acaena microphylla**   This is a very pretty plant for the front of the border producing bronzy mats of foliage and crimson burrs in the summer. It is evergreen and likes a position in full sun.

**Acanthus spinosus**   This is another evergreen plant. Leaves are dark green and deeply divided and it produces soft mauve flowers in June to July. It is about 60cm (2ft) and it is a very accommodating plant because it is equally happy in full sun or full shade.

**Achillea** (*Yarrow*)   The achilleas or Yarrow are beautiful plants for cutting, and their flat heads produced in June to August are most striking. 'Coronation Gold' has bright golden flowers and the most attractive silver foliage. It attains a height of just over 60cm (2ft) and likes a position in full sun.

**Aconitum** (*Monk's Hood*)   This has most eye-catching helmet-shaped flowers produced on long spikes in July to August. One of the best varieties to use is 'Bressingham Spire'. This has beautiful violet blue flowers, and the plant grows over 60cm (2ft) high.

**Agapanthus** (*African Lily*)   This is a lovely plant for the border, producing flowers on long stems from July to August. The strap-like leaves are attractive too. In the Middle States it is wise to give some protection in the winter and it is best situated in a very sunny border. In the North, plant Agapanthus in tubs which can be wintered in a shed or cellar. Height 60cm (2ft) or more.

# Choosing flowers

**Ajuga**  This is a very handy plant to have as it is low growing and covers the ground well. Flowers are usually blue to pink and produced from about May to June. It is another plant which likes full sun. The variety *A*. Multicolor is an evergreen with delightful, variegated bronzy red foliage, and the plant grows to a height of just under 15cm (6in).

**Alyssum** (*Gold Dust*)  Another excellent plant for the front of the border. It is a useful plant to have for spring color and it likes a sunny position. The variety *A. saxatile compactum* has golden yellow flowers and nice grayish foliage. Height is about 15cm (6in).

**Anaphalis triplinervis**  This is a really delightful plant to have in any border scheme. It has white starry everlasting type flowers produced in August and September. It grows to a height of about 30cm (12in). The leaves are delightfully woolly, and form gray domes.

**Anchusa**  This is one of the best plants for a brilliant blue flower display. It has a useful long period of flowering from about May to August and prefers a sunny position. The variety 'Opal' has sky blue flowers and grows to a height of 90cm (3ft).

**Anemone**  The Japanese Anemones are excellent for a late display in an herbaceous border. The flowering display is produced from about August to October, and plants thrive equally well in full sun or even full shade. Three particularly lovely varieties are 'Bressingham Glow', which has semi-double ruby rose flowers and grows about 30cm (12in) high; 'Louis Uhink', a very unusual name, which is a beautiful white flowering plant growing just over 60cm (2ft) in height; and for a plant approximately 45cm (18in) in height 'September Charm' is a really lovely pink form.

**Anthemis tinctoria**  An evergreen plant which has marguerite-like flowers of a pale lemon color which are produced from June to August. It likes a sunny position and is a must in the collection because it is so excellent for cutting. It grows to a height of just over 60cm (2ft).

**Aquilegia** (*Columbine*)  This is a most graceful plant with attractive fern-like foliage and spurred flowers. The display is produced from May to June, and a sunny position is important. The McKana hybrids are excellent and these grow to a height of just over 60cm (2ft).

**Armeria** (*Thrift*)  The thrift is an evergreen plant. For an early summer display of flowers from May to June in a sunny situation this plant is hard to beat. It produces dense cushions of leaves with attractive round flower heads. The variety 'Bees Ruby' is an excellent acquisition, with beautiful pink globes, and the height of the plant is about 30cm (12in).

**Artemisia** (*Wormwood*)  This plant has lovely silver foliage. It likes a fully sunny position, but will do quite well in partial shade. The height of the variety 'Silver Queen' is about 45cm (18in) and this particular variety has delicate silver foliage with a spreading habit.

**Aster** (*Michaelmas Daisy*)  No border could be complete without the wide range of Hardy Asters, also called Michaelmas daisies. They prefer a sunny position and are useful for the end of season flower display from September to approximately October. The *A. novi-belgii* group are excellent for the borders and also for cutting.
　　Here are some beautiful varieties in the Aster range: 'Ada Ballard' has double lavender blue flowers and grows 60cm (2ft) high; 'Crimson Brocade' has intense ruby

*Right : Campanula isophylla is a pretty dwarf form for the front of the border.*
*Below : perennial asters, or Michaelmas Daisies, are among the most popular perennial plants, and much work has gone into the production of new and improved varieties. Here they make a strong splash of color in the late summer border.*

red double flowers of the same height; 'Eventide' has deep blue flowers which are semi-double and the same height; 'Marie Ballard' has powder-blue flowers and grows about 90cm (3ft) high; 'Royal Velvet' is mildew-resistant and grows about 45cm (18in) high.

The dwarf hybrid types are excellent for the front of the border growing some 15–23cm (6–9in) in height. These are bushy plants and flower from about September to October. Delightful varieties to try include 'Lady in Blue' with semi-double, rich blue flowers; 'Rose Bonnet' with double pink flowers; and for a gorgeous cyclamen red flower 'Starlight' must not be omitted.

**Astilbe**   These are great character plants for any border. They like full sun or full shade and they produce most attractive feathery plume-like spikes of flowers from about June to August.

Here are some excellent varieties to consider: 'Bressingham Beauty' has rich pink flowers, very freely produced, and the plant grows just under 60cm (2ft) high; 'Fire' has salmon-red flowers and grows to about 45cm (18in) high; 'Red Sentinel' has glowing red flowers and grows nearly 60cm (2ft) high; and 'Rhineland' produces pink flowers and grows about 60cm (2ft) high.

**Aubrieta**   Very useful spring flowers in shades of blue, pink, purple and red. They grow to a height of about 15cm (6in) and are excellent for the front of the border.

**Bergenia**   Another character plant, with large round glossy leaves. It is an excellent ground cover subject and flowers usefully early in March to May. It likes sun but will do quite well in partial shade. The variety 'Ballawley' is evergreen with red stems and rose-red flowers and grows about 30cm (12in) high. A lovely dark purple red flower is produced by the variety 'Evening Glow', another evergreen plant which grows about 25cm (10in) high.

**Campanula** (*Bellflower*)   This plant prefers a deep well-worked soil which is moist. It likes full sun, or partial shade. The variety 'Loddon Anna' grows about 90cm (3ft) high and has large lilac-pink bells. 'Pritchards Variety' produces flowers from June to July. These are deep blue in color and the height of the plant is just over 60cm (2ft). There is a very attractive dwarf form of the campanula called 'Stella' which has very bright blue flowers and grows to a height of only 8–10cm (3–4in).

**Catananche coerulea major**   This plant has rather wiry stalks which bear lavender-blue daisy-eyed flowers. It likes full sun and is very useful where there is a problem of a rather dry soil or site. An excellent plant also for cutting. Height is about 30cm (12in).

**Ceratostigma plumbaginoides**   Flowering from August to October, this is a very useful plant for autumn which has blue flowers and bright red leaves later in the season. It grows about 30cm (12in) high and likes full sun.

**Chrysanthemum maximum** (*Shasta Daisy*)   The Shasta Daisy is an excellent plant for cutting. It likes a sunny position and flowers from about June to August. Two lovely varieties should be incorporated in any planning scheme; these are 'Jennifer Read', with white flowers and yellow centers, growing to a height of 60cm (2ft); and 'Wirral Supreme', which also has white flowers but with anemone centers.

**Cimicifuga cordifolia**   This is a plant which flowers from August to October and is very useful for the back of the border as it grows to a height of 1–2.5m (3–8ft). It has creamy white plumes and branched stems, and likes full sun.

*Above: Eryngiums are grown mainly for their gray foliage which forms an attractive muted background for the brighter colors in the border.*

**Convallaria** (*Lily of the Valley*)   A gem of a plant to include in any border scheme. It has exquisitely scented white flowers in April to May. It is happiest in a moist position in sun or shade.

**Coreopsis**   The variety *C. grandiflora* 'Mayfield Giant' is one of the best to use, with deep yellow flowers which are produced throughout the summer. It is an excellent subject for cutting and likes a sunny situation. Height is about 60cm (2ft).

**Delphinium**   Excellent plants for the back of the border are the delphiniums. There are many beautiful types such as 'King Arthur', which is royal purple with an attractive white central eye, and 'Blue Jay' with slightly lighter blue flowers. They like full sun and will do best in a well-prepared soil. The 'Belladonna' group are slightly smaller-growing plants as compared to those so far mentioned which are all 120cm (4ft) or more. The smaller group grow between 60cm (2ft) and just over 90cm (3ft) in height. Varieties such as 'Blue Bees', with pale blue flowers, and 'Pink Sensation' are invaluable types to have.

**Dianthus** (*Pinks*)   The pinks are essential ingredients for a border because they are the front row plants. Heights are from about 15cm (6in) to about 30cm (12in) and their very popular flowers are produced from about June onwards. They like a sunny situation. Of the many varieties available, 'Pink Mrs. Sinkins' has glorious double pink flowers and 'White Ladies' is another beautiful double white variety with very deep fragrance.

**Doronicum** (*Leopard's Bane*)   These flower from April to June according to climate and are happy in sun or partial shade. They are very handy as they provide early color in a border, 'Spring Beauty' is specially fine with double deep yellow flowers which grows to a height of about 45cm (18in) or more.

**Echinops** (*Globe Thistle*)   A great character plant for a border with lovely globe-shaped flower heads and gray green foliage. The heads are produced in June to August and the plant likes full sun. The species *E. ritro* is especially useful, with steel-blue flower heads and a height of just under 90cm (3ft).

**Erigeron** (*Fleabane*)   Growing to a height of between 30cm (12in) and 60cm (2ft), this plant with its daisy-like flowers is excellent for planting toward the front of the border. The display is produced from June to July and a sunny site is important. 'Darkest of All' is a beautiful dark violet-blue flower and 'Foerster's Liebling' has large semi-double pink flowers.

**Eryngium** (*Sea Holly*)   A very attractive foliage plant which does well during the winter. It likes a sunny site. The variety *E. oliverianum* has very attractive jagged-edged leaves and the blue shade of the stems is observed from July to September. Approximate height is just over 60cm (2ft).

**Euphorbia** (*Spurge*)   The Euphorbia likes a sunny or semi-shaded position. The species *E. myrsinites* has very pretty trailing stems with gray foliage. The very unusual lime-green flower heads are produced in late May. It is a small plant attaining a height of only 15cm (6in) or more.

**Geranium**   The plants do well in either full sun or partial shade and their foliage is very attractive. The variety 'Russell Pritchard' flowers from June onward and the display can be continued until the autumn. Flowers are a magenta pink and the height is about 15–20cm (6–8in). Another variety is 'Johnson's Blue' with very bright blue flowers in June or July and a height of about 60cm (2ft).

**Geum** For a long season of flowering from about May to August in a very sunny position, this particular plant is ideal. It has thick foliage which covers the ground and makes it a very useful weed suppressor. The variety 'Mrs Bradshaw' has deep double scarlet flowers and 'Lady Stratheden' has golden-yellow blooms. Both plants attain a height of about 30cm (12in) and possibly more.

**Gypsophila** This has a very dainty effect in a border and is also a great plant for flower arranging. The flowering period is July to September. The variety 'Bristol Fairy' produces huge masses of double white flowers and grows to about 90cm (3ft) upward.

**Helenium** This plant is very easy to cultivate and its daisy-like flowers are very eye-catching in July to September. A sunny position is important and the height of growth is about 60cm–2m (2–6ft). An especially lovely variety is 'Moerheim Beauty' with very deep red flowers. For a welcome touch of yellow the variety 'Butterpat' should be included.

*Below: Hosta ventricosa. Bottom: Hosta fortunei Albo-marginata. Below right: Helianthus 'Loddon Gold'.*

**Helianthemum** (*Sun Rose*) Flowers from May to July in full sun. It is low growing, about 15cm (6in) in height, and is therefore excellent for the front of the border. The variety 'Ben Nevis' has yellow and orange flowers, 'Red Orient' deep single red flowers and 'Wisley Primrose' has gray foliage and very large flowers.

**Helianthus** (*Sunflower*) Growing to a height of about 90cm (3ft) or more, the perennial sunflowers are excellent for the back of the border planting schemes. The variety 'Loddon Gold' has very attractive golden yellow flowers produced in the late summer from July to September.

**Helleborus** (*Christmas Rose and Lenten Rose*) These flowers are important for winter and early spring displays in a border. They will cover the ground well, thus smothering weeds. They are also problem solvers as they will grow in semi-shade or even full shade. The species *H. niger* is the popular Christmas Rose and grows to a height of about 30cm (12in). *H. orientalis*, the Lenten Rose, may flower from late November into April. Colors of these blooms vary from white to purple.

**Hemerocallis** (*Day Lily*)   This plant grows to a height of about 60cm (2ft) or so and flowers in late summer from July to September. The flowers are particularly attractive as they are trumpet-shaped. There are some particularly lovely varieties which do well in full sun or partial shade: 'Dorothy McDade' has light yellow blooms, 'Golden Orchid' is deep orange and there are several shades of pink such as 'Pink Charm', 'Pink Prelude' and 'Pink Damask'.

**Heuchera**   This flowers in June to September and likes partial shade. Heucheras grow to a height of between 30cm (12in) and 60cm (2ft). The variety 'Coral Cloud' has coral red blooms, 'Pretty Polly' has delightful pink flowers, and for a deeper color 'Shere Variety' has scarlet flowers.

**Hosta** (*Plantain Lily*)   Likes semi-shade and flowers from July to August approximately. Heights are from 30cm (12in) to 60cm (2ft) and a particularly good variety is 'Royal Standard' with white flowers which are pleasantly scented.

**Incarvillea delavayi** (*Trumpet Flower*)   A good plant for an early summer display bearing beautiful bright rose-red blooms in May to about July. It appreciates full sun and its height is up to 30cm (12in).

*Incarvillea delavayi bears rose-pink flowers whose form explains the common name of Trumpet Flower.*

**Iris**   An invaluable group of plants for the herbaceous border are the Bearded irises, *Iris germanica*, (described on page 103) which have heights from about 60cm (2ft) to 90cm (3ft). They flower in June and there are many beautiful varieties. A few examples of the range are as follows: 'Golden Alps', white; 'Jane Phillips', blue; 'New Snow', white; 'Party Dress', pink; 'Right Royal', red; 'Top Flight', deep apricot.

**Kniphofia** (*Red Hot Poker*)   This plant flowers from summer into fall, thus giving a welcome late summer and autumn display. Full sun is appreciated and heights are from approximately 30cm (12in) to as much as 90cm (3ft). 'Royal Standard' has yellow flowers with a scarlet top, 'Snow Maiden', as its name implies, is a very nice white type, and 'Jenny Bloom' has salmon peach flowers.

**Lavatera olbia Rosea**   This is also known as Mallow and has hollyhock-like flowers in rose colors. As it attains a height of 60–90cm (3–4ft) approximately it is an excellent plant for the rear of the border, producing its displays from June to October.

**Lupinus** (*Lupin*)   The popular lupins produce a welcome display from about May to July. If the first flush of flowers is cut hard back after flowering it is sometimes possible to have a second display in September. Heights are from about 60cm (2ft) to just over 90cm (3ft), and the Russell and Mixed hybrids produce a wonderful display of color if they are established in a sunny border.

**Lychnis chalcedonica** (*Campion*)   These flowers are about 75cm (2½ft) high and the display is produced in the late summer from July to August. Foliage is a very attractive rich green and the plants have clusters of bright scarlet flowers which they produce on stiff stems.

**Monarda** (*Bergamot*)   This is especially useful for its aromatic foliage. The flowers are produced from about July to September and a semi-shaded position is appreciated. Heights are about 60–90cm (2–3ft). The variety 'Adam' has deep red flowers and 'Croftway Pink' has rather unusual soft pink flowers.

**Nepeta mussinii** (*Catmint, Catnip*)   The Catmint, as it is occasionally called, is a

*Left : a white form of Phlox, one of the most useful herbaceous plants, which is available today in a wide range of colors.*
*Below : Papaver orientale, the Oriental Poppy, flowers in midsummer and likes bright sun.*

very useful front of the border plant, and with its gray foliage and small blue flowers during the summer it is an excellent edging subject. Maximum height is about 30cm (12in) and it appreciates a sunny border. Cats are attracted by the smell of these plants and may cause damage by rolling on them.

**Oenothera** (*Evening Primrose*)   The Evening Primroses produce a lovely display from July to August, and if they can be sited where they receive plenty of sun an excellent display can be had. They arc attractive plants attaining a maximum height of about 75cm (30in). The variety 'Fireworks' is really beautiful with its clear yellow flowers.

**Paeonia** (*Peony*)   The paeonias are essential plants for any border, producing an intriguing display of color from June to July. They are mid border plants growing to a height of approximately 60cm (2ft). There are many beautiful double-flowered varieties such as 'Sarah Bernhardt' which has pink blooms and 'Auguste Dessert' with semi-double flowers of salmon color with an edging of white. If a good red color is required then 'Karl Rosenfield' should be included. For a white variety, 'Mme. Emilie Lemoine' is a gem.

**Papaver orientale** (*Oriental Poppy*)   These have really large flowers, unusual in form, which are produced at the height of the summer in June to July. Like the peonies, they should have a sunny position. The variety 'Perry's White' is an excellent plant, growing to a height of about 75cm (2½ft), and 'May Sadler' has salmon blooms.

**Penstemon barbatus**   This plant flowers June to September and has a height of about 60cm (2ft) maximum. It does well in either a sunny or partly shaded border and its attractive bright pink flowers are borne on graceful spikes.

**Phlox paniculata**   The Phlox are a popular mainstay of any good border scheme. They are a late summer flowering plant producing most of their display from late July until mid September. Average height is 60cm (2ft) or more and they are best grown in a semi-shaded situation. There are many lovely varieties such as 'Brigadier', orange red; 'Star Fire', bright carmine; 'Eventide', mauve; 'Annie Laurie', pink; 'Sandringham', pink; 'White Admiral', white.

# Choosing flowers

**Physostegia**   This plant has very pretty tubular flowers carried on stiff stems. The flowering time is late summer and some displays can go on as late as October. There are two outstanding varieties, 'Summer Snow' and 'Vivid', the latter being a pink flower. Height is about 60cm (2ft).

**Polygonum**   Flowers from about August to October and is accommodating enough to grow in both full sun and semi-shade. The variety 'Donald Lowndes' only grows some 15cm (6in) high and is therefore a good ground cover plant and one for the front of the border too. It has pretty little red spikes with copper autumn foliage. Another good polygonum is *P. vaccinifolium* which has a creeping habit with clear pink spikes of flowers produced in late August.

**Potentilla** (*Cinquefoil*)   Likes sun or semi-shade and is an excellent main summer flowering plant. As it grows only to about a height of 30cm (12in) it is another good front row plant. The variety 'Gibson's Scarlet' is excellent, and an exception to the dwarf habit is 'William Rollison' with orange-yellow flowers. This plant grows to a height of about 60cm (2ft).

**Primula**   These plants like shade and a moist soil preferably. They flower according to variety from about March to late July and grow from about 15cm (6in) to about 60cm (2ft) according to variety. 'Wanda' has purple flowers and *P. denticulata* bears pale violet flowers.

**Pulmonaria** (*Lungwort*)   This is another front of the border plant with a height of only about 10–15cm (4–6in). It grows well in semi-shade or full shade and is an excellent ground carpeting plant. The varieties 'Munstead Blue' and 'Mrs Moon' with rose flowers are excellent subjects.

**Pyrethrum**   These flower from May to June in full sun and are excellent for cutting. Heights are about 60cm (2ft) and there are three particularly excellent varieties which are 'Scarlet Glow', 'Brenda', which is pink, and 'Eileen May Robinson', also pink.

**Rudbeckia** (*Coneflower*)   The rudbeckia likes sun or semi-shade, and it flowers usefully in the early autumn from August to approximately September. The variety 'Autumn Sun', which has nice yellow flowers, grows to a height of about 1.2m (4ft) and the variety 'Goldsturm' has orange flowers, but grows only to a height of about 60cm (2ft).

**Salvia** This plant grows in full sun or semi-shade and according to the variety produces a pleasant display of bluish flowers from May to as late as September. The height is about 30cm (12in) to a maximum of 60cm (2ft). The variety 'East Friesland' has blue flowers, and 'May Night' has lilac-blue flowers.

**Saponaria ocymoides** This plant has an interesting trailing habit and produces flowers of dark pink from May to June. It grows to a height of about 8–10cm (3–4in) and is a splendid front of the border subject.

**Saxifraga umbrosa** (*London Pride*) An attractive plant with splendid rosettes of green foliage which form fascinating mats. Usually in April or May it throws out nice spires of pink flowers which make a delicate floral display. Maximum height is about 23cm (9in), and the plant grows well in full sun or semi-shade.

**Scabiosa** (*Scabious*) The scabious flowers from July until late into November and is a mainstay of any border planning display. Full sun is essential, and the height is about 60cm (2ft). The variety 'Clive Greaves' is a very established one, which bears violet-blue flowers. As a complete contrast the variety 'Miss Willmott' should be included with its white display.

*Below : Sidalcea malvaeflora is a lovely subject for the midsummer border. Below, right : Salvia 'May Night' is one of the many attractive varieties available today.*

**Sedum** (*Stone Crop*) The Stone Crops are similar to the London Pride in that they form pillows or mats of foliage. They grow well in full sun or partial shade, and heights are from about 5–8cm (2–3in) to as much as 30cm (12in). The variety 'Coral Carpet' has pink flowers, 'Ruby Glow' ruby red flowers, and 'Brilliant' has white flower heads.

**Sidalcea** Flowers from July to August and has very attractive spikes of rose or deep rose colors. Height is about 60cm (2ft) and the varieties 'Croftway Red' and 'Rose Queen' are two excellent types to include in the border.

*Above : the pretty blue-flowered Veronicas come in a wide range of heights and flowering times. These two dwarf forms are Veronica whitleyi (left) and Veronica teucrium (right).*

**Solidago** (*Golden Rod*)   The Golden Rod easily attains a height of 60–120cm (2–4ft). It flowers from July to August in a sunny border. 'Golden Mosa' has lovely yellow flowers, and for a primrose-yellow 'Lemore' should be considered.

**Stachys** (*Lamb's Ears*)   This is a most unusual plant. It has very pretty gray foliage, and the variety *S. lanata* 'Silver Carpet' is a particularly good one to plant.

**Thalictrum**   A very graceful plant with ferny foliage and lovely purple flowers which are produced from June to about August. A sunny or semi-shaded position is ideal. The species *T. aquilegifolium* 'Thundercloud' grows to a height of about 60cm (2ft), and for a very useful tall plant with a height of about 90–120cm (3–4ft)

**Thymus** (*Thyme*)   A low-growing plant only an inch or so high, making an excellent front row plant. It is happy in sun or partial shade and produces its mauve or white flowers from June to August according to the variety. *T. lanuginosus* and *T. serpyllum* Albus are particularly good, and Coccineus has deep red flowers.

**Trollius** (*Globe Thistle*)   This tall-growing plant has globular flowers which are produced from May to June in a sunny or semi-shaded situation. There are two very nice varieties, 'Golden Queen' and 'Orange Princess'.

**Verbascum** (*Mullein*)   A plant for the back of the border which has a full growth of 90cm (3ft) or more. It likes a sunny position and flowers in summer. Three extremely good varieties are 'Cotswood Beauty' with amber flowers, 'Gainsborough' with yellow flowers and 'Pink Domino' with deep pink flowers.

**Veronica**   According to variety these plants can produce a display of beautiful color from May to September. Heights are from about 15cm (6in) to as much as 90–120cm (3–4ft) according to variety, and they like a sunny situation. The species *V. gentianoides* has light blue flowers and glossy foliage, *incana* has dark blue flowers and silver foliage, *prostrata* has blue flowers and it is low growing and spreading, and *V. teucrium* 'Royal Blue' is also delightful.

**Viola**   For ground cover these are excellent and are very accommodating as they can be planted in full sun, partial shade or even full shade. They grow to an approximate height of 5–8cm (2–3in), and the variety *V. hederacea* has lovely violet flowers with white tips.

# ROCK GARDEN PLANTS

Rock plants (or alpines as they are often called) are ideal subjects to use in the planning of a beautiful garden. They are, in fact, extremely versatile plants, being equally at home on the rock garden, in or on walling, and also in the crevices or joints of paving. Another useful feature is the fact that all the plants are perennials so that once they are established in the garden they will go on flowering and growing year after year.

Although most of the rock plants can be classed as hardy, some can be affected by dampness in winter, and plants which are especially affected are those which have very downy foliage such as the androsaces. The problem, however, can be overcome quite easily if they are protected by small sheets of glass or even plastic supported on a suitable wire framework. This forms an umbrella over the plants and sheds the wet or dampness. Vulnerable plants should be protected in this way during the cold winter months.

One of the fascinations of rock plants is the fact that most are quite tiny and dainty and an excellent display can be achieved in even the smallest of gardens. Quite often containers can be used in which to establish a small collection of alpines. If an old sink can be obtained a very eye-catching feature can be the construction and planting of a sink garden which contains a range of these pretty little plants.

**Purchasing plants** The most popular and easiest way to obtain rock plants is to buy them from a local source or from a specialist nursery. The plants are grown in

*A rock garden can be a most effective way of exploiting a steeply sloping site, though one on this scale will be initially very expensive to create.*

*Opposite, top: Dianthus and Sedum scramble naturally down a steep rock face. Opposite, bottom right: the pinks should find a place in every rock garden. Many lovely dwarf forms are available. Opposite, bottom left: 'Riverslea', a late-flowering aubrieta hybrid.*

*Right: Alyssums are easily grown rock plants. This is Alyssum saxatile citrionum.*

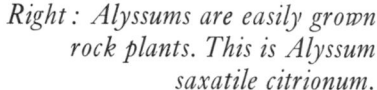

### ROCK GARDEN PLANTS FOR SHADE

Most rock garden plants or alpines are at their best and happiest in full sun. Where it is impossible to give them these ideal conditions, there there are still some which will tolerate shade or half-shade, provided that there is good drainage. The following are particularly recommended:

*Cyclamen neapolitanum*
*Omphalodes verna*
Primula
Ramonda
Saxifraga—'mossy' varieties
*Tiarella cordifolia*
Trillium

### CREVICES AND DRY WALLS

One of the amazing properties of the rock garden plants is the ability of certain varieties to exist and even thrive in the tiniest pockets of soil. The following are recommended for planting in crevices in paving or in pockets in an old wall:

Dianthus—cushion varieties
Ramonda
*Saponaria ocymoides*
*Saxifraga lingulata*
*Sedum cauticolum*
*Sempervivum tectorum*
*Thymus serpyllum*
*Veronica prostrata*

tiny containers and it is possible to plant them out at practically any time of the year provided the soil and weather conditions are suitable. Plants grown in this way have a very good root system and once they are planted out in their permanent quarters they become established very quickly and give an early display in most cases. The best way to remove the plants from their small containers, if the container happens to be a plastic or clay pot, is to turn the pot upside down, inserting two fingers one on each side of the plant, and gently tap the rim of the container on a hard surface. This should eject the plant with its soil ball and it can then be planted out in its quarters.

**Sites for planting** The obvious site for rock plants or alpines is a rock garden, which makes a most attractive feature in any garden. Wherever they are planted they must have excellent drainage. If a rock garden is being made, the base should be formed of masses of small rubble over which some good turfy loam is placed to a depth of at least 30–45cm (12–18in). Mix with this soil some peat or composted vegetable waste; if the soil is inclined to be heavy some sharp sand should also be worked in. Many of the trailing or creeping types of rock plant are especially useful for planting in the crevices or gaps of rocks so that eventually they trail over the rocks in a most natural way.

The plants can also be used for planting in the crevices or joints in paving, and here the soil should be excavated at the planting site and if necessary filled with some good quality loam mixed with some peat. When this form of planting is contemplated it is essential that the plants are sited so that one can walk down the pathway easily without treading on the plants.

Plants can also be established in walling, either dry walling or walling with soil joints. Here gaps between the walling stones can be planted with some of these plants, filling in the gap with some good soil and making sure also that this soil goes right through to the soil behind the wall. Many plants can also be established along the top of the wall, in the soil behind the wall, so that eventually the plants can grow over the top of the wall and trail down in a most attractive fashion.

Rock plants can be used to form an attractive mini-garden in a trough or a container. Old sinks are ideal for this purpose and even a modern glazed sink can be camouflaged by treating the surface with a mixture of two parts peat, one part sand and one part cement. This is mixed with water to a stiff paste and the sink is then coated with a strong adhesive. When the adhesive is tacky this mixture is then applied to create a natural rough face.

Rock plants can also be established in other containers and even old barrels are ideal for this purpose. Make sure that all containers have adequate drainage holes in the base and it is a good idea to place old broken crocks over these drainage holes to prevent them from becoming blocked in time with soil.

# A SELECTION OF ROCK GARDEN PLANTS

One of the problems facing the gardener when it comes to the choice of rock plants is to decide from the vast numbers available exactly what to plant. To start with, therefore, a short collection of easy varieties is given, and these are not only easy to grow but easy to raise from seed. The seed is usually sown in the late spring or early summer in a sunny position outdoors, working in some moist peat before the seed is sown.

**Alyssum montanum** This is a pretty little plant because it has very attractive gray-green foliage and lots of pretty little yellow flowers which are on display from March to May. Like many alpines, it is a dainty little plant growing only 8–10cm (3–4in) high.

**Arabis rosea grandiflora** This has two popular names—Pink Arabis and Rock Cress. It has a useful flowering period from May to July, the flowers are a delightful pink and the plant grows about 15cm (6in) high.

**Aubrieta** No rock garden plant collection could be complete without this useful plant. The modern varieties now have larger flowers and there is a useful range of color which includes lavender, lilac, rose and carmine. It has a long flowering display from March to June, and the height is about 10–15cm (4–6in).

**Campanula carpatica** One of the attractions of this particular plant is its fascinating cup-shaped blooms. These are produced from June to August and the shades are blue, lavender and white. The height is little taller than the other plants, about 23cm (9in).

**Cerastium tomentosum** (*Snow in Summer*) What a delightful popular name this plant has. It produces virtual carpets or dense mats of fascinating, silvery white foliage and it is an especially useful subject for trailing over rocks and banks. Flowering time is a little later in the season, from June to August, and the height is 15–20cm (6–8in).

**Dianthus allwoodii** (*Pinks*) What rockery would be complete without the dainty pinks? These have fringed flowers in useful colors of pink, crimson and white. The flowering time is from June to August, and heights are from 23–30cm (9–12in),

# Choosing flowers

*Below : saxifrages are ideal
subjects for a dry wall. Bottom :
rock plants grown in paving
look pleasantly informal.*

according to variety. The type *Dianthus deltoides* has beautiful small pink flowers which are peppered or speckled with crimson. It is a most beautiful plant to acquire as it flowers from June to October, a useful long period of display, and the height is 15cm (6in).

**Gypsophila repens rosea**   This is a trailing type of plant, very handy for edges of walls and rockeries. It has rose pink flowers from June to August.

**Helianthemum** (*Rock Rose*)   This plant has a dwarf evergreen habit and flowers are available in a wide range of colors from yellow through to orange, pink and scarlet. It is a problem solver too, as it is one of the few plants which can do really well in a dry, hot position. Height is 30cm (12in) with a long flowering time from May to July.

**Iberis sempervirens**   Another beautiful trailing or cascading plant with beautiful white flowers and evergreen leaves. It is an ideal partner for the aubrieta and the alyssum. Flowers are produced from May to July and the plant grows about 23cm (9in) high.

**Saponaria ocymoides**   An ideal subject for planting in crevices in walls or in path joints. It tends to trail delightfully and has beautiful pink flowers. It has a display in the mid to late summer period of June to August.

**Saxifraga** (*Saxifrage*)   If you want a change of form then this is the plant for you. It has rosettes of leaves which are of a silvery color. Flowers are white or pink and it is ideal for planting in walls or in paving. The flower display is from May–July; height 10–15cm (4–6in).

**Sedum** (*Stonecrop*)   The stonecrop is another plant with a difference. This is because it has fleshy leaves and yellow, pink or white flowers. Height in a useful range of 8–30cm (3–12in).

**Silene schafta**   Here is a very handy little plant for a late display of color up to October. It has tufty leaves and purple flowers. Height is about 15cm (6in).

So much for a range of popular, easy plants. Now let us take a look at some other varieties which are fascinating to grow and will make your alpine feature one with a difference simply because you have introduced a few less common plants.

**Androsace chumbyi**   This is a lovely little plant which has rosettes of woolly foliage and lots of bright rose colored flowers which are produced in late spring. Heights are from 2–10cm (1–4in) and spread about 20cm (8in).

**Cyclamen neapolitanum**   Why not try some miniature cyclamen? These are not dependable in northern tier States, but well worth trying. They have attractive, large ivy-shaped leaves and rose colored flowers in autumn.

**Geranium dalmaticum** (*Crane's Bill*)   These are extremely useful plants to have in the rock garden. Geraniums produce pink, lavender and crimson flowers from June until October if other species such as *G. sanguineum*, *G. cinereum* and *G. subcaulescens* are used. Height variation is from 15–23cm (6–9in).

**Phlox douglasii**   It is always handy to have a carpeting type of plant and with its spread of about 45cm (18in) this particular plant is very useful. It flowers from May to June, and produces lavender shades which are most restful.

**Ramonda pyrenaica** If you want a change of foliage then this plant with its rosettes of dark green, crinkly, hairy leaves is ideal. The flowers are especially delightful too, being a soft lilac blue with golden centers. It is a useful plant because it is happier in crevices and with a north aspect. Flowers are produced from May to June, and the plant's height is about 15cm (6in).

**Sempervivum tectorum** Another handy plant for a change of foliage. This has green leaves with purplish tips and its red flowers are produced in July. The height is only 5–8cm (2–3in) and the plant does well in a sunny position, thriving best in a dry wall or situated in paving.

**Thymus serpyllum** The wild thyme, with sweetly scented foliage. A gem of a plant to include especially as it has rosy purple foliage. Flowers are produced from June to August and height is only 2–8cm (1–3in).

**Veronica prostrata** This plant has a prostrate or carpeting habit. It flowers in late spring—early summer, bearing beautiful deep blue flowers. Height is 8–20cm (3–8in) and it will spread easily over an area about 45cm (18in) wide. They are accommodating plants which will grow happily in sun or light shade, and are especially useful for planting in dry walls or in paving.

*Below, left : Silene schafta is a useful low-growing plant for a late summer display. Below : the Sempervivum or Houseleek flourishes in crevices in a dry wall.*

# The vegetable garden

This is a very important part of the garden, and increasingly so in these days of self-sufficiency. The cultivation of a vegetable plot is a very satisfying undertaking: there is nothing like growing your own food, and in addition to having delicious fresh produce all through the summer, you can preserve and store your crops in many ways for out-of-season use.

In a small garden it may be difficult to plan easily for vegetable crops but, even so, there are certain vegetables which give good yields for minimum area. For example, one could grow salad crops such as lettuce and radishes, and even a short row of carrots will produce a useful number of roots for the table.

On the larger scale, quite comprehensive cropping schemes can be evolved which still give the gardener a tremendous variety of vegetables and of course very much larger yields. How does one plan a vegetable garden? Obviously a certain amount of personal preference must creep into the scheme of things, but the wise gardener makes careful plans so that there is something to be had for most weeks in the year.

Do not forget the deep freezer. Here is an excellent aid to the vegetable grower because he can store away any surplus produce to eat out of season when fresh vegetables are scarce. Good examples are snap and lima beans and peas, which he can grow for fresh picking, freezing as much of the crop as he wishes. These

*Well-grown vegetables in Britain's Royal Horticultural Society garden at Wisley, Surrey.*

will be available for use at Christmas time and in the new year when it would be impossible to have such crops from the garden. There is also another interesting point—that is, that home grown crops from your freezer will save you a considerable amount of money.

### Choosing the site

The position for the vegetable plot must be selected with care. There are several important factors to consider such as shelter from winds and the amount of light and sunshine received. Of course the site must have plenty of air movement, otherwise there could be problems with damp.

Some gardeners are conscious of the fact that a vegetable garden can look a little untidy at times, and one must admit that at certain periods of the year, such as the late autumn, the plot is not always at its best. The tendency therefore is to hide the plot away. Concealment can be achieved if the vegetable plot is divided from the rest of the garden by, say, a hedge of fruit. For example, brambles and raspberry canes can be trained against a suitable wire support, or dwarf apple trees can be established.

Another consideration is access to water or to a tap because there will be many occasions when the crops will need watering. It is also a good idea to situate the plot near a greenhouse or frames because many plants will be raised under glass for the vegetable garden.

Depending upon the size of the area it is a good plan to incorporate paths, and on the larger plot there should certainly be several main paths to connect up the various beds. Do not forget that some area should be devoted to the compost heap or heaps, as the addition of composted material is invaluable when the ground is being prepared for the crops.

### New site clearance

Quite often the gardener is confronted with a piece of virgin ground and it is necessary to clear this and prepare it for the vegetable garden. Conventionally the best time to start work is in the autumn, or winter in mild areas, since then many plants have died down and at least any growth is at its lowest ebb. Starting work at this time also means that the soil can be prepared in good time for the important spring start to sowings and plantings.

The first thing to do is to cut long grass or weeds down as close to the ground level as possible. Care must be taken to remove debris, and possibly the best tool to use for the initial clearance is a good scythe. If the ground is reasonably free from obstacles and the grass not too tall, a tough rotary mower will be able to cope with the short grass.

Digging can now commence, and the grass should be cut off with a spade and stacked upside down in a neat heap where it will eventually rot down. You can encourage quicker rotting down of the heap if a commercial rotting agent is sprinkled over each layer.

The method of digging will depend a great deal on the soil conditions. On badly neglected sites the ground should be double dug, and this entails the removal of the soil in each trench to a depth of 25cm (10in) or so. The bottom of the trench is loosened up with the fork. Actually weeds can be cut off and placed in the bottom of each trench as work proceeds. Here they are rotted down and provide valuable organic matter for the plants.

Where the site has not been too neglected single digging can be practised, making sure that as the spadefuls of soil are thrown forward into the trench so the soil is reversed and the weeds are at the bottom of the trench. Leave the surface of the soil as rough as possible so that the frosts and weather can work on it and break it down during the winter.

The use of mechanical cultivators or tillers is increasing in popularity and this can save a tremendous amount of time and energy. They can be used on fairly rough neglected ground, but it is better to remove coarse grass etc., before work commences. In some cases it may be necessary to go over the site several times with the machine in order to break the soil up really well. There is a lot to be said for the use of mechanical aids because a quicker turn-round of crops can be achieved. For example, a crop can be harvested, and within a very short time the bed can be prepared with the machine ready for new planting or sowing.

As cultivation proceeds, it is important that some plant food should be worked in, and this can take several forms. Fresh manure can be incorporated in the winter so that by springtime it will have matured and will not be fresh and harmful. If manure is unavailable the alternative is composted vegetable waste or horticultural waste. There is much to commend the use of special or prepared manures. These are usually dried concentrated products. In general they are excellent and have a useful high organic content.

## Planning

**Crop rotation** A successful vegetable garden depends on careful initial planning so that there is always something to pick or store, according to the seasons. It is important to combine in this plan some form of crop rotation. This is essential so that a correct feeding or manuring program can be maintained according to the types of crop grown. For example, the root crops such as carrots and potatoes are happier in a plot which has received a good manuring the season before. The root crops should never be grown in freshly manured ground because, in the case of carrots for example, the roots may become badly twisted and forked.

Usually a three year rotation is planned and the vegetable crops are grouped under three main sections. The first contains the salad crops and the peas and beans. In the first year this ground is manured well. The second crop consists of the root crops and here the ground is not manured but is given dressings of fertilizer. The last crop holds the cabbages etc. (brassicas), and here fertilizer and lime only are applied. If the crops are planned in this order, each crop or section is moved one plot forward every year. In the fourth year the crop which started on a plot in its first year will return to that plot.

**Planning for continuity** Planning also requires the use of rotations so that there is plenty to harvest not only in the summer months but also in the more difficult

*Right : rows of lettuces and brassicas at different stages of growth will provide a continuous supply for the kitchen. The space between the brassicas is intercropped with carrots. Far right : a water supply on the spot can be very useful for a large vegetable plot.*

| CROP ROTATION—3 YEAR PLANT | | |
|---|---|---|
| | **Bed 1** | **Bed 2** | **Bed 3** |
| **1st Year** | MANURE (Crops needing rich condition) Peas, Beans, Onions Celery, Spinach, Beet Lettuces, Tomatoes Leeks<br><br>OTHER CROPS | FERT & LIME (Soil is very acid)<br><br>BRASSICAS | FERTILIZER<br><br>ROOTS |
| **2nd Year** | FERTILIZER Beetroot, Carrots Parsnips, Potatoes<br><br>ROOTS | MANURE<br><br>OTHER CROPS | FERT & LIME<br><br>BRASSICAS |
| **3rd Year** | FERT & LIME Cabbages, Broccoli Cauliflowers, Savoys Brussels Sprouts Kale, Swede, Turnips<br><br>BRASSICAS | FERTILIZER<br><br>ROOTS | MANURE<br><br>OTHER CROPS |

*Left: crop rotation chart for a three-plot system. Gardeners who do not have the space to practise a full three-year rotation program should, at least, try to move crops around, which prevents the spread of diseases such as blight and club root, and remember never to sow root crops in freshly manured ground.*

winter and early spring period. This means that careful planning of crops is necessary so that seed is sown in good time for the winter plants to become established and over-winter successfully. For example, for cutting in the spring, seed of suitable cabbage varieties has to be sown in July or August in the warmer areas, but for cutting in the winter, seed is sown quite a lot earlier in the year to mature quicker. The secret of regular pickings is regular sowing of certain crops, and this applies particularly to lettuce. The answer is to sow little and often. A pinch of seed sown once every two weeks should provide a continuity of plants for planting out.

Another important crop which requires careful sowing for continuity of picking is the pea. The dwarf quick maturing varieties are ideal, and these should be sown fairly frequently to ensure a continuous supply. These early varieties are usually ready for use about eight weeks after sowing, whereas the main crop types are ready nine or ten weeks after sowing.

The planning should also take into consideration what is known as the 'lean period' in the vegetable garden, and this is generally the late winter and early spring months even in the South. Here the root crops can play a most important part. Some, like the carrot and beet, can be lifted and stored away, whereas others like parsnips, can in most areas be left in the ground to be used as required. Of course, if one has a generous area of vegetable plot, the provision of vegetables for most of the year is not too much of a problem. It is the small plot, however, which could give us problems and here the gardener needs to be a little ingenious and practise intercropping and catch-cropping. These are both methods of exploiting limited space to the full, and particularly in the small garden where space is at a premium it is possible to practise really intensive planting and get much higher yields.

# The vegetable garden

**Inter-cropping** Inter-cropping is the method of growing a quick maturing crop close by a slower growing crop, so that the quicker maturing one is harvested before it is over-shadowed by the slower crop. For example, there is usually wasted space between the row for the pole beans and the next crop by its side, because eventually the beans will grow several feet high and over-shadow the surrounding ground. There is no reason, however, why a quicker maturing crop, such as lettuce or radishes, cannot be grown in this space, and these crops will be gathered before the beans get too high.

Another example of inter-cropping, is where a single row of carrots is sown and a row of lettuce is planted on each side. Carrots are slow growing if they are the main crop type, and the lettuce will be cut away long before the carrots are ready for pulling.

**Catch-cropping** This is a similar system of making full use of spare areas of ground, such as the area near the celery trench before the soil is used for earthing up. The radish is probably the most versatile plant for this kind of use, because it occupies very little room even when mature and its progress to maturity is so rapid. It is an excellent vegetable for broadcasting thinly in odd sunny warm areas or corners of the vegetable plot to provide delicious pickings for the salad bowl.

Hotkaps and cold frames are invaluable for vegetables because they promote more rapid growth and are excellent for bringing along tender plants in cooler and more exposed gardens. It is surprising what a difference shelter from a cold wind can make, and covering a sowing or planting strip a week or two before work takes place means that the soil is pre-warmed to a certain extent and is always ready for use despite bad weather conditions.

Planning also depends on the returns one might expect from different crops. Here are some very approximate guides to the average yield one can expect from a 3m (10ft) long row of some of the following popular crops:

| | | | |
|---|---|---|---|
| Broad beans | 1kg/2.4lb | Onions | 5.5kg/12lb |
| Snap beans | 7kg/15lb | Parsnips | 6.5kg/15lb |
| Pole beans | 22kg/48lb | Peas | 1–1.5kg/2–2½lb |
| Beets | 5.5kg/12lb | Turnips | 5.5kg/12lb |
| Brussels sprouts | 7kg/16lb | Lettuce | about 10 heads |
| Carrots | 6kg/13lb | Maincrop potatoes | 9kg/20lb |
| Leeks | 4.5kg/10lb | Early potatoes | 6kg/13lb |

It is helpful to be able to time crops well, though any calculation can only be taken as a rough guide as weather conditions may vary so much. Nevertheless, within reason one can ascertain the time it takes a crop to be ready for picking from the day the crop was sown. Take peas for example: the first early types are usually ready about eight weeks after sowing but the main crop or late varieties are slower in growth and about nine or ten weeks can elapse before the crop is ready.

To have a continuous supply of crops is not always possible if the garden is relatively small. On the grander scale, however, there are no problems, because there is plenty of room to have various rows of the same crop at different stages of growth. For example, the ideal way to grow peas is to have a crop ready for picking with another row where the pods are still forming, followed by another row which is only a foot above the ground. The frequency of sowing must also depend on the personal requirements of the family. It may well be that a large proportion of a crop is earmarked for the deep freezer. On the other hand, there is a lot to be said for picking crops as fresh as possible; so in the larger garden one can have a special area set aside for block growing where crops such as peas and beans are grown en masse to be harvested at a close period and deep frozen quickly, while another area provides pickings for immediate use.

*Opposite, top: well-grown asparagus spears tied in bunches ready for cooking. Opposite, bottom: these broad beans are reaching maturity, and the pods at the base of the plants are ready for picking.*

# VEGETABLE CROPS

It should be appreciated that vegetable varieties are always being superseded by interesting new ones, but it is comforting to know that there are many old faithfuls which still keep going on and on.

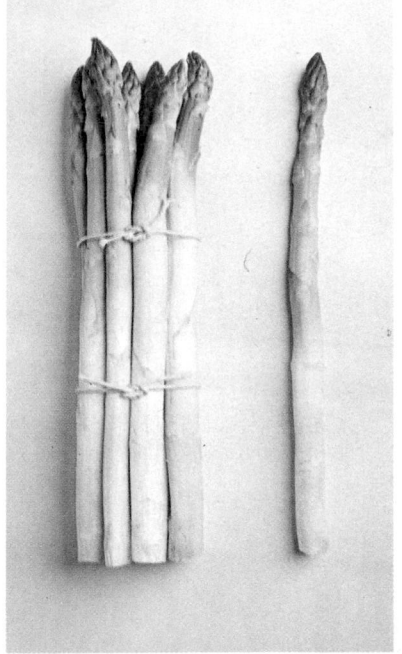

**Asparagus** This can be termed a luxury crop, which everyone would like to try to grow, but unfortunately it is not the easiest of vegetables to cultivate as it does require a well-prepared soil, and quite a rich one too. It also takes up quite a bit of ground, but where there is room it is a crop well worth trying, and one which is well worth cultivating for the deep freezer. The quickest way to grow the crop is to purchase three year old crowns which are planted in the spring. They are planted about 45cm (18in) apart in the row and usually a four row bed is built up with a spacing of about 90cm (3ft) between beds. As drainage is vital, it is a good plan to make raised beds for the crop about 15cm (6in) above ground level.

One can raise the crop from seed sown in 4cm (1½in) drills in spring in a prepared bed. Germination is a slow business and the ground must be kept nicely moist. One must be patient with plants raised from seeds, however, because one must not start harvesting the delicious heads or spears until the plants are in their third year. Good varieties are 'Paradise' and 'Mary Washington'.

**Beans, broad** The earliest crops are sown in late October and November in milder climates. The main sowings are made from about March under glass, May outdoors. The beans are sown in double rows, spacing these about 23cm (9in) apart, and if more than a double row is required, a spacing of 75–90cm (2½–3ft) should be provided between the rows. The depth to sow is about 8cm (3in) and the seed itself should be spaced 23–25cm (9–10in) apart along the row. Those beans which are over-wintered should preferably be given some protection under glass. This will bring them along slowly but surely, and frames or Hotkaps will be invaluable for those gardens which are exposed or situated in colder areas. When the beans have reached the tops, or near the tops, of the protection, it can be removed, by which time danger of frosts should have passed. This method is declining in popularity in the U.S.

On clay soils the beans can be placed on the surface and the soil ridged up to cover them. As these soils tend to be cold and heavy this method can assist germination. Good named varieties include 'Green Windsor', 'Saville Longpod', 'Early Longpod', 'Masterpiece', 'Green Longpod', 'Bunyard's Exhibition', 'Harlington White' and the American 'Frostproof'. Broad beans are less commonly grown in the U.S. than snap and pole beans.

Main cultural requirements are to grow in ground well enriched by very old manure or with a high organic content provided by peat or material from the compost heap. The tops or growing points of all the plants should be nipped out when they are in full flower. This seems to reduce attacks by aphids and will encourage the quicker swelling of the pods.

**Beans, pole** This is a very important crop and, like the previous crop, is an excellent one for the deep freezer. The plants require a soil which is very retentive of moisture, and plenty of organic matter must be worked in. It is, however, a tender crop, so sowings cannot be made too early. The earliest possible sowing requires raising the plants in a greenhouse, and then they are planted out in mid to late May, keeping Hotkaps over them until the danger of frosts is past, which will vary from region to region. The main outdoor sowing without protection is in May. Seed should be sown about 5cm (2in) deep, 15cm (6in) apart in the row, using a double row in the trench and spacing the rows 30cm (12in) apart.

As pole beans grow quite tall it is necessary to allow about 1.5m (5ft) between every double row if a lot of beans are to be grown. There are many modern training systems possible, and a system which consists of a metal frame supporting plastic netting is an excellent one.

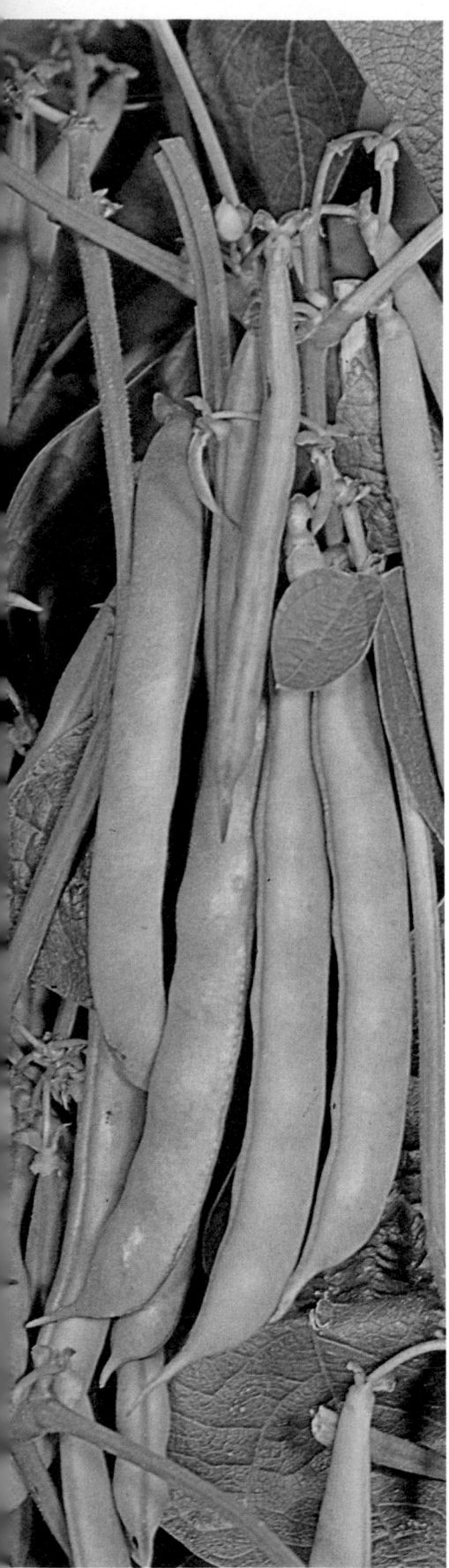

Plenty of water is vital for this crop, and during dry weather the setting of flowers can be assisted if the plants are sprayed overhead in the evenings with water. If the weather is cold then naturally pollination by bees can be reduced simply because the bees will not venture out during poor weather conditions. The crop should be given the occasional feed during the growing season, using either a granular or liquid formula, which is applied approximately once every fourteen days.

Quality is important in pole beans to ensure that they are not stringy when cooked, but this will not only depend on the variety grown but also on the way in which they are cultivated. Plants which are allowed to dry out badly will produce tough stringy beans. As far as varieties are concerned, there are two old faithfuls: 'Kentucky Wonder' and 'Kentucky Wonder Wax'. A variety which is also supposed to be fairly stringless is called 'Blue Lake'. Occasionally grown for extremely long pods, many of which can attain a length of 45cm (18in), is 'Yard Long'. This is the sort of variety which will appeal to the exhibitor. All the varieties mentioned are excellent for deep freezing as well as for immediate use.

**Beans, snap**   A very useful crop and especially so for the smaller garden because, grown well, they will give good returns from a small area. Like the pole beans they are tender plants so cannot be sown too early without some form of protection. For an extra early crop, seed can be sown under glass ahead of time. The seeds should be sown in peat pots or wafers which can be set out without disturbance later. Grow plenty of young plants for a good early crop with a head start. It should be safe in most areas to set them out by late May, but a watch should be kept for late frosts which could damage or even kill the tender plants. For main crops seed can be sown in May onward, spacing the rows this time 60cm (2ft) apart.

One of the old varieties is 'Bountiful', which will give very heavy crops from good soils. 'Stringless Greenpod' is another old faithful. It is a variety which does well anywhere. Other newer varieties include 'Tendergreen' and 'Topcrop'. Both of these are excellent for the deep freezer. An interesting variety is the wax bean, which has a full meaty flavor, and good varieties to try are 'Kinghorn Wax' and 'Pencil Pod Wax'. These too are excellent types for the deep freezer.

Among the Dwarf beans one must not forget the invaluable varieties which can be dried for use during the winter period. The pods are allowed to mature and turn brown on the plant before they are pulled up and hung upside down to dry completely in a cool airy shed. A good variety is 'Royal Burgundy'.

**Beets**   These are a valuable vegetable crop to grow because they provide fresh pickings during the summer months, especially for salads, and the roots can also be stored to provide useful vegetables for the winter period. A start is usually made in late April when seed is sown thinly in drills about 38cm (15in) apart and about 1–2cm ($\frac{1}{2}$–$\frac{3}{4}$in) deep. Sowings continue in this way until the middle of June or later. It is important that sowings are made as thinly as possible, but even so some thinning to about 13cm (5in) apart will be required, and a final thinning to about 23cm (9in) apart in the row. For a late crop a sowing can be made in late July, and the best variety for this purpose is either 'Early Wonder' or 'Detroit Dark Red'.

Of the other varieties for general sowing 'Early Red Ball' is excellent. Where there is a good depth of soil it is worth growing the long varieties, and a good one to choose is 'Green Top Bunching'.

The beets for winter use are lifted before the ground freezes, and great care must be taken not to bruise the roots. They can then be stored in deep boxes filled with sand or dry peat and kept in a cool frostproof place. For salad use the beets are ideal if they are lifted when they are the size of a table tennis ball. The flesh is deliciously sweet and tender.

**Broccoli**   A most important crop is the broccoli or sprouting broccoli. It is a really tough vegetable, withstanding really severe weather conditions. Seed is sown in two periods as for Brussels sprouts, sowing as thinly as possible, and later on, when the young plants are large enough to handle, they are planted out in their permanent quarters. Space the plants 60cm (2ft) apart each way. Useful varieties include 'Spartan Early', 'Green Comet', 'Italian Sprouting', 'Waltham' and 'Premium Crop'. Most of these start to produce their delightful sprouting side shoots rather early.

**Brussels sprouts** Again a very valuable late crop and a vegetable which should always find a place in the cropping scheme. Seed sowing can be divided into two sections: March to April indoors in the North (outdoors where weather permits), and during May outdoors for a main crop. Plants are generally planted out in their final quarters by or in May and they require a generous spacing of 60–90cm (2–3ft) between the plants in the row. In the South they are also a winter crop.

It is helpful to use some of the dwarf varieties where the garden is exposed as the tall sprouts can be blown about badly by strong winds unless they are staked. For a small variety growing to a height of only about 45–60cm (1½–2ft) 'Early Morn' is excellent. Other varieties which are ideal include 'Long Island Improved' and 'Green Pearl'. A specially early variety is 'Jade Cross', and all are usually ready for picking late in the year.

Brussels sprouts are ready for picking when the bottom or lower leaves turn yellow. Picking should only take place within that area and never higher up into the green stems or foliage until these too begin to die down. Cut the sprouts off cleanly with a sharp knife. If you are just taking a few sprouts from each plant this helps to prevent the entry of disease spores.

**Cabbages** In keeping with our varied climate there are three convenient sections to the cabbage family to provide heads for cutting at specific times. For the earliest cutting spring cabbage should be sown; and these are sown during the summer. They should be ready for planting out during September and October, spacing the plants about 30cm (12in) apart with 45cm (18in) between the rows.

*Opposite : French beans should be harvested regularly as the pods ripen to ensure a continuous supply.*

*Below, left : purple sprouting broccoli. Below : this semi-dwarfing Brussels sprout is ideal for the smaller garden, and will provide pickings over a long period.*

When the ground is in a suitable state in March or April make a main sowing, using two varieties, one for early use and the other for winter storage. If, by chance, you overfeed the plants causing the heads to grow too fast and split, slow the growth down. Tip the plants over to break the roots off on one side, then right them. Heads of winter cabbage may be cut and stored in barrels in a cold fruit cellar or the plants may be pulled up whole and hung by their roots.

Good early varieties include 'Copenhagen Market', 'Early Jersey Wakefield', 'Emerald Cross Hybrid' and 'Early Green'. Mid-season varieties include 'Allhead Early' and 'Stein's Flat Dutch'. Late kinds include 'Penn State Ballhead', 'Jumbo' and 'Savoy King Hybrid'.

Red cabbage, also known as pickling cabbage, is usually sown in the same way as other cabbage varieties, and thereafter treated in the same way, although it is better to plant out 90cm (3ft) apart to get better heads. Varieties usually have the word 'Red' as part of their name, and include 'Mammoth Red Rock', 'Red Acre' and 'Ruby Ball Hybrid'. The latter two are early varieties, whereas 'Mammoth Red Rock' is usually treated as a late or winter variety.

Also gaining in popularity is Chinese or Celery Cabbage. Good varieties to try are 'Burpee Hybrid' and 'Michihli'. Ornamental cabbage is an interesting novelty, and it is not always realized that the plants are edible as well as being popular with flower arrangers.

**Capsicum or Peppers**   These are fun to grow and are useful vegetables too. Seed is sown under glass from March to April and the plants are eventually planted out from late May or June onward. They should be sprayed occasionally with tepid water and regular picking of the mature fruits is important to keep the plants bearing well. Suitable varieties to try are 'Early Hybrid', 'California Wonder', 'Pennbell' and 'Early Canada Bell'.

**Carrots**   This is not always the easiest crop to grow, since carrots prefer a deep soil and one that is not too heavy. However, the development of intermediate and stump-rooted varieties has meant that the gardener has a much wider choice.

Sow early crops thinly in drills about 2cm ($\frac{3}{4}$in) deep and 30cm (12in) apart. Main crop sowings can begin around May. The plants should eventually be thinned to about 15cm (6in) apart in the rows. Carrots can be stored in layers of dry sand or ash in a cool shed until they are required.

Among reliable shorthorn carrots are 'Earliest French Horn' and 'Early Nantes'. Stump-rooted varieties include 'Nantes Half Long' and 'Danvers Half Long'. A good intermediate variety is 'Chantenay', and for an excellent maincrop try 'Waltham Hicolor'.

**Cauliflowers**   With the introduction of carefully bred new varieties the cultivation of this crop is much easier than it used to be years ago. Cauliflowers can be divided conveniently into two sections: these are the summer and autumn varieties and the winter varieties (in warm areas). For the former, seed is sown in early spring and the plants are planted out about a month later, giving them spacing of about 60cm (2ft) apart each way. For an exceptionally early crop seed can be sown in heat in the greenhouse in February or March, the plants are hardened off and planted outdoors later in spring, about April or May. Varieties used for the summer and autumn include 'All the Year Round', 'Super Snowball' and 'Dominant'.

'Stokes Early Abundance' is a quick maturing variety and ideal for the early sowings in heat. Another good variety is 'Whitehouse'.

The planting distance should be about 60–75cm (2–2$\frac{1}{2}$ft) apart each way. All the brassicas, which includes the cabbages, sprouts, sprouting broccoli and cauliflowers, must be planted on firm ground and must be planted firmly. Loose planting encourages poor growth. Of the winter varieties 'Igloo' is ideal, 'Super Snowball'

*A healthy row of winter cabbages ready for harvesting.*

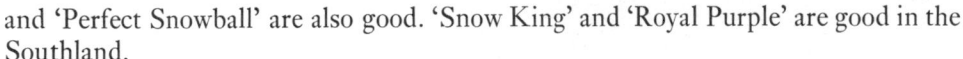

and 'Perfect Snowball' are also good. 'Snow King' and 'Royal Purple' are good in the Southland.

**Celery**  This is not an easy crop and demands careful attention to soil by deep digging. Moisture retaining soils are the best, but not the heavy ones. It seems to pay if the gardener incorporates plenty of moist peat or composted vegetable waste when preparing the ground initially. Seed is best sown under glass and heat in a temperature of at least 16°C (60°F) during February in the North. The seedlings are eventually pricked out into deeper boxes and then hardened off before they are planted out in early June about 25cm (9in) apart in a single row. They are best planted in a trench 30cm wide by 45cm deep (12in wide by 18in deep), the bottom 15cm (12in) or so being well enriched with old manure or composted vegetable waste. Some good soil is returned to the trench until the trench is about three inches below the level of the surrounding ground. The plants must be kept watered at all times—dry weather or a check to growth will cause them to run to seed.

As they grow the stems may be blanched or whitened by either drawing up soil either side of the row or by wrapping paper collars around them as the plants progress. To save a lot of time a self blanching variety can be grown.

There are also green varieties which need no earthing up such as 'American Green' and 'Non-Bolting Green'. One self blanching variety is 'Golden Self Blanching'. Other desirable varieties are 'Florida 683', 'Improved Utah' and 'Beacon', all of which are reliable varieties of good flavor.

**Cress**  Mustard is included here because mustard and cress is a delightful salad crop. The seed can be sown upon a damp surface such as matting (which has to be kept wet) or it can be grown in boxes of soil. The seed can be sown at any time of

*Above, left: fully ripened peppers are brilliant red or yellow and slightly sweet to the taste. Above, top: Celery 'American Green'. Above: the summer cauliflower is distinguished from the winter kind by its more spreading leaves.*

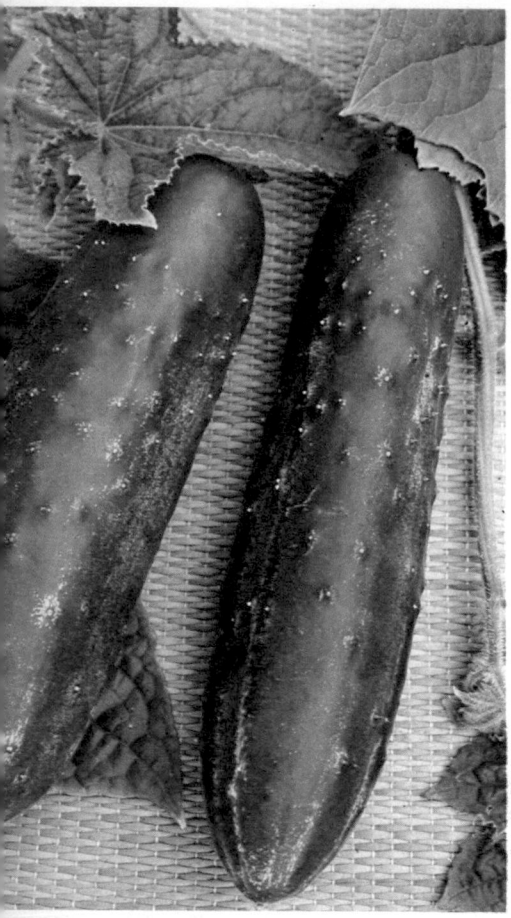

*Above : cucumbers are invaluable for crisp summer salads. Above right : when lifting leeks it is important to insert the fork well away from the plants to avoid damage.*

the year under glass. As it is slower in growth the cress should always be sown about three days before the mustard so that both crops are ready for cutting at the same time. A good variety of cress to use is American or Land Cress. Both can be grown outdoors in summer.

**Cucumber**   The warm summer weather experienced in most parts of the United States makes cucumber culture outdoors a relatively simple matter, although gardeners must still keep an eye out for late spring and early fall frosts, especially in the northernmost states.

Seeds can be started in the greenhouse or cold frame in conventional pots or peat pots, and the plants set out after the danger of frost is past: May 15 in the latitude of Boston or Chicago. However, this is rarely necessary. In general, the seeds are sown outdoors a week in advance of this date, or about 3 weeks earlier if protected with waxed paper Hotkaps.

The bed should be well-drained and fertile. The application of a mulch of garden compost just prior to planting out is helpful. The plants should be spaced about 90cm (3ft) apart. Plants growing on the flat are pinched out when seven true leaves have formed. This encourages the production of sub-lateral shoots. Tie the new growth of climbing plants to the supports and pinch out at approximately 2m (6ft). The plants should be given a feed of liquid manure when the first fruits set, and they should be kept well watered at all times. Fertilization of the female flowers is necessary so do not remove the male blooms. Harvest the cucumbers regularly to encourage more flowers to set.

Good slicing varieties include 'Victory', a dark green cylindrical gynoecious hybrid which is highly tolerant to many of the most serious cucumber diseases such as scab and cucumber mosaic. 'Burpee F1 Hybrid' is also highly resistant to disease and has crisp white flesh of excellent flavor. Among the good combination varieties, equally good for slicing or pickling, are 'Improved Long Green' and the snow-white variety 'White Wonder'. For pickling try 'Burpee Pickler' or 'West India Gherkin' which produces small bright green burr-like fruits covered with fleshy prickles and only about 8cm (3in) long.

**Garlic**   A favorite vegetable now that people like seasoning in their food, especially in salads. Garlic is purchased as cloves or bulbs and these are planted out in April or May about 30cm (12in) apart in the row. The crop can be lifted in the early autumn and dried to be used as required.

**Leeks**   A delicious vegetable to have during the lean period, even in winter where climate permits. The seed is sown in 1cm (½in) drills, spacing these about 23cm (9in) apart. This is done indoors in February and March, and when weather permits, the young plants are planted in their growing quarters. The best method of planting is to make a hole with a dibber about 13–15cm (5–6in) deep, spacing the plants 30cm (12in) apart in the rows with 45cm (18in) between the rows. A plant is placed in each hole and a little water is added from the watering can, which helps to settle the roots and cover them with some soil. Outdoors plant April to June in the North. Later on the stems may be blanched or whitened by drawing up the soil on either side with the draw hoe. The leeks can overwinter in the milder areas and can be lifted as required. One of the most outstanding varieties to use is 'Musselburgh'. Another excellent one is 'Elephant' and a winter variety which produces heavy crops is called 'Unique'.

**Lettuce**   The mainstay of everyone's salad bowl. It is also an easy crop to grow provided care and attention is paid to the selection and use of the varieties. The early varieties for the spring can be grown either under glass or outdoors. For work under glass, which means greenhouse or frame cultivation, special varieties are essential otherwise complete success cannot be expected. For growing under glass the soil should be forked over so that good drainage is provided, and seed can be sown in late August to the end of September or again in October for transplanting in November. Seed is sown in seed trays, seedlings pricked out, and the young plants eventually planted out in the beds. Space them about 30cm (12in) apart each way minimum. Plenty of ventilation is important and only the minimum of watering should be given, just enough to keep the soil nicely moist. A good movement of air is essential to prevent mildew. Although lettuce can be grown successfully in an unheated greenhouse in some areas, better results are obtained if heat can be provided, and an ideal variety for this purpose is 'Kwiek'. A variety which can be grown quite well in unheated conditions is 'May King', and this is especially useful for growing in a frame or greenhouse. For growing under protection 'Arctic King' and 'Deci-Minor' are especially good, and in milder areas where there is little danger of severe frost it is worth while chancing some of these outdoors unprotected. The later sowings of these winter and spring lettuces, say from early October, will produce cuttings of lettuce heads in the early spring months, a very useful time indeed.

For late spring and general summer work there are lots of very good varieties to choose from. Seed is sown either thinly indoors around March or outdoors in April and May and the plants planted out in their permanent quarters about 30cm (12in) apart each way, or seed can be sown very thinly in shallow drills where they are to grow, thinning from time to time until the final plants stand at this distance. Some of the thinnings can be used for salads.

It is important to keep lettuce growing as steadily as possible to encourage succulent, crisp leaves and stems, and it is essential therefore that the soil is never allowed to dry out. For spring sowing the variety 'All the Year Round' is excellent and looseleaf 'Domineer' is worth a trial for the early sowings too. For the main late spring and

*Lettuces should be sown at regular intervals throughout the summer for a continuous supply.*

*Above: crisp heart varieties of lettuce are slower maturing and usually more bolt-resistant than butterhead types. Both are forms of the cabbage lettuce. Above, right: the 'loose-leaf' varieties are very popular in America and Australia. Individual leaves can be pulled from the plants as required.*

summer work there are plenty of good varieties to choose from such as 'Buttercrunch', 'Ruby' and 'Great Lakes'. A particularly good variety to try is called 'Jack Frost', which makes a very neat compact head, more frost-resistant than most. Other good varieties are 'Salad Bowl', and 'Oak Leaf', a variety which has serrated leaves very much like a dandelion leaf. Both can be cut regularly by pulling off the leaves only and as the plant is cut or pulled more leaves are produced. They do not produce a head but the leaves are surprisingly tender. Quite often trouble can be experienced with lettuce because they bolt or run to seed during hot dry weather but 'Oak Leaf' is very drought and hot weather resistant, so well worth a trial. Another excellent looseleaf lettuce is 'Green Ice'.

There are also the tall or cos lettuces and of these the varieties 'Parris Island', and 'Valmain' are excellent. For summer greenhouse production use the variety 'Ostinata'.

**Marrow or Squash** The seed can be sown early under glass in 8cm (3in) or 10cm (4in) pots using a good seed mixture. A temperature of 10°C (50°F) minimum will produce quick germination. The plants are tender and must be hardened off before they are finally planted out at the end of May (or early June in colder Northern gardens). Seed can also be sown where the plants are to grow, sowing seed in late May in the North and covering the young plants with an upturned flowerpot to protect against possible late frosts. Plants should be planted out on a slight mound of soil well enriched with old manure or composted vegetable waste and the plants should be spaced (if more than one is being grown) at least 1.2m (4ft) apart.

The plants require plenty of moisture at all times, and the trailing types should be pinched when they have produced about five leaves. The plants will then produce several side shoots or laterals and when these have produced about seven or eight leaves the ends of these should be pinched in turn. Where the garden is small it is a good plan to grow the bush varieties which are more compact as opposed to the trailers which can occupy quite a lot of ground when growing well. It is important that the female flowers are pollinated by the male flowers to ensure a good set of fruit. Plants must be kept well watered at all times, and liquid feeding every ten to fourteen days is very important too. Of the bush varieties 'Vegetable Marrow Bush' or 'St. Pat Scallop' are ideal, and of the trailers 'Green Delicious', 'Butternut' or 'Golden Delicious' are good varieties, well worth a try.

Tiny marrow fruits are extremely delicious and the zucchinis are excellent for this purpose. Fruits are best cut when only about 20cm (8in) long or even less, and regular cutting will encourage the plant to produce a good crop.

**Onions**   Although onions can be grown from seed (the seed is sown from March to April under glass and the plants hardened off and planted out in rows 30cm (12in) apart with 23cm (9in) between plants), it is a much easier method to grow onions these days from onion sets. These are in fact specially prepared small immature onions in an arrested stage of growth. The onion sets are planted out during April spacing them about 23cm (9in) apart in the row, and the rows should be 30–38cm (12–15in) apart. The sets are pushed into the soil to about half their depth and the area should be kept watered to ensure quick rooting. It is wise after a week or two to go down the rows to examine the sets and refirm any which may have been loosened. Late in August the tops will start dying down, and this is a sign that before long the onions will be ready for lifting. It should be pointed out that quite large onions can be produced by the use of these sets. When the tops are completely yellow and have practically died down the bulbs or onions should be lifted carefully, the soil shaken out from the roots and, if the weather is kind, the onions can be left on the soil surface for a day or two to dry out and ripen thoroughly. If the weather is inclement at the time the onions should be brought into a frame or even into a greenhouse or outhouse to complete their drying. Eventually the onions can be stored away in a frostproof place to be used as required. A well proven variety is 'Stuttgarter' and there are many new varieties coming along each season.

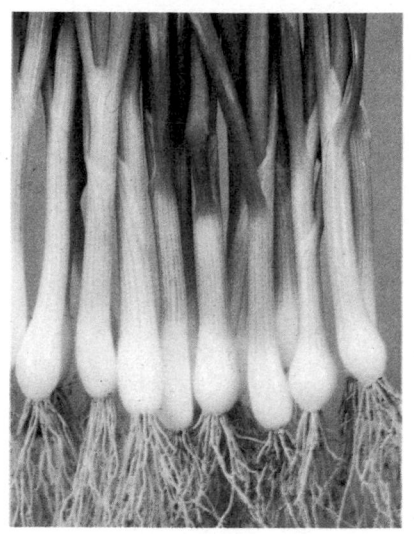

*Below: scallions should be harvested when small and mild-tasting. Bottom: onions should be harvested when the tops have died down and roped together in strings to hang in a dry place until needed.*

*Parsnips are among the hardiest vegetables and require minimal attention.*

*Scallions:* These are a useful crop to complement the salad bowl and very easy to raise too. Seed is sown from March onward in drills 30cm (12in) apart, the seed being sown as thinly as possible.

**Parsley** It is surprising how many gardeners overlook parsley. The seed is sown in March indoors or late April outdoors to provide pickings for the summer, and in June for winter pickings. Seed is sown thinly about 1cm (½in) deep in drills spaced 30cm (12in) apart if more than one drill or row is being used. The young plants should be thinned out to about 15cm (6in) apart eventually. It is most important that the soil is kept moist at all times because the parsley seed takes quite a time to germinate. A good variety to use is 'Deep Green'.

**Parsnips** An extremely valuable crop to have for the winter period. The ground must be deeply dug to encourage the production of reasonably long roots, and sowing can be made in April or May, sowing the seed in pinches about every 30–45cm (12–15in) and spacing the rows about 45cm (15in) apart. Alternatively, the seed can be sown as thinly as possible continuously down the drill, but in either case thinning is necessary later on to leave the plants finally 20–25cm (8–10in) along the row. Water must be given, especially during the early stages, to keep the seedlings growing strongly. The roots can either be left in the ground and lifted as required during the winter, or some roots can be pulled up, the surplus soil taken off carefully, and the roots stored in deep boxes of dry sand or peat in a frostproof place. It is reckoned that exposure to frost improves the flavor, converting the starches to sugar. There are several good varieties to select from such as 'Hollow Crown Improved' or 'Harris Model'. A particularly good new variety is resistant to canker, a disease which attacks and browns the top or crown of the plants, and the variety is called 'Avon-resister', a British variety now available in the U.S.

**Peas** These are the mainstay of any vegetable garden, especially where there is adequate room to grow several rows to ensure continuity and plenty of pickings for the deep freezer!

There are three main 'divisions' of peas and these are sown at certain periods of the season to provide that important continuity of harvesting. The first section is the First Early peas. These are the quickest maturing types and can be used at the start of the season and towards the end of the season where they will grow quickly before the colder weather sets in. The First Earlies are generally ready for picking some 8 weeks after sowing.

The next section is the Second Early pea where the period of maturity is a little longer—about 9 weeks. The final section is the Maincrop type which takes approximately 10 weeks to become ready for picking. The First Earlies are the dwarfest types, growing about 30–60cm (12–24in), according to variety. The second division peas have heights from about 60–90cm (2–3ft), and the Maincrops are from about 75cm (30in) to as much as 2m (6ft).

All peas must have a well prepared, shallow trench with lots of composted vegetable waste placed in the bottom—peat will do, or very well rotted manure. This organic matter is vital in order to conserve moisture—so important for the swelling of the peas in their pods.

The First Earlies are sown from November onwards according to the location of the garden. These will be ready for harvesting possibly from about May onward. The

*A good crop of dwarf early peas ready for picking.*

main sowing of the Earlies, however, usually takes place from mid-March onward. The Second Earlies and Maincrop types are sown from April to mid-May. In late summer one may again use the First Earlies to get that quick growth at this late stage in the season for a fall crop in certain favorable areas.

There are many excellent varieties of peas to choose from today.

*First Earlies:* 'Kelvedon Wonder' is a heavy cropper growing to a height of about 60cm (2ft). 'Little Marvel' is an exceptionally good pea for late sowings and very early sowings and the flavor is especially sweet. Height is 45cm (18in). 'Alaska' is good, among the very earliest of varieties, and grows about 45cm (18in) high.

*Second Earlies:* 'Early Onward' is a good cropper with well-filled pods of sweet peas. Height is 60cm (2ft). 'Thomas Laxton' grows 1m (3ft) high and has 8cm (3in) or longer pods, well filled. 'Improved Laxton's Progress' is rather early, of good quality, and bears long pods which are often filled with 7–9 peas each. Flavor is excellent. One of the best for freezing is 'Freezonian', which is hardy, productive and resistant to fusariam wilt.

*Maincrops:* 'Alderman', also known as 'Telephone', is a variety of long standing reputation and grows about 1.5–2m (5–6ft) high. Obviously plenty of staking is required. Heavy crops are produced of 15cm (6in) long pods. Another good variety is 'Lincoln', some 75cm (2½ft) high, and quite disease resistant. Large well-filled pods are produced. 'Green Arrow' is a good one too, with a height about the same and some of the longest pods produced by any pea. It is also downy mildew and fusariam resistant. 'Onward' is another very reliable variety which bears blunt-nosed pods well filled with good flavored peas. Height is about 75–90cm (2½–3ft).

**Potatoes**  This is a crop which needs thinking about because you do need plenty of room to reap a reasonable harvest. If there is a restriction on space, then the Earlies are the best type to go for.

Potatoes like a well prepared site with plenty of organic matter worked into the drills. Adequate moisture in the soil is vital. A limy soil or a very heavy soil is not suitable for this crop and good drainage is essential too. There are, like the peas, three divisions of potatoes: the Earlies, Second Earlies and the Maincrops. There are even types to suit cooking requirements such as ideal ones for French fries, boiling and salads!

The Earlies are usually planted in April, but keep an eye on late frosts as the plants are tender. In early May, the Second Earlies are planted, and, finally, the Maincrops can go in in late May or early June.

Potatoes are planted out as seed potatoes—small potatoes specially raised by seed potato firms. Ideally, these seed potatoes should be encouraged to send up little shoots or sprouts, as they are called. This is done by placing the small potatoes eye-end uppermost in seed boxes and in a warm place with a minimum temperature around 7°C (45°F). Do not keep in full light, but adequate light is important. The 'eyes' are the small bud areas situated at one end of each potato. This is known as the rose end. This sprouting gives you a good start and is also a handy check on the health or vigor of each seed potato.

Potatoes are planted out in shallow drills taken out with the draw hoe or even the spade. A depth of about 10–15cm (4–6in) is adequate. Space the seed potatoes 30cm (12in) apart with rows 60cm (2ft) apart for Earlies; 38–45cm (15–18in) apart with rows 75cm (2½ft) apart for the Second Earlies and Maincrops.

After planting cover over with a slight mound of soil. This will protect from late frosts. As the tops grow, more soil is drawn up either side of each row to keep the swelling tubers below blanched and to give them adequate soil to retain valuable moisture. Top-dressings can be applied down the rows and worked in at earthing up times.

The First Early potatoes should be ready for lifting in early summer. Late July is probably the harvesting time for the Second Earlies, and Maincrops later. The fork is the ideal tool to use for lifting but the prongs or tines must be inserted well away from the plants to avoid piercing the tubers.

The Maincrop potatoes are the ones to store. After they have been lifted, leave them on the surface of the soil to dry for a few hours. They can then be stored in deep boxes or sacks in a cool, dry frostproof place. During very cold weather it is as well to add extra protection in the form of burlap or straw to prevent frost damage. Examine the stored crops from time to time to remove any tubers which may be rotten or damaged.

*First Earlies:* 'Irish Cobbler', the standard early, is dependable and grows in nearly every state. 'Early Ohio' is a good cooker and especially suited to gumbo soils. 'Norland' is oblong, deep red, shallow-eyed and very early. 'Early Gem', a russet Idaho type, keeps well.

*Second Earlies:* 'Cherokee' is round, smooth, creamy white and resists late blight, scab, necrosis and mosaic. 'Chippewa' is a good, standard, shallow-eyed sort especially suitable for muck soils. 'Kennebec' is ideal for French fries and chips.

*Maincrop:* 'Katahdin', the standard of quality for years, is a good late cooker. 'Houma', from Louisiana, is particularly good in the Gulf states. 'Russet Burbank' is an excellent keeper and especially suited to the Northwest. 'Shoshoni' is a good, round Idaho sort.

**Radishes**   Here again we have a most important crop for the salad bowl, a crop which is very quick maturing and extremely easy to grow. Seed is sown very thinly either in drills or broadcast over a small area or seed bed where the plants are allowed to mature ready for picking. The early sowing can be made in March in a hotbed, continuing outside when warm enough, for a continuous supply. A sowing once every three weeks will produce an adequate supply of succulent roots for the salad bowl. Water is of prime importance to this crop, not only to keep it growing strongly, but also to produce crisp succulent roots which are not too hot to eat. There are several varieties to choose from such as 'French Breakfast' which produces a symmetrical root, or 'Cherry Belle' with globe-shaped roots. For a winter crop the 'Chinese Rose' variety is useful. Seed is sown during August, lifted in the autumn and stored in sand or dry peat until ready for use.

**Shallots**   This is a crop well worth growing in most gardens to produce small onions for pickling. The sets are planted from late February onward spacing them 15cm (6in) apart in the rows with the rows about 30–45cm (12–15in) apart. Do not allow the soil to dry out especially in the hot weather. When the foliage turns yellow it is a sign the clumps are ready for lifting. The surplus soil should be carefully shaken out and the shallots allowed to dry out in the sunshine or, in inclement weather, indoors. They should then be stored in a cool dry frostproof place and the individual shallots

*Opposite: sprouting and planting potatoes. The seed potatoes are sprouted in a warm place, and when the small purplish shoots are growing strongly, all the healthy tubers are planted 30cm (12in) apart in drills, which are covered with soil, using the hoe, to a depth of 10–15cm (4–6in.)*

*Left: these summer radishes are ready to be pulled within three or four weeks of sowing.*

can be removed from the clumps. Shallots are less commonly grown in the U.S. and so varieties are not readily available.

**Spinach**   It is a pity that this is not as popular as it should be but it is a vegetable which is not to everyone's taste. It is however a crop well worth growing, if only for the reason that it is very nutritious and rich in iron. There are two main periods of sowing: at the beginning of March, and about every month for continuity of supply until late spring, and for winter use during August and into September. A good variety to use for the summer work is called 'America', and for winter use the variety 'Cold Resistant Savoy' is excellent as it is extremely hardy.

A cultural point about spinach is that it must be kept moist especially during dry weather, and regular picking is important to encourage the plants to produce fresh young tender leaves.

**Swedes (Swedish turnips, Rutabagas)**   This is another vegetable which unfortunately seems to be sadly neglected by the average vegetable grower. Again it may be a matter of taste but it is a vegetable which is so useful for winter use. Seed is sown in June in the North shallowly in single rows spacing the rows about 45cm (18in) apart. Later on the seedlings must be thinned to about 30cm (12in) apart minimum. They are left there until required during the winter. It is important to select a variety which produces the most tender and best flavored flesh and the variety 'American Purple Top' is well recommended.

**Sweet corn**   An extremely delicious vegetable and one which is ideal for the deep freezer to provide lovely vegetables for the out of season period, especially at Christmas time. The main sowing period is in May, after danger of frost is past in most areas, since this crop wants a good early start. The seeds are sown at two per station spacing them about 60cm (2ft) apart along the rows and the rows spaced about 45cm (18in) apart. The strongest seedling is allowed to remain and the weakest one is pulled up later. It is important to grow the plants in blocks rather than single solitary rows. The reason for the block planting system is to ensure good pollination throughout the crop, and usually at least four or five rows are planted.

Good varieties to grow are 'Golden Miniature', 'Golden Cross Bantam', 'Seneca Chip' and 'Northern Belle'. One of the best sweet corn varieties is called 'Extra Early Super Sweet'. As its name implies, it is exceptionally sweet and tender and a variety which is worth a trial in every garden. Another new one is the late 'Golden Sweet', with a sweet tasting ear which lasts well after picking.

**Turnip**   For the early crops in the summer seeds should be sown in late April in drills 2cm (¾in) deep, spacing the drills or rows 38cm (15in) apart. It is important to sow thinly, but despite this some thinning will have to be undertaken so that the plants finally stand about 23–25cm (9–10in) apart along the row. These turnips can be pulled when quite young and are delicious for the main vegetable course. Some people like them quite young, cold and sliced for salads.

It is a nice idea to have some turnips for pulling later on in the season, and for this purpose seed can be sown toward the end of July and possibly again in August in more favored warmer gardens. This crop must be kept growing quickly and steadily and to this end the soil should never be allowed to dry out. For an early sweet flavored variety 'Milan White' is excellent, and so is 'Model White'. For a good flavor and a sweet flesh 'Tokyo Cross Hybrid' cannot be bettered, and 'Purple Top White Globe' is good.

**Tomatoes**   Once considered poisonous and unfit to eat, tomatoes are now the most popular vegetable in American gardens. Further, there are as many types as there are uses. They vary from the tiny 'Pixie' to giant 'Lincoln' which has been recorded

*Below: a popular form of spinach is perpetual spinach or spinach beet (top). New Zealand Spinach (bottom) is less commonly grown. It looks like a large-leafed form of mint and can withstand much drier and hotter conditions than other forms of spinach.*

*Above, top: sideshoots should be removed from tomato plants as soon as they appear. Above: these tomatoes are cordon-trained to avoid vertical staking and tying. The ripening trusses rest on a bed of dry straw. Above, right: these plants are trained on a fence of stout stakes with lines of twine stretched between them. Black plastic sheeting is used as a mulch to retain moisture and make weeding unnecessary.*

tipping the scales at three pounds. There are yellows and pinks to glamorize salads as well as the reds. Some are round, some flat, some low-acid and others highly acid. Some are meaty for slicing, others are ideal for making paste and sauces, and there are commercial varieties for canning.

Since tomatoes are frost tender the usual practice is to start them in pots or flats in the house, greenhouse or hotbed in March in the North. Still easier is to put two or three seeds each into peat pots or wafers, thinning so only the strongest remains. When the time comes they can be set outdoors without a setback. Before planting out, usually late May in the North, for then danger of frost should be past, they are hardened off by gradually exposing them to outdoor temperatures in a cold frame. For germination a temperature of 16–18°C (60–65°F) is needed, but for growing on 10–13°C (50–55°F) is sufficient and will produce stronger plants. In the South, too, they are planted early so that the crop is harvested before the hot weather arrives.

When ready to transplant, set out in well-prepared and fertilized soil at least 1m (3ft) apart each way. More fruits will result from letting the plant sprawl, but larger, better and cleaner fruit which is less likely to rot from contact with the soil results from tying the plants upright to stakes at least 1.2m (4ft) tall above the soil level. Protect from frost, if necessary, with Hotkaps when first set out. Then mulch, feed and water as necessary. If diseases have been troublesome, select disease-resistant varieties. These are frequently indicated as VFN (verticillium, fusarium, nematode resistant). Newly-set plants are also endangered by cutworms which sever the stems near the ground. Control these by scattering a slug, snail, or cutworm bait. It has no effect on birds or pets.

In cold climates those with greenhouses can also produce early crops indoors. For indoor culture the start will depend on whether the greenhouse is heated or not. For greenhouses which cannot be heated a March or April start is advised, though where a minimum temperature of 16–18°C (60–65°F) can be maintained sowings can be made as early as January. Indoor tomatoes must have all the side shoots removed regularly, and the plants are stopped or pinched out when they reach the tops of their training material or the top of the greenhouse.

For outdoor purposes try the varieties 'Pixie', 'Ultra Girl VFN', 'Burpee's Big Boy', 'Floradel', 'Veebrite', 'Ponderosa', 'Orange Queen', 'Manalucie' and 'Rutgers'. Small-fruited kinds include 'Tiny Tim' and 'Red Cherry'.

Many varieties are F1 hybrids, which are special crosses produced by the breeders or raisers. These tomatoes cannot be raised from home-saved seed, since the resultant plants will not grow true to type or true to the original variety.

For greenhouse culture select indoor forcing varieties such as 'Tropic', 'Tuckqueen', 'Michigan Ohio Forcing Hybrid' or 'Ohio MR7 Pink Forcing'. If you wish to grow a fall crop indoors use 'Vendor', a fall forcing variety.

# Fruit growing

In most gardens it is possible to grow some form of fruit. Fruit trees and bushes are perhaps the most accommodating of plants because somewhere in even the smallest garden one can find a suitable site for them. On a larger scale a garden solely devoted to all types of fruits can be very rewarding, providing the household with quantities of fresh fruit all summer long, with a surplus for preserving and deep freezing.

Many gardeners fail to appreciate the variety of sites where fruit can be grown. For example, why not make use of walls or fences where fruits such as peaches and nectarines, or even outdoor vines, could be grown? Fences can also support cane fruits such as brambles, loganberries and of course the popular raspberries. There is no reason too why fruit cannot be used as a division or fence in the garden. This can be easily carried out by erecting a suitable strong support such as wooden or concrete posts through which are fastened strong galvanized or plastic covered horizontal wires. Then suitable fruit trees such as apples and pears can be trained against them in fan or cordon form. Some fruits, such as the strawberries, can be grown in containers. There are now special jars or 'strawberry barrels' for this purpose, and the plants can be positioned both around the top of these containers and in holes in the sides. Even an old beer barrel can be put to good use by drilling out large holes around the sides, filling with a good rich soil mixture and planting a strawberry plant in each hole so that eventually the strawberries cascade down the sides. Therefore even a solid paved area can accommodate some fruits grown in suitable containers.

It is well to appreciate that fruit embraces many different types of plants. Usually fruit can be conveniently classified into two sections: the tree or top fruits and soft

*Below: a late summer harvest of tree fruits.*

fruits. In the former case these include peaches, nectarines, cherries, apples, pears, plums, damsons, etc. In the latter category fruits include the blackberries, gooseberries, blackcurrants, redcurrants, white currants, strawberries, etc. There is some argument about the classification of crops such as melons and rhubarb, but melons certainly are or should be classed as a fruit and there is no reason why rhubarb should not be included although it is generally relegated to the vegetable garden.

**Top fruits**  In the tree or top fruits there are different forms available. There are for example **bush trees**, and these are grafted on a dwarfing or semi-dwarfing rootstock which influences the type of growth produced by the main body of the tree (the main stem and the branches). Their average height is in the region of 2.5–3m (8–10ft) and their spread is very similar, so this is a most accommodating type of tree fruit to have even in the relatively small garden. There is no point really in going for the taller **standard** or **half standard** trees unless the garden is fairly extensive. Obviously the larger the eventual spread and height of the tree the greater the planting distance required between individual trees, so to accommodate quite a few trees a large area is vital. The standard trees have a spread and height of 6–11m (20–35ft), and the half standards have height and spread of 4.5–6m (15–20ft).

One desirable type of fruit tree is the **cordon**. This is particularly suitable for the small garden. They are limited in height and also in spread. They are trained against a suitable horizontal system of wires, or of course they can be trained against a suitable wall or fence. They have a height of about 2m (7ft) but the trees are planted at an angle of about 45°. The spread from side to side of individual cordon trees is in the region of 3m (10ft). This form of tree can of course be restricted in growth and kept within bounds by careful pruning. In appearance the cordon has a main stem with few spreading branches on either side whereas the next type called the **espalier** has a single central stem but pairs of horizontal branches arising either side of the main stem. These plants also have to be supported against either the horizontal wire system or against a suitable wall or fence. Their height is about 2.5–3m (8–9ft) and they spread some 3.5–4.5m (12–15ft). Again they can be kept within bounds by careful pruning. If one wants to go to quite a bit of trouble in the pruning and training and one is looking for rather an eye-catching and very attractive tree form then the **fan** shaped tree is ideal for this purpose. They are trained like the cordons and the espaliers and they do require quite a bit of area as they grow to about 3m (9–10ft) in height and have a spread of some 4.5–5.5m (15–18ft).

The age of the tree purchased is an important consideration. A maiden tree is one which is only one year old and will require training carefully for the first few years of its life. A second year tree will have more growth, and third and fourth year trees will have a well formed framework or skeleton of branches. The older trees will not transplant quite so well. Very basically, a maiden tree has simply its main stem or trunk, a second year old tree has a few side branches from its main growth and a third and older tree has many more branches arising from the basic framework. Obviously, as far as labor and time saving is concerned, the older tree is much better as a lot of the basic training has been done for you at the nursery.

### Site and soil preparations

The site for fruit must be selected with some consideration to light, especially sunlight, which is very important for good and rapid fruit ripening. Under no circumstances should fruit be situated in low-lying ground which can be waterlogged; this would result in very poor root growth, and these low-lying areas can also be frost pockets, which means that early blossom can be seriously affected or killed with the resultant loss in fruit production.

The site must be thoroughly prepared for all types of fruits because in most cases the fruit is a pretty permanent feature of the garden. It is difficult (in fact well nigh impossible) to rectify mistakes or lapses in the initial basic preparations of the site.

Basically, fruits require very good drainage, and to this end the site (whether new or established) should be deeply dug and the drainage improved wherever necessary. A high organic content is also vital, and this can be provided by incorporating very well rotted manure or composted waste material. A slow acting fertilizer is helpful for the early stages and for this purpose sterilized bonemeal or superphosphate can be scattered over the site a few days before planting at the rate of application 90–120g per sq. m (3–4oz per sq. yd). A balanced or general fertilizer should be scattered at 90g per sq. m (3oz per sq. yd) and thoroughly worked in with a fork or garden rake.

It is important where closely planted fruit is being grown to remove perennial weeds during the initial soil preparations. It will be much easier to keep the ground weed-free once the canes or bushes have become well established. The planting time is any suitable mild period in fall and early spring. If there is an ideal time then late March and early April seem to be the best, provided the soil is in good condition. Trees or bushes grown in containers can be planted at most times of the year if the roots are not disturbed and weather and soil conditions are suitable. If by any chance fruit arrives which is not grown in containers and the weather makes it impossible to plant quickly then the plants should be heeled in.

## Planting

It is important not to cramp the root systems of any fruit. Therefore when the hole is being taken out for them it should be wider than the actual spread of the root system. Make sure that the base of the planting site is well broken up beforehand with the fork. This is an important operation if the site has been prepared for some time before the fruit is planted. In the case of tall plants the planting stake or support must be driven in securely towards the center of the hole before the fruit tree is put in position. This prevents any damage which would occur if the stake were driven in after planting had taken place. A substantial stake is necessary, especially for the apples and pears, and a wooden stake at least 2.5cm (1in) square should be used. Make sure that the base of the stake—in fact preferably the whole stake—is suitably treated with wood preservative to prevent rotting. If bought stakes have not been treated when purchased use a safe preparation such as a horticultural grade of Cuprinol and allow this

*Above : mature espalier-trained fruit trees in an attractive setting of grass and spring bulbs.*

*Right : the cordon system is an intensive, yet decorative, way of growing fruit.*

*Above, left : a fan-trained apple is a beautiful sight in the fall.*

*Above : fruit trees are trained over a pergola here to form a decorative arch.*

to dry out thoroughly for a few days before the stake is used. Place the tree in position and spread the roots out carefully around the planting hole, then trickle in some fine soil which has been made up beforehand of a mixture of 3 parts soil to $1–1\frac{1}{2}$ parts moist peat. As this soil is worked around the roots, carefully firm with the fingers or the feet and then replace the main body of the excavated soil, firming again gently with the feet. Then tie the plant to the stake using some soft material.

The correct depth to plant is to the old soil mark from the nursery. Plant the tree no deeper than this. Make sure also that the tree roots are not dry before planting, and if necessary soak in water for an hour or so beforehand; if the weather is dry at planting time and afterwards make sure too that the soil is well watered and kept nicely moist.

Many gardens out in the country can have an additional hazard to contend with, and that is rabbits. It is very important therefore that some protective device is arranged around the stems of newly planted fruit trees, otherwise the rabbits may gnaw the bark and kill the plants. Usually an encirclement of strong wire netting is sufficient, making sure that this is taken at least 15–20cm (6–8in) below the soil level.

Where fruit trees are being specially trained, such as the cordons, espaliers and fan trees, the supporting material must be erected well before planting time. Usually the basic system of training consists of a series of strong wooden or metal posts inserted in the ground along the run of the planting line, making sure that these main supports are firmly anchored into the ground. Where necessary some concrete should be placed in the hole and allowed to set around the base of each post. Then a series of horizontal training wires are attached to the supports, using strong galvanized wire or plastic covered wire. The wires should be arranged so that the first wire is about 30cm (12in) above ground level, the next wire about 90cm (3ft) above ground level, the next one 1.5m (5ft) above ground level, with if necessary another horizontal one about 2m (6ft) above ground level. This is a suitable spacing for the cordon trained trees but where others are planted, such as espaliers and fans, the spacing between the wires will have to be closer to accommodate the larger number of branches which this type of training produces. For the espaliers the wires should be spaced about 40–45cm (16–18in) apart and for fan trained trees about 30cm (12in) apart.

Where fruit is trained against a wall the training wires should be placed in position beforehand. Special vine eyes or hooks can be screwed or rawlplugged into the mortar courses of a wall, or threaded screws or screw eyes can be inserted in a wooden fence. Then training wires can be stretched between these, spacing them at the distances previously mentioned. It is possible to train many fruits against a wooden trellis but this must be thoroughly treated before erection.

**Apples** With careful selection of varieties it should be possible where facilities are available to virtually have apples from the beginning of the year to the end. This is achieved by planting some varieties for fresh picking and others for their good keeping qualities so that the fruits can be stored away and used as required during the winter period. Obviously special consideration must be given to special varieties which have their own special features such as good keeping, cooking and eating qualities. It is also vitally important to plant varieties which will pollinate well so that the maximum amount of flower set is achieved, which results in a good fruit crop.

Most apples produce a fairly good crop with their own pollen but for maximum results it is a good plan to have one or two other varieties planted close by to ensure maximum pollination. It is also important to plant at the correct distance, and here it is better to err on the generous side. However there are recognized and accepted distances for the various types of fruit tree. For half standard trees plant about 6m (20ft) apart, for the bush trees plant 3.5–4.5m (12–14ft) apart, for espalier and/or fan trained trees plant 4.5–5.5m (15–18ft) apart. Cordons can be planted at much closer spacing, about 60–90cm (2–3ft) apart in the row. These last plants are of course planted at an angle of about 45°.

How many fruit trees should one plant to provide the household with a sensible amount of fruit? This is unfortunately a most difficult question to answer as so much will depend on the soil, the type of tree and variety, and also on the way in which it is cultivated, especially with regard to its pruning. However if bush trees are grown and there is a family of four to five then about six to eight trees should be adequate, for the espaliers five and for cordons about fourteen. This, however, must only be taken as a rough guide.

It is probably most convenient, and perhaps more sensible, to suggest certain really good varieties which should provide pickings at certain key periods of the season. For the very earliest harvesting, around August, the variety 'Stark Earliest' is ideal. Bringing the harvesting time a little later toward the winter we have the late varieties, and for a gorgeous dessert apple the red 'Baldwin' is ideal, although it tends to crop bi-annually if allowed to overbear in any one year. For the main crop it is a good idea to have a dessert and a culinary apple, though most U.S. varieties are dual-purpose, an excellent example being 'Rome Beauty'. For a strictly cooking apple 'Rhode Island Greening' cannot be bettered, and it makes an excellent pollinator for practically any other variety. Most U.S. varieties come into bearing reasonably early, though 'Northern Spy' is a later dessert variety well worth waiting for. In addition we have the crab apples such as 'Cardinal Hyslop', 'Red Dolgo' and 'Whitney', which are decorative trees with fruits ideal for making delicious crab apple jelly.

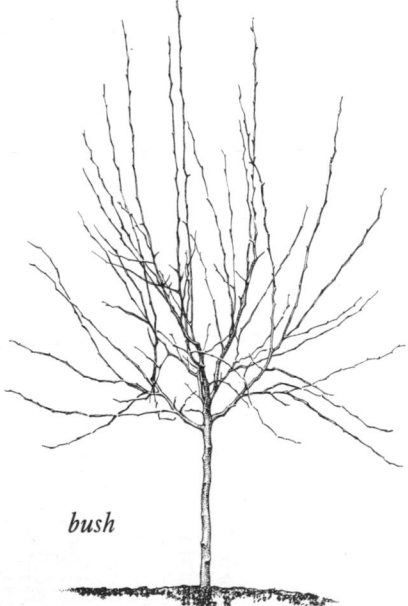

*bush*

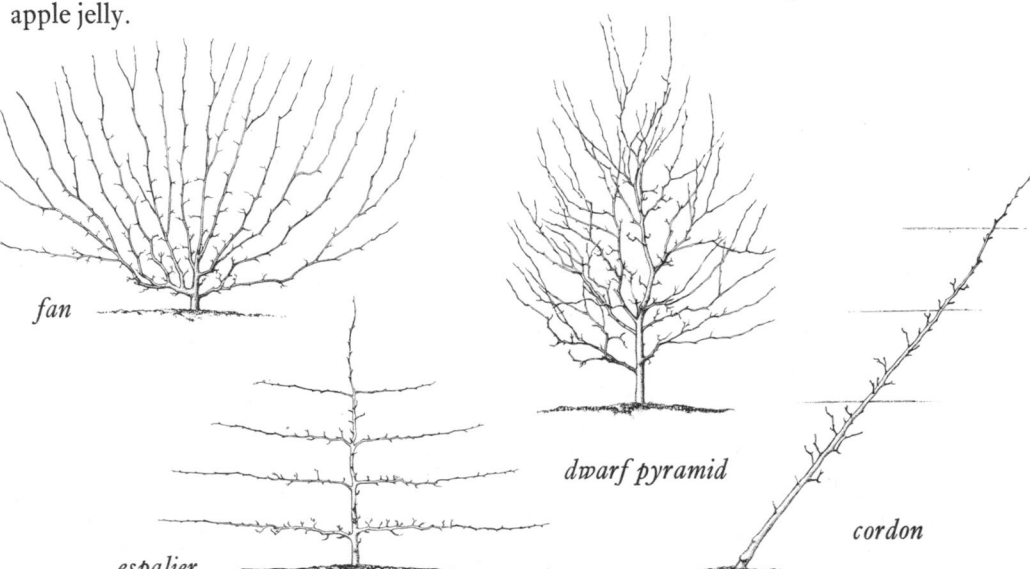

*fan*

*espalier*

*dwarf pyramid*

*cordon*

**Cherries** An ornamental fruit tree is the Cherry tree. These are extremely useful to have as they provide sweet or sour cherries from the garden, and these are usually available from about June to September according to variety. The only problem with cherries is the fact that birds are attracted to them and a great loss of fruit can occur unless it is possible to tie in suitable bird scarers in the branches or to cover the tree or even part of the tree with fine mesh netting. It is important to have a pollinator with cherries, so get your supplier's advice.

Planting should be carried out only in the spring in colder states, and the fairly minimal pruning is best confined to spring and early summer, when infection from leaf disease is least likely. Among the sweet cherries, popular and reliable varieties include 'Bing', 'Van', a good pollinator, 'Lambert', which has extra large dark fruit, and 'Schmidt's Biggareau', one of the best crack-resistant varieties. Good yellows are 'Stark Gold' and 'Napoleón' (also called 'Royal Ann'). Sour cherry varieties include 'Early Richmond' for an extra early crop, 'Montmorency' and 'Suda Hardy'. Fruiting periods vary with local conditions.

**Peaches and Nectarines** These are lovely fruits to have in a garden but need a sheltered aspect and a site which is warm; they may be trained against a wall. These trees are widely grown in areas with a Mediterranean climate and do not stand temperatures below zero; but like other deciduous trees, they need a dormant period and their cultivation is only possible where there is winter cold. The ideal condition is a moderately cold winter, followed by a warm frost-free spring. Peaches may be grouped by the color of their flesh, white being best for flavor, yellow popular for canning. Nectarines are a sport of peaches, with smooth, plum-like skin. The trees are less hardy.

Of the nectarines there are two outstanding varieties: the first is 'Mericrest' which is exceptionally reliable and hardy and the second is 'Stark Delicious' which has very richly flavored fruits.

Of the peaches 'Redhaven' is a renowned variety, bearing medium-sized fruits which are delicious both for eating and freezing.

**Pears** No fruit garden is complete without the pears. These can be selected to give pickings from about August well into October in mild areas. One of the earliest is 'Colett'. This is a newly introduced dessert variety with fruit which is of excellent quality. It can be planted with other varieties for pollination purposes, and the varieties 'Beurre Bosc', 'Bartlett' or 'Doyenne du Comice' are ideal for this purpose. For a picking in October the varieties 'Beurre Bosc', 'Beurre d'Anjou' or 'Doyenne du Comice' are excellent. All have high quality fruits and the trees are easy to cultivate. Of the three the latter is the variety which is the favorite on the West Coast and it does require a very well-drained soil and a warm location. These trees can be pollinated with any of the others mentioned.

**Plums and Damsons** These fruits are not as popular in American gardens as they should be because they are easy to cultivate and grow well in a reasonably wide range of soils. They do however like good drainage, and on heavy soils particular attention should be paid to this point. Of the plums the following varieties can be recommended: 'Burbank Elephant Heart' which fruits in about August and is self fertile; the Japanese 'Ember' which also fruits in August and is self fertile; 'Hybrid Sapa', an early variety which has black fruits and starts its bearing in July onward. Another good dessert is 'Giant Cherry Plum', and when grown in good soil this can bear very heavy crops. It is self fertile. 'Fellemberg' is probably the most famous of the prune plums, another self fertile variety, and can produce very heavy crops indeed. These are available for picking in approximately September. Of the damsons very few are grown in the U.S. However, they are a nicely flavored fruit which grows well in most situations and is available for picking from about September.

*Opposite: a triple cordon apple grown against a wall.*

*Below: dessert cherries ready for picking.*
*Bottom: this is 'Kirke's Blue', a European dessert plum with dark reddish skin. It is ready for picking in September.*

**Blackberries and raspberries** It is very useful to be able to grow fruit against walls or fences and for this purpose the blackberries and raspberries cannot be bettered. In the blackberries section there are some very interesting hybrids. Of the pure blackberries the best is the new 'Darrow' which fruits late July or August. It has very sweet and juicy berries and is a very vigorous grower. Another variety is 'Himalayan Giant' which is a useful variety to have but one that is not hardy in the East. Now we come to the interesting hybrids. One is called 'Oregon Thornless' which, as its name implies, is completely free from those prickly thorns and is therefore the most pleasant plant to pick fruit from. Fruits are quite large, beautifully sweet, and available from September to October. A new variety is called 'Smoothstem', another thornless type which is exceptionally vigorous. It crops from late August and can produce its large berries even as late as October under some conditions. Another new one is 'Thornfree' which is very similar to the previous variety and fruits at the same time. An interesting hybrid between the loganberry, blackberry and raspberry is known as the 'Thornless Boysenberry'. It is a particularly useful variety for the lighter soils as it resists dry conditions quite well. It can bear heavy crops of large fruit from about July to August. Another nice plant to have is the Thornless Loganberry. This produces extremely large fruits which are a cross between the wild blackberry and the raspberry. The fruits ripen late July or August and cropping is very good indeed.

There are many more fascinating varieties of raspberry than many gardeners appreciate. For convenience they can be divided into the one-season types and those which flower later on in the autumn. Of the one-seasons the following varieties can be thoroughly recommended. 'Canby' is a variety which fruits in mid season, a heavy cropper on good soils. The berries are easy to pick and nice and firm. 'Gatineau' also ripens early and can be a very heavy cropper in good soils, though its flavor is not as good as the previous one. Another new variety is the black 'Morrison' which bears medium sized fruits which are nice and firm. 'Golden Queen' is a heavy yielding yellow variety which is one-season. Fruits are medium to large and of good flavor.

In the autumn or 'everbearing' section of raspberries, the variety 'September'

*Below: Raspberries ripe and ready for picking.*

has good quality fruits, and a new one, 'Heritage', is perhaps one of the most out-standing varieties to date.

**Currants** These can be divided according to their colors: black, red and white. Unfortunately there are very few varieties in the black range, and this is because they are the most susceptible to the white pine blister rust and, for practical purposes, are not generally available in American nurseries. In fact, even the red and white varieties may not be grown where white pines are native and plentiful.

**Gooseberries** The gardener should not omit gooseberries from the soft fruit section of the garden, though unfortunately in some areas it is not permitted to grow them, again because of the white pine blister rust. The selection of varieties is once again very limited for this reason. Best known is probably 'Pixwell', a fairly new, almost thornless variety with fruit which hangs free of the branches, which makes picking easy. Also available in some nurseries is the old, reliable 'Poorman' and the newer pink-fruited 'Nelarme' introduced by the University of Minnesota.

**Grapes** Vines can be grown successfully outdoors in most parts of the United States. The preferred time for planting them is early spring before their growth commences, depending on local soil and weather conditions. Select a warm, sunny site with good air circulation.

In the North the favored type is the bunch grape. Popular varieties include the following. Blue or purple: 'Concord', 'Sheridan', 'Concord Seedless', 'Brighton', and 'Buffalo'. White grapes include: 'Niagara', 'Ontario' and 'Interlaken Seedless'. For reds choose 'Catawba', 'Yates', 'Delaware' or 'Agawam'. In addition to these some new hybrids such as 'Baco No. 1' have also been introduced, permitting one

*Strawberries grown in barrels are decorative enough to adorn a terrace or patio.*

to grow European types in the East.

In the South are grown the vigorous muscadines including 'Hunt', 'Wallace' and 'Yuga', while California grows the European *vinifera* type such as 'Muscat of Hamburg', 'Muscat of Alexandria', 'Ribier', 'Thompson Seedless', etc.

**Melons**  Mention must be made here of cantaloupes and muskmelons, which are grown in much the same manner as marrows, squash and cucumbers although classed as fruits. In the North seed should be sown indoors 4–6 weeks ahead of safe planting-out date. Preferred varieties include 'Burpee Hybrid' and 'Honey Rock'. In warmer areas try white-fleshed 'Golden Beauty Casaba' and green-fleshed 'Honey Dew'.

**Raspberries**—see Blackberries and raspberries.

**Strawberries**  No fruit garden could possibly be complete without its strawberry beds, and great strides have been made in recent years in the production of some excellent new varieties, but of course some of the old favorites are still going strong. The strawberries can be divided into two convenient groups: those which produce their fruits in the main summer period of June to July, and the 'everbearers' which fruit as late as October.

Perhaps the most popular variety grown is 'Catskill', which is classed as a midseason, and does really produce very heavy crops. Another popular variety is 'Fairfax', another midseason, which also bears heavy crops of fruit and is reasonably resistant to disease.

For the Middle Atlantic states choose 'Blakemore', 'Jerseybelle', 'Pocahontas', 'Sparkle' or 'Tennessee Beauty'. Farther South one's choice should run to 'Dixieland' and 'Surecrop' as well as 'Pocahontas' and 'Tennessee Beauty'. In the Prairies and Plains States grow 'Arrowhead', 'Howard 17' and 'Radiance', while Northwesterners should select 'Marshall', 'Northwest' or 'Puget Beauty'.

Among the later fruiting or everbearing varieties, most useful because they can continue to crop right up until the first heavy frosts, are 'Evermore' and 'Ozark Beauty'. For heavy crops mulch well and in dry summers water frequently.

### A quick guide to planting distances

*Blackberries:* may be trained against fences or walls and they are best spaced about 2–2.5m (6–8ft) apart in the row. *Raspberries:* these should be planted about 45cm (18in) apart in the row and if more than one row is grown the spacing between the rows should be about 2m (6ft). *Blackberries and their hybrids:* these are planted about 2–3m (6–9ft) apart, and if more than one row is grown then a distance between rows of 2m (6–7ft) should be allowed. The more vigorous varieties of the blackberries and hybrids can be spaced even further apart in the rows and a distance of some 3–3.5m (10–12ft) will not be excessive. *Currants:* if grown, space at least 1.5m (5ft) apart and where more than one row is grown a distance of at least 2m (6ft) between rows must be allowed. *Gooseberries:* space the plants about 1.5–2m (5–6ft) apart. If more than one row is grown a distance between rows of at least 2m (6–7ft) should be allowed. *Strawberries:* the plants should be spaced about 30–45cm (12–18in) apart in the row, and the rows should be not less than 90cm (2ft) apart. *Grapes:* the vines are usually grown on trellises or arbors by homeowners, but if grown on posts or wire supports these should be spaced 2.5–3m (8–10ft) apart for bunch grapes, about the same for European types, and up to twice this distance apart for muscadines.

### Soil preparation and planting for soft fruits

The blackberries, loganberries, raspberries, etc. will grow quite well in a wide range of soils but where the soil is poor or dry plenty of organic matter must be worked in beforehand. These fruits are also quite accommodating as far as situation is concerned, and will do well in either a sunny or partly shaded position. Good drainage is vital and the site should be dug to at least the full depth of the spade. Where necessary the subsoil should be broken up with a fork, working composted vegetable waste at the rate of a good bucketful to the square meter (square yard) or well rotted manure at the rate of a bucketful to 1.5 sq. m (1½ sq. yds). If manure or compost is not available in large quantities one or two shovelfuls of the compost or manure can be worked in to each planting site. A few days before planting takes place apply a general or balanced fertilizer at the rate of 90g per sq. m (3oz per sq. yd) and rake this in thoroughly. When the plants are planted in their quarters make sure that the roots are spread out in the planting hole or trench. Work some fine soil around the roots, first firming gently with the feet, then return the rest of the soil and firm this also with the feet.

The currants (black, red and white) will also grow well on quite a wide range of soils, but they should not be planted where the ground is exceptionally damp. As the crop flowers early on in the season they are liable to early frost damage so avoid also a low lying area or a situation which is exposed and liable to frost attacks. All these fruits like a rich soil so the area should be deeply dug and plenty of organic matter worked in at the rate of at least a bucketful to the square meter (square yard). A dressing of a balanced fertilizer should be applied a day or two before planting and this should be scattered on at the rate of 60–90g per sq. m (2–3oz per sq. yd) and then raked in thoroughly. When the plants are put in their planting hole make sure that the roots are not cramped and that they are spread out carefully along the bottom of the hole. As with the cane fruits, trickle some fine soil between the roots first of all, firm this, then return the remainder of the soil and firm this also with the feet. The same planting advice applies to the gooseberries.

Grapevines require similar treatment outdoors, but if grown under glass a special border should be prepared. This should be enclosed with brick or concrete to restrict the roots and prevent them penetrating into soil in other borders. An alternative is to plant the vine outside the greenhouse in a similarly prepared border and take the main stem into the greenhouse itself through a suitable hole made in the side of the greenhouse walling. Very good drainage is required for vines, and the bed should be dug to a depth of at least 60cm (2ft) with the base of the bed broken up well with the fork. To ensure perfect drainage some small rubble should be placed along the bottom of the bed to a depth of 5–8cm (2–3in). There is nothing like an old fashioned formula for the soil in a vine border to obtain the best possible results. This special mixture can be made up as follows: 8 parts of chopped turf, 1 part of old mortar rubble, ½ part wood ashes and ¼ part of charcoal broken to the size of peas. To each bushel of the mixture add 240g (8oz) of sterilized bonemeal. A bushel, incidentally, is contained in a box with inside dimensions of 55 × 25 × 25cm (22 × 10 × 10in). All these ingredients should be mixed thoroughly together and then applied to the prepared area. Of course, cultivation of grapes under glass is rarely practised now even in cooler parts of the U.S. except where it is desirable to have fruit out of season, when the extra effort involved may be considered worthwhile.

The plants are best planted indoors when the buds begin to break, which will be February or early March. The roots should be spread out well in the planting hole (which should be fairly shallow) and then some fine soil trickled in around the roots, firmed, and the remaining soil replaced and firmed also with the feet. Very firm treading is necessary. Make sure also that the vines are well watered in, and an eye must be kept on watering until the vines become established. This is especially important where the vines are planted inside the greenhouse and are not naturally watered by rainfall.

### Pruning apples

Before pruning is discussed in any detail it is important that the gardener appreciates

*Below: an outdoor vine, well trained and pruned like this, can be allowed to fruit in the third season from the time of planting.*

the meaning of certain terms. Pruning is carried out by cutting back growths to certain types of bud, and there are two main types of bud growth on a fruit tree: these are the *fruit bud* and the *growth bud*. A fruit bud, as its name implies, will produce the bloom or blossom which in turn becomes the fruit. The fruit bud is usually large and round whereas the growth bud which produces only the extension growth or new branches is smaller and generally lies flatter to the stem.

Certain types of growths or branches have particular terms such as *leaders* and *laterals*. The leader is the leading shoot or growth of a branch, whereas a lateral is a side growth or shoot from this type of branch.

Other common terms are *spurs* and *tips*. In certain cases some fruit trees bear their fruit on short growths which are technically called spurs, other varieties produce their fruit buds on the ends or tips of the growth made the previous summer. These are known as the tip bearers.

Cuts must be made with a sharp bladed pair of pruning shears as with rose pruning, immediately above an outward pointing bud so that the new growth is encouraged to grow outward and not in toward the center of the tree, thus making the tree overcrowded and rather tangly. All pruning cuts should be made in the same direction as the bud and in a slope.

*Right : pruning tools include 1. saw for removing large branches ; 2. parrot-nosed saw for awkwardly placed wood ; 3. budding knife for those who wish to graft their own roses and fruit trees on suitable rootstocks ; 4. pruning knife. 5, 6 and 7 are all types of pruner, the only essential tool for the amateur.*

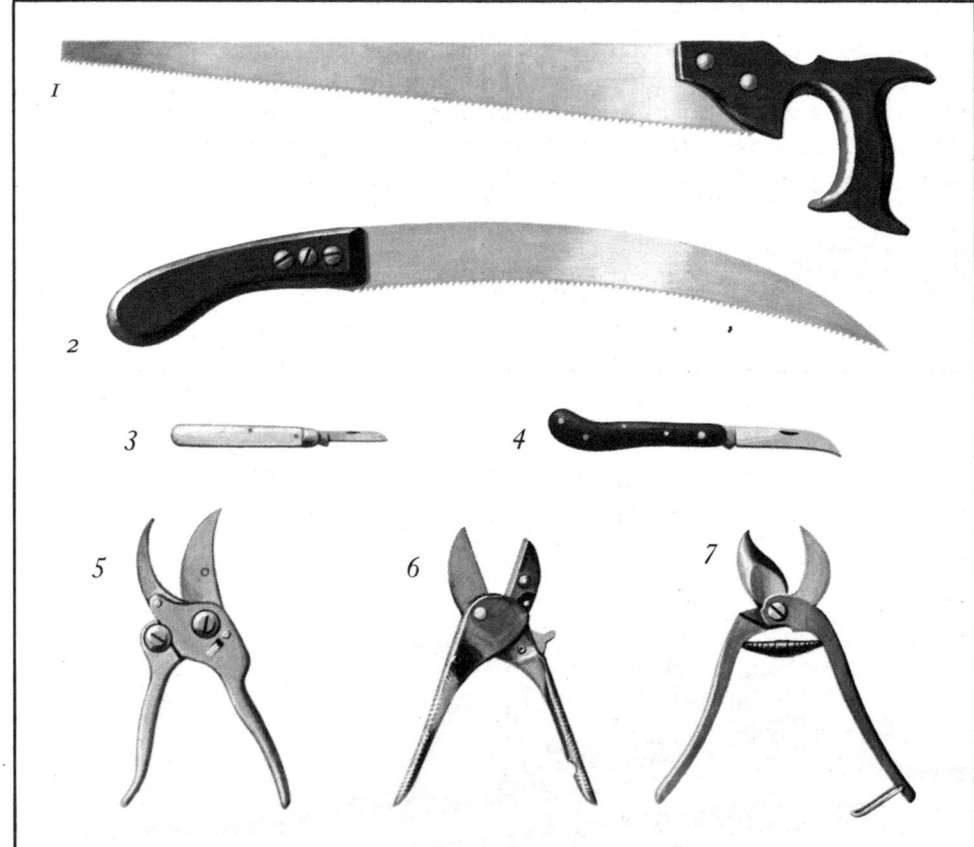

**Pruning spur forming trees**   The aim of pruning here is just to encourage as much new growth as possible which will replace some of the growth which has produced the fruit. It is important to appreciate the fact that it takes three years for a spur forming bush tree to produce fruit on its fruiting spurs. In the first year the growth bud produces a growth or shoot and in the second year this starts to produce the fruit buds. It is not until the third year or summer that these fruit buds form spurs on which the fruit is produced that year. Another important factor to appreciate is that in its second year a shoot will produce new growth from its tips as well as fruit buds. Of course in its third year there will be one year old *and* two year old extension growth arising from the shoots. In the renewal system of pruning a small number of the two year old and three year old shoots are pruned back, the aim being to prevent an overcrowded tree. It is really a matter of the gardener looking at the bush tree and deciding just how many of the various growths he wishes to remain and those which he wishes to cut out to keep a nice open tree.

**Pruning trees which are tip bearing**   This type of fruit tree produces its growth in a similar fashion to the spur forming bush tree, but the difference here is that a large proportion of the one year old growth will produce a fruit bud at the tips. Fortunately the tip bearing trees require less attention to pruning and therefore, as far as the gardener is concerned who requires minimum upkeep and maintenance in his fruit garden, the tip bearing apple trees are the best to purchase. Pruning consists of pruning back the shoots which have no fruit bud at their tip, and the pruning cut should be made to the fruit bud which is toward the top of the growth. If a fruit bud is not conveniently placed higher up, the pruning cut should be more severe, cutting back to about four growth buds from the base of the growth.

**Dealing with a neglected tree**   Sometimes gardeners take over a neglected garden in which there are badly overgrown fruit trees. How does one deal with trees in these circumstances? Most of the problems will be concerned with dead, diseased or badly overcrowded branches. Take a look at the general framework of the tree and then cut out carefully all these offending branches. Cut out all the branches growing too close to other branches. Where wounds or cuts are large, these are best painted over or sealed with a commercial tree wound paint to prevent the entry of disease spores. All such pruning should be burnt afterwards. The main aim is to keep a nice open center, spacing branches about 60cm (2ft) apart each way. Other branches can be cut back to an outward pointing bud so that the tree is kept open and there is a good movement or circulation of air amongst all the branches. In a very badly neglected tree pruning should be quite severe and ruthless. What you are aiming for is to encourage new healthy sturdy growths to arise from the older cut back branches.

**Pruning a cordon**   These trees are planted against their training material at an angle of about 45°. Pruning basically consists of cutting back mature laterals to three leaves from the basal cluster of leaves, and this is done at the end of July. The mature side shoots which grow from the laterals or spurs should be cut back to one leaf from their basal cluster. If there are any small secondary growths these should be pruned back to one bud later on. What happens when the cordon reaches beyond the top of its supports? The tree is carefully untied and lowered still further to an angle of not less than about 35°. After this the tree is not moved at all but is restricted to its training material by cutting back any new growth at the tip to about 1cm ($\frac{1}{2}$in) above a bud. This pruning is usually carried out in May.

**Pruning espaliers**   This is a fairly simple system. With a one year old tree, this should be cut back as soon as it has been planted, the cut being made to a bud or a convenient shoot which will be about 38cm (15in) above ground level. Make sure that the selected bud or shoot is 2.5cm (1in) or so above the first horizontal training wire. Then you must choose three other buds: one which will grow upwards to continue the height of the espalier tree and the other two buds conveniently placed to the left and to the right of the main stem so that they will produce growths which can be trained along the wires to the left and right of the main stem. Any other buds or growths below these three buds should be carefully removed with the fingers. Sometimes it is necessary to encourage the bottom bud to grow strongly, and this can be done by making a small notch in the bark just above the bud. The next year the shoots which arise from these three buds should be trained along canes or along wires, allowing the top shoots to grow upward and training in the other two shoots to the left and to the right horizontally along the wires. It is often convenient to use some thin canes tied to the wires and the new young growths are tied in turn to these canes. The young growths cannot be trained completely horizontally left and right of the main stem and it is wise to train them first at a lesser angle along the canes and then, during the following winter, pull them back carefully to lie horizontally on either side of the main stem and fasten them to the horizontal training wires. Pruning now consists of cutting back the main central growth to about 5cm (2in) or so above the second strand of horizontal training wire. Then turn your attention to the growths to the left and right of the main stem. These should be cut back to just over half their length or, if weak, they should be cut back more ruthlessly.

You now wish to encourage some more arms left and right of the main stem so you look for two more buds just below the pruning cut on the main stem. These should be selected so that their growths can be trained conveniently along the second run of horizontal training wire, and all buds below these should be carefully cut off. It may be necessary to make the notch in the lowest bud. In the following summer the new growth should be trained along canes at an angle of about 45°, and then in the following winter these are unfastened and carefully pulled back to run straight along the horizontal training wires. The current year's growth should be pruned about late July, and this is done by cutting back the mature laterals to about three leaves above their basal cluster. A little later on in the summer, around September, the secondary shoots from the July pruning need cutting back and these should be pruned back to about one bud. In subsequent seasons the training and pruning continues in this fashion until the required size or framework of the espalier tree has been formed.

**Pruning a fan shaped apple tree**   Pruning consists of training or guiding suitable growths to form the very attractive fan shape. If you like to involve yourself in some fascinating work in forming a tree from its very early stages then you will start with a one year old or maiden tree. After planting the main stem is cut back to about 60cm (2ft) from ground level above two suitably placed buds, which, ideally, should produce growth left and right of this main stem. In the next season or the following summer these two buds will produce some nice healthy shoots which, when they are about 30cm (12in) long, should be fastened to some thin canes which are then attached to the horizontal training wires at an angle of about 45°. It should be pointed out that when the initial two buds have been selected and the main stem has been cut back to its 60cm (2ft) length, all buds below these two should be carefully removed with the fingers. What you are aiming for is a clean stem below these two buds.

In the second winter the two growths made during the summer should be pruned back so that they are about 45cm (18in) long. Make sure that the pruning cut is made just above a growth bud. From this pruning cut several new growths will arise from buds along the original stem. There will be a continuation or extension growth at the tips of the original stems, and these growths should be trained along canes, maintaining the same angle as the original two growths. Then lower down the stems there will be other growths and only two of these on the upper part of the stem should be allowed to continue. They too should be trained against thin canes which in turn are fastened to the horizontal training wires. One, and only one, side growth should be allowed to grow below the main stem and this too is fastened to a suitable thin cane. All other shoots along the main stems should be carefully removed. The selected shoots should be trained to form an attractive fan shape. By the third winter you should have eight growths, four on each side: one extension growth, two growths growing upward and one growth growing downward on each side. These should now be pruned back to leave about 60cm (2ft) of growth and the cut again should be made just above a growth bud. During the summer of the following season the training procedure is very similar to that of the second year's work: three nicely spaced growths on each of the original shoots are allowed to grow on, selecting two to grow above the branch and one below as before, all other unwanted shoots being carefully removed.

*Left, top : a pear tree is given a light summer pruning to encourage the formation of fruit buds for the following spring. Center : the side-shoots are shortened to about five leaves from the base. Bottom : an old blackcurrant bush can be severely pruned almost to ground level.*

**Pear tree pruning**  The pruning of these trees is exactly the same as for the apples. The only slight exception is for the summer pruning of the pears which is best done at the beginning of July.

## Cherry tree pruning

Here again, we are placing the emphasis on training trees to fit the small garden rather than full-sized orchard trees. In the case of young trees pruning has to be carried out fairly hard to form a nicely shaped tree. Usually the leaders are cut back to about a half or two-thirds their growth and pruning cuts should be made to outward pointing buds to keep the center of the tree open. Where fan trained trees are grown they should not be allowed to form a central stem, but should be cut back to about 40cm (16in) from soil level so suitable branches are formed near the base.

For general pruning the cherries are classified into two types: the sweet cherries which form spurs in a similar way to apples, and the sour cherries such as 'Montmorency' which do not form these spurs quite so easily but fruit on the previous year's growth. Generally speaking, all pruning should be carried out as lightly as possible and it will consist of cutting out badly placed or diseased branches, which is done in March. In the case of trained trees the sweet cherries should be summer and winter pruned in a similar way to apples except that young laterals should be kept at full length, provided of course there is sufficient room on the wall or fence. Usually the summer pruning is carried out in June. Winter pruning is done in March. The sour cherries are disbudded in summer. This consists of taking out young side shoots when they are only quite small but retaining about two on each fruiting growth near the base and another at the tip. In the early spring the old growth which has fruited is cut out and the young shoot is retained to take its place.

## Training peaches and nectarines

The pruning of 'dwarf' or 'bush' trees is relatively simple. Where a one year old is grown the central growth is cut back to about 75cm (2½ft) above ground level, and this is done in May, making sure the cut is made just above a growth bud. To form the basic framework of the bush tree the four buds below the cut are allowed to produce the growth and all other buds or small shoots must be removed. In subsequent years pruning basically consists of the careful removal of badly placed growth, cutting it back hard to the original source of growth. No shoots or growths should be allowed to grow below the bottom branches of the main stem; this is done to keep a nice stem on the plant and to encourage bushy growth in general. Unfortunately peaches in particular have a habit of producing dead shoots at the tips. This is known as 'die back', and this growth should be cut out to a good bud. In subsequent years try and maintain as much healthy new wood as possible even though in some cases it may be necessary to cut out a lot of the older wood which may not be quite so fruitful. The training for a fan shaped peach tree is as for sour cherry training. For the initial training prune when growth starts in the spring.

## Pruning plums and damsons

Where half standard or bush trees are grown the building up of the initial framework is carried out in a similar way to that of apples. Pruning from then onward consists mainly of the removal of dead and badly placed branches, and this should be done in June. Also any weak growth should be thinned out or removed in the late summer when the crop has been gathered. In March the leaders can be shortened back by about one-third, making sure that growth is cut back to an outward pointing bud. Where a variety tends to produce a drooping habit then an upward pointing bud should be selected, and for those varieties which have an upright habit an outward pointing bud should be selected. It is very important to paint over large pruning cuts with a tree wound dressing. This prevents the entry of disease spores.

Where the trees are trained against a trellis or fence quite hard pruning is necessary.

The ends or tips of young side shoots should be pinched back when they have produced about eight leaves, and this work is carried out in about July. In early spring older shoots should be shortened to any fruit buds which have been made, and at the same time leaders should be cut back by about one-third.

A fan trained tree is trained right from its early one year old stage by cutting it back in early spring to about 45cm (18in) from ground level. When this has been done, about four new growths are allowed to grow on, spacing them out in a fan shape. In the following November these shoots are shortened to about 45cm (18in) in length and the thinning and pruning process is carried out every spring until the fence is suitably covered with a fan shaped growth.

## Pruning soft fruits

**Cane fruits**   Here we come to a much simpler system of pruning. For the blackberries and loganberries all the canes should be cut back after planting to about 30cm (12in) of ground level. It is wise not to allow fruiting in the first year, the object being to encourage the canes to produce really strong growth. In later years, as soon as the crop has been gathered, all the old fruiting canes should be cut right out to ground level and the young canes should be trained in their place. According to variety the number of new canes produced may vary, but never allow more than about eight new canes per plant each year.

In subsequent years canes which have fruited should be cut right out to ground level and the new canes trained in their place. Some varieties tend to make rather tall growth, and these are best tipped back in early spring to about 2m (6ft) from ground level. Autumn fruiting types of raspberry should be pruned with great care cutting out only old canes which have fruited for the second time, i.e. fall and then early summer. Leave about six good strong canes per plant.

**Pruning currants**   Blackcurrants are pruned in October, and pruning can continue until the end of January according to weather conditions. Pruning is carried out to remove as much as possible of the growth which has just borne the fruits but care must be taken not to cut out too many of the young shoots which will bear the following year's crop. New blackcurrant plants should be cut back to about 5–8cm (2–3in) of soil level when they have been planted.

Red and white currants are pruned twice: once in the summer, and again in the winter. Summer pruning is done around July when side growths should be cut back to about five leaves each. Winter pruning is carried out from the end of October until the end of January, and side shoots are cut back still harder to about three dormant buds. Leaders are cut back by about one-third of their length. A careful eye should be kept on some varieties which tend to produce poor shoots, some of which can be dead; these should be cut right back to strong buds.

**Pruning gooseberries**   Summer and winter pruning is also carried out for this fruit and the system is exactly the same as for the redcurrants. The center of the bushes should be kept as open as possible to facilitate picking (this applies also to the other currants). There are some varieties of gooseberry which tend to make a rather drooping or arching growth, and in the autumn these growths should be cut back to a bud which is pointing upward and near the top of the arch or droop. This will keep the branches away from the soil in the following season.

**Pruning grapes**   Most gardeners grow grapes on trellises or arbors, and hence will find it necessary to adapt the following advice as it fits their needs. When the shoots have produced about five or six leaves their growing point should be carefully pinched out, but the leading one should be allowed to grow on as this is to form the extension growth to the shoot or rod. Any secondary laterals which are produced should be pinched out above the first leaf. Then turn your attention to the leading

*Below: a severely pruned blackcurrant bush produces vigorous new growth in spring. These new shoots should be thinned (bottom) and the strongest growths retained.*

growth which, when about 2m (6–7ft) long, should have its growing point pinched out. Also look at the side growths produced. These should be pinched above the first leaf, all except the top one which is allowed to grow on. Any other shoots made on the leading growth should be left until winter when they too should be pinched. Lateral growths that have been produced should be pinched out also. In the winter, all the side growths should be cut hard back to the main stem and the leading growth should be shortened to within about 120cm (4ft) of ground level.

In the vine's second year unwanted side growths should be removed. The idea is to produce a trunk or rod and two permanent arms on each side on both the eastern or fox grapes and the southern muscadines. The latter, being much more vigorous, are allowed to grow longer and produce more bearing side shoots. The European or vinifera grapes, on the other hand, are often grown with one strong trunk and a wheel-like arrangement of branches radiating from its summit.

With any type of grape no cane or shoot is allowed to grow rampant. Each year after the basic or permanent structure is formed the canes are cut back in winter or early spring to within just a few nodes or joints of where they started growing the previous spring. This limits the number of fruit clusters to what the vine can bear well and without strain. The muscadines, since they produce such few-berried clusters, are allowed to produce correspondingly more of them.

### Aftercare for strawberries

If a few cloches such as the barn type are available, an early crop of strawberries can be produced. The cloches are placed over a few plants in fairly early spring and the cloches remain on the crop until the fruit has been picked. If you do this the plants are encouraged to fruit a week or two earlier than unprotected plants in a garden. Another advantage is the fact that the fruit is protected from rain and also from the attention of birds. Another method of producing out of season strawberry fruits is to select strong runners in June and pot them singly in 13cm (5in) pots in August, using a fairly rich potting mixture. The pots should be placed in a shaded part of the garden or plunged up to their rims in a bed of ashes in a frame. In October the pots should be protected with a cold frame and then the pots brought into the greenhouse from January until March where a temperature of at least 7–10°C (45–50°F) should be maintained. It will be necessary to hand pollinate the flowers when they open using a camel hair brush for this purpose. When the plants come to flower the temperature should be increased gradually up to a maximum of about 18–21°C (65–70°F). When the fruit begins to swell the temperature can be lowered to about 16–18°C (60–65°F).

**Propagating strawberries**  Many gardeners make the mistake of keeping strawberry beds too long. After their third year the fruiting capabilities are reduced, so it is a good idea to make or remake one third of the bed each year.

It is an easy matter to increase one's stock of strawberries by means of the runners which are thrown out by the parent plants every year. It is most important though that only the best or healthiest plants are selected for propagation purposes; about five runners per plant should be used and the remainder cut off. The tips of the runners where the little plantlet is forming should be pegged securely into the soil, after the surface has been broken up and loosened with a hand fork and a little moist peat and some sharp sand incorporated The plantlet can be retained close to the soil by a bent piece of wire forming a pin. Another system is to peg the plantlets in small flower pots filled with a suitable mixture and plunge the pots up to their rim in the soil nearby. The only snag with this form of propagation is that the pots can dry out and they do require watering occasionally. The best propagating time is between June and July. The pegged down runners must be kept moist all the time. By late August they should have rooted and will be ready to be lifted and potted up into larger pots or planted out in their final fruiting positions.

*Below: propagating strawberries from runners is a simple process. It sometimes helps to remove excess leaves with a sharp knife before pegging the runners down where they are to root.*

# IMPROVING THE SOIL

The soil is the most important factor in the whole garden. The rate of growth of plants and their flower display (or the yield in the case of fruit and vegetables) is dependent on the fertility of the soil they grow in. It is important, therefore, to spend a little time in the preparation and improvement of one's soil because it is very difficult in later years to rectify mistakes, particularly once you have put in permanent plants such as trees and shrubs.

### Organic manures

Basically soil is improved by deep digging and by drainage, and also by incorporating certain materials into the soil which not only supply nutrients to the plants but also help to maintain the structure of the soil itself. For example, a light or sandy soil is beautiful and easy to work but it is a soil which dries out very quickly and as a result plants suffer. To reduce this tendency or to prevent it completely the soil should be enriched with plenty of material which can act like a sponge and retain every vestige of moisture. There are several materials which can be used for this purpose and these include manure, peat, and composted vegetable waste. The manure can take several forms such as farmyard manure (usually cow manure), horse manure from stables, and concentrated manures which are a dry or prepared manure, usually from cattle feed lots. These are very pleasant to handle since they are often dry and virtually odorless, and are very good as far as nutrients and soil conditioning is concerned.

Where ground is vacant at the time and will remain so for a month or so before seeds or plants are put into the ground, fresh manure can be dug in. By the time planting or seed sowing times come along it will have rotted down sufficiently. Fresh manure is known as 'hot' and can burn plant roots badly. Chicken manure is especially caustic in its fresh state and should be incorporated in good time, or should be rotted down for several months like the manure if to be used just before seed is sown or plants are put out. The manures are generally stacked in a convenient heap where they will rot down quite quickly.

Another useful form of organic matter is composted vegetable waste which is obtained from the stacking and rotting down of all sorts of garden waste material

*Below : waste organic matter is rotted down in heaps to make compost. The vegetable matter can be sprinkled with an activator, followed by a layer of soil, every 15cm (6in) or so to speed up the process of decomposition and prevent unpleasant smells. Below, right : autumn leaves can be collected separately in a wire enclosure and rotted down to make leafmold.*

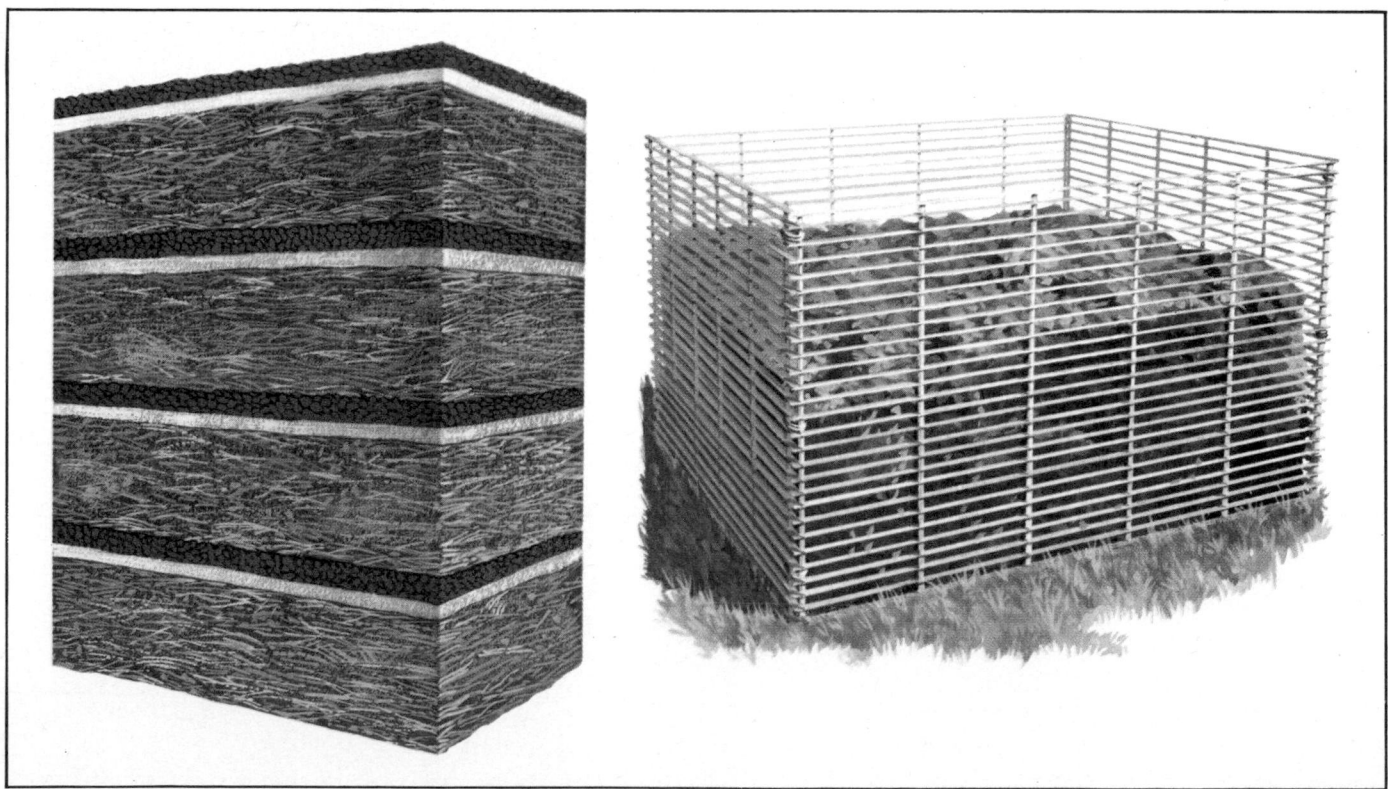

such as lawn mowings, the trimmings from the vegetable plot, flower heads, leaves and of course the autumn leaf fall. There are neat compost bins or containers which can be purchased these days to keep the heap neat and tidy and there are accelerating materials which can be applied to hasten the decomposition process. These also help to produce a sweeter smelling material.

The average dressing of manure is about 50kg (one hundredweight), or an average size barrow load, to about 6.5–8 sq. m (8–10 sq. yd). This composted vegetable waste has not quite the same high food value, and therefore a barrow load of this material should be applied to every 2.5–3.5 sq. m (3–4 sq. yd). Another way of improving the soil is to grow a green manure, which is usually either mustard, rape, annual lupins, soybeans or buckwheat. These are sown in the spring quite thickly and are dug into the ground when about 20–23cm (8–9in) high. As they are dug in, sulfate of ammonia is applied at about 45g per sq. m (1½oz per sq. yd) to hasten the decay. Used more commonly in home gardens, however, is winter rye, which is planted in the fall and turned under in spring.

The prepared or concentrated manures should be applied according to the manufacturer's instructions, but usually the approximate rate is about a couple of handfuls to the sq. m (sq. yd). Another valuable material is seaweed, which can be gathered and dug in at the rate of about 50kg per 6.5 sq. m (1cwt per 8 sq. yd). There are several types of seaweed but the most useful are bladder and driftweed. Horticultural peat, which can be purchased in large bags, is also ideal for soil improvement. It has no food value but is very high in organic matter. The rate of application should be a good bucketful to the sq. m (sq. yd) on light soils and for average soils about three quarters of this amount can be applied.

In many cases, especially where one has a large garden and the outlay on manures could be prohibitive, they can be applied only where plants are to be planted. In time, by moving plants around (especially in the vegetable garden) the whole of the plot will be manured.

*Organic manure can be incorporated one spit deep when a new plot of land is being trenched. On well-cultivated land it is usually sufficient to fork it into the topsoil in the fall.*

## Fertilizers

These are important as they act as a booster to many crops, but they are also invaluable for the initial preparation or improvement of the soil, especially those soils which have been sadly neglected for several seasons. It is possible to buy individual fertilizers which provide specific plant foods, but it is also possible to purchase what is known as a complete or balanced fertilizer which contains a mixture of different nutrients to provide the plants with a 'well-balanced meal'.

In many cases specialist firms supply specific plant foods, for example for roses, for vegetables, for fruit and for the lawn. Let us first of all take a look at some of the most useful and popular individual fertilizers. Where a steady and slow-acting fertilizer is required then hoof and horn meal is invaluable, but this is, unfortunately, rarely available in the U.S. It is used outdoors at the rate of 60g per sq. m (2oz per sq. yd). Another useful slow acting fertilizer which provides phosphates has long been bonemeal, but so much is extracted from it today that it is no longer as beneficial as it was. The rate of distribution is up to 120g per sq. m (4oz per sq. yd). Another soil improver is lime. Hydrated lime is the quickest acting, and is used at rates up to 500g per sq. m (1lb per sq. yd), but is likely to burn and is no longer recommended. Instead use ground limestone at twice the amount. This also helps to improve the condition of the soil and helps to break down the heavier soils though it should not be used on eastern limy or western alkaline soils. It is best applied in the autumn or winter. Gypsum or calcium sulfate can be used where lime would not be suitable, and this should be applied at about 250g per sq. m (½lb per sq. yd). A very quick acting fertilizer which gives a boost to plant growth, especially to leaf formation, is nitrate of soda. This is rather caustic and must be kept away from foliage and stems. It is applied at the rate of not more than 15g per sq. m (½oz per sq. yd) or 8g (¼oz) in 4.5 litres (one gallon) of water.

*Above : tomatoes grown in containers can be topdressed with a suitable artificial fertilizer when the fruits are beginning to ripen.*

*Right : you can get a rough guide to your soil type in a new garden simply by looking at it and feeling a sample.*

It has about 16% of nitrogen. Another useful fertilizer is sulfate of ammonia which provides high nitrogen and encourages rapid growth. It is also caustic and needs application with care—rates should not exceed 15g per sq. m (½oz per sq. yd). It is best used in the apring or early part of the summer. It contains about 20% of nitrogen. Sulfate of potash provides the very important potash to encourage sturdy, strong plant growth and can be applied at about 15g per sq. m (½oz per sq. yd). It contains about 14% of potash. To apply phosphates to the soil and to encourage good root formation superphosphate can be applied at 30–60g per sq. m (1–2oz per sq. yd). It is applied in the spring or early summer and an averege analysis is 18% phosphoric acid. Today it is preferred to bonemeal by progressive growers.

These then are the individual fertilizers. One can purchase these in quantity and make up one's own fertilizer for specific crops. For example a good potato fertilizer is made up as follows: sulfate of ammonia 3 parts by weight; superphosphate of lime 4 parts by weight; sulfate of potash 2 parts by weight. The ingredients are mixed well together and applied just before planting at rates up to 90g per sq. m (3oz per sq. yd). For roots such as carrots, etc. the following can be made up: sulfate of ammonia 1 part by weight; superphosphate of lime 4 parts by weight; sulfate of potash 2 parts by weight. Use just before sowing or planting and apply at the rate of 90g per sq. m (3oz per sq. yd). For peas and beans the following is excellent: sulfate of ammonia 1 part by weight; superphosphate of lime 3 parts by weight; sulfate of potash 2 parts by weight. These are mixed together as for the others and applied just before sowing at the rate of 60g per sq. m (2oz per sq. yd).

For a general or balanced fertilizer for most garden plants the following is an excellent mixture: sulfate of ammonia 5 parts by weight; superphosphate of lime 7 parts by weight; sulfate of potash 2 parts by weight; steamed bone flour 1 part by weight. Apply at the rate of 90–120g per sq. m (3–4oz per sq. yd).

## Soil types

There are of course many different types of soil which are encountered and the type of soil or its condition can vary quite considerably within a small area. Basically there are three main types or divisions of soil: these are light, medium and heavy. The difference depends on the amount or proportion of sand or clay that is in them, and there is another classification as to the alkalinity or otherwise of a soil which is

known as the pH. The acidity and alkalinity is usually measured as far as the gardener is concerned by a scale known as the pH. A pH of 7.0 indicates that the soil is neutral—in other words it is neither acid nor alkaline. If however the pH is above 7.0 it is alkaline and below the figure of 7.0 the soil is acid. Plants will not grow well on a very acid soil, probably because the phosphates in the soil become unobtainable to the plants and the potassiums and magnesiums are easily lost from this type of soil. Also iron and aluminum are released in rather large amounts and this can actually cause poisoning of the plants. The acid soils can be corrected to a certain extent by the use of lime, in the form of ground limestone, chalk, or hydrated lime. On the other hand, alkaline soil can be corrected by giving generous dressings of peat or leaf mold or the use of acidifying materials like sulfate of ammonia. It is possible to purchase a very simple and cheap soil testing kit so that the pH content of one's soil can be checked from time to time. There are more complex or comprehensive soil testing outfits which will not only assess the pH content but also the deficiency or otherwise of some basic chemicals in the soil. By color chart comparison corrections can be easily made following the instructions provided with these kits. Of course you can tell a great deal about your soil just by looking at the color, looking at the plants already growing in it, and crumbling a sample through your fingers to feel the texture. But getting your soil tested scientifically is well worth a little effort and expense.

The sandy soils are the light soils which tend to dry out badly and which are known as hungry soils because they need plenty of feeding. They are soils which can be worked on at most times of the year and even during reasonably wet weather drainage is so good that the soil can be walked on very shortly after heavy showers of rain. The light sandy soils require plenty of organic matter or humus working into them in order that this material will act as a sponge and retain as much valuable moisture as possible and also provide a good rooting medium for the plants to grow into. Limestone soils can be difficult because they are often sticky and hard to work, but they too require plenty of feeding. To keep them nice and open plenty of organic matter should be worked in regularly. The peat soils are easy to work, like the light sandy ones, and they are particularly good for growing celery. One of the main problems with a peat soil is that it may be too acid. A peat soil is also a hungry soil and needs good feeding.

The clay soil is heavy because the soil particles are fine and closely packed together and these are perhaps the most difficult soils of all to work because they bake hard in dry weather and become wet and sticky during wet weather. In many cases they are only fit to work on during infrequent periods in winter, and one has to choose one's opportunity when the weather is reasonably dry and a cooling dry wind is prevalent, which helps to dry up the particles to a certain extent and facilitates the breaking down of the large resistant lumps. A clay soil, however, is a reasonably rich soil with a lot of plant food locked in it. The clay and heavy soils are usually poorly drained and therefore tend to become waterlogged. Particular attention should be paid to drainage and also to the working in of plenty of organic matter and sharp sand or well-weathered gritty cinders, which helps to open up the soil particles and keep them open so that they can be broken down more easily.

There is of course the ideal soil if one is lucky enough to have a garden with this type of soil in it. It should be a mixture of equal parts of sand and clay with a nice amount of organic matter included to make it nice and workable. A garden soil which has been well cultivated for years and years will generally be this kind of fertile, friable loam, but it is something that will not be achieved overnight.

Whatever type of soil you have in your garden make sure that you examine it thoroughly to begin with to assess the type and then treat it accordingly. Careful initial preparations pay off with handsome dividends of good crops, and frequent attention to soil improvement will in the course of a few seasons produce a soil which is much easier to work and which is rich in the essential plant foods. And if you are sensible about choosing plants, rather than trying to grow carrots on stony ground, or lime-loving plants on acid soil, you will be assured of successful gardening.

*There are many soil-testing kits on the market which will not only give you the pH value of your soil but will also let you know if it is deficient in certain basic chemicals.*

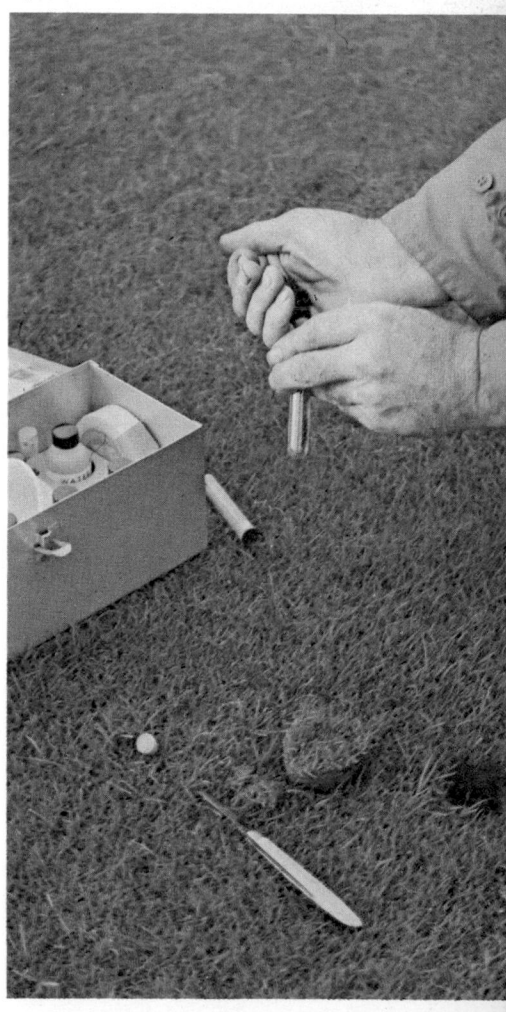

Unfortunately from time to time our fruit, flowers and vegetables can be attacked either by pests or by virus or fungus disease. The nature and intensity of these attacks varies from season to season. In the average garden the damage caused is of no great consequence, but it is a wise gardener who is prepared to combat either of these problems. For convenience, the attack is defined in the following list by the part of the plant which is affected.

However, at all times bear in mind that the U.S. Department of Agriculture and the Environmental Protection Agency change their regulations frequently. Likewise, each state has its own set of regulations. Therefore, the information which follows is to be regarded merely as a general guide. Follow the spray charts issued by your own state Extension Service and the materials available from your local dealers.

### Irregular areas or holes eaten out of leaves
This can be a sign of attack by one or two different types of insect. Caterpillars can cause a great deal of damage and the period of attack is normally from about March onward.
**Control:** Spray with Sevin, derris or malathion.
Earwigs can also cause irregular holes in foliage and these are generally seen during the period between May and late summer.
**Control:** Spray or dust the foliage with Sevin or malathion.

### Scalloped edges on leaves
The scalloped effect is an indication that the plant has been attacked by either leaf cutting bees, vine weevils or the pea and bean weevil. The period of attack is from early to late spring as far as the pea and bean weevil is concerned and from about then onward for the leaf cutting bee and the vine weevil.
**Control:** Spray with malathion.

### White flies on leaves
Masses of tiny white flies on crops such as cabbages and also indoor plants such as tomatoes are a sign of whitefly attack. The period of attack is from about early May into September in the north, longer southward.
**Control:** Spray with Sevin, pyrethrum or malathion. There are also special fumigating preparations available for use in greenhouses. Also attract to yellow cards coated with sticky material such as Jack Trap.

### Insects on leaves and young shoots
Lots of tiny flies of black, green, pink or even red color are indications of aphid attack. The spring and early summer are the critical periods outdoors, but under glass these creatures can attack during any part of the gardening year.
**Control:** Use pyrethrum, Sevin or derris.

### Woolly or mealy white covering on foliage
This is a sure sign of attack by the mealy bug. These insects can attack at any time.
**Control:** Use a systemic insecticide for ornamental subjects only. Follow local recommendations for food crops.

### Leaves practically reduced to a skeleton of veins
This is an attack by the gooseberry sawfly, and the period of attack is likely to be from about April to late August.
**Control:** Spray with derris or malathion.

### Chocolate colored spots on leaves
There is a disease which affects broad beans known as chocolate spot. The trouble

*Below, top: caterpillars attack many plants, especially brassicas. Center: black spot on roses. Bottom: gooseberry sawfly.*

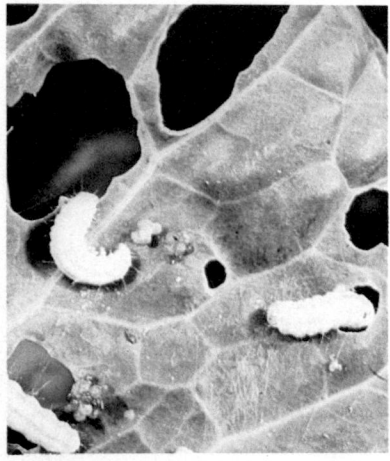

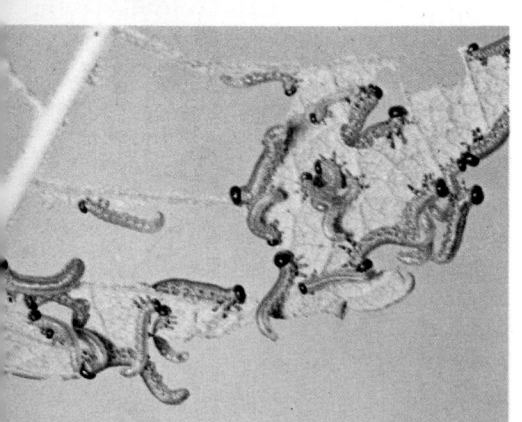

usually affects plants grown during the winter.

**Control:** Apply potash in the form of sulfate of potash to encourage sturdier and healthier growth at the outset.

Dark spots on rose leaves are an indication of black spot, a virus disease which is less common in city gardens than in the country.

**Control:** Spray with a recommended fungicide or systemic Benlate. One control is just to burn affected leaves and prunings.

### Brownish mould spots or areas underneath leaves

This is the leaf mould disease which chiefly affects tomatoes in the greenhouse. It can occur early on in the year in May, but is more prevalent in the middle of the summer. The cause is poor ventilation and general damp conditions.

**Control:** Allow more ventilation, leave plenty of spacing between plants, and grow the modern, more resistant varieties. Plants can also be sprayed with a copper preparation such as zineb or whatever is approved locally.

### Leaves with white tunnels in them

This is a sure sign of the chrysanthemum leaf miner. It affects plants from early July to late autumn, and it can affect several other plants as well as chrysanthemums.

**Control:** The badly affected leaves should be removed and burnt, and spraying with diazinon or locally approved chemical, preferably a systemic, should effect control.

### Frothy areas on foliage

This is a sign of the "cuckoo" or "snake" spit caused by the frog hopper. It can affect a wide range of plants and is usually found during the height of the summer.

**Control:** Light attacks are fairly harmless, but a spray with malathion will be effective if the trouble is serious.

### Leaves wilting badly or drooping

This can just be a sign of dryness, and it can also be a sign of some check to growth due to root damage. A distinct wilting of foliage in tomatoes, however, is a sure sign of a disease called verticillium wilt. The plants can be affected at any time of the growing period.

**Control:** The best control is the severest—pull up and burn the affected plants, and at the end of the season thoroughly sterilize the soil. Some plants not badly affected may be encouraged to grow on by top dressing with moist peat around the base of the stems. This action encourages roots to form higher up the stems in that area and it may save the plants. Resistant varieties are available.

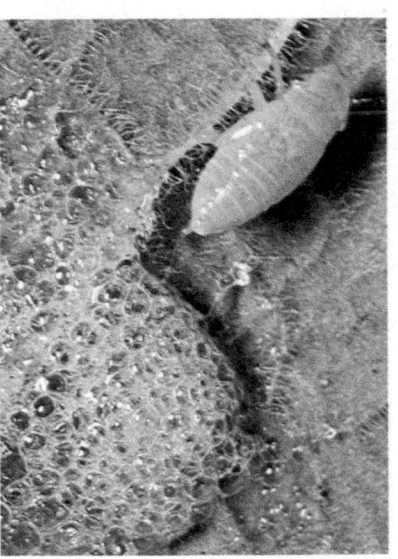

### Streaks and black and brownish marks on foliage

This could well be a virus disease and can occur at any time of the year on plants both indoors and outdoors. Quite often too the markings continue into the stems.

**Control:** There is unfortunately only one sure treatment, and that is to dig up and burn the affected plants and to sterilize the soil where the plants have been growing.

### Leaves badly curled

This can affect many plants and is usually an indication of attacks by aphids. The usual period is from about late spring to late summer.

**Control:** Spray frequently with derris, nicotine sulfate or Sevin.

### Elm foliage dying

It is important here to make mention of the Dutch elm disease. It is identified by the foliage which turns yellow and then brown, and then hangs from the branches which are themselves slowly killed. The time it makes itself known is from about May to late September, and it is vital that the affected trees are destroyed. It is in

*Above, top: aphids are probably the commonest garden pest. Center: these tell-tale white trails are left by the chrysanthemum leaf miner. Bottom: frothy areas on foliage are a protection for the frog hopper larva.*

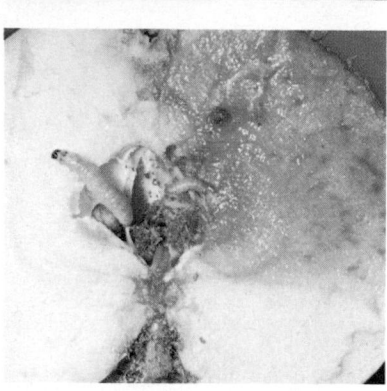

*Above, top: the petals of chrysanthemums can be badly damaged by earwigs. Center: codling moth caterpillar in apples. Bottom: apple scab.*

fact important to notify the local authority at once if a tree on your property is suspected of having this trouble.

### Stems rotting at ground level
This chiefly affects seedlings in their very early stages but can also affect more mature plants. It is a disease which is called 'damping off', and eventually the affected plant collapses and dies.
Control: One of the best ways to avoid the trouble is always to use sterilized seed mixtures and to make sure that receptacles such as pots and trays are scrupulously clean. It pays to dip these in a 1 to 9 solution of Clorox, or any other suitable sterilizing preparation for horticultural use. Also seedlings in boxes can be watered with a dilute preventive solution.

### Buds failing to open
This can affect fruit and flower buds and is caused by a weevil. The period of trouble extends from about April to late May. Usually apples are badly affected, and in this case the apple blossom weevil is responsible.
Control: The best preventive measure is to spray as recommended by your state just before the buds begin to open.

### Buds grossly enlarged
This is usually seen on blackcurrant bushes and is caused by the blackcurrant gall mite. It is usually seen in early spring, if at all.
Control: The buds should be picked out and burnt as quickly as possible, and the plants sprayed with lime sulfur as soon as the first flowers open. A repeat spray should be given about three weeks later.

### Flower petals badly eaten
Many flowering plants are affected but especially dahlias and chrysanthemums. The culprit is the earwig. The damage is usually seen from about May to late September.
Control: Spray frequently with malathion or other recommended material. The pest can also be trapped in rows of corrugated cardboard or flowerpots stuffed with straw and the pots placed either near ground level or on top of canes by the plants. The contents should be examined each day and destroyed.

### Caterpillars found in the center of fruit
The trouble usually affects apples and pears, and is caused by the caterpillar of the codling moth. The period of attack is from about June to late August.
Control: Prevention here is better than cure. Spray as recommended by your state Extension Service.

### Young fruit eaten into the center by caterpillars
This is a type of damage which occurs obviously much earlier in the fruit formation stage and chiefly affects apples. The attacks occur in spring.
Control: Apply a recommended spray as soon as the petals have fallen.

### Raised areas or bumps on fruit
This usually affects apples and is caused by the apple capsid. It affects the fruit from about April to August.
Control: Use a recommended dormant spray, which kills the eggs. You can also spray just before the flowers open, following the recommendations of your state's spray chart.

### Brown or black scabs on fruit
This is closely allied to the visual type of damage of the previous apple problem. It

is caused by a disease known as scab and can affect the fruits during the whole of the growing period.

**Control:** The treatment is to give frequent spraying as soon as the flower buds are formed, using captan, lime sulfur (but take care that lime sulfur is not used on those varieties of fruit that are known as 'sulfur shy'), or any recommended spray.

*Below, top: brown rot on apples. Center: maggots of the pea moth caterpillar. Bottom: narcissus fly grub.*

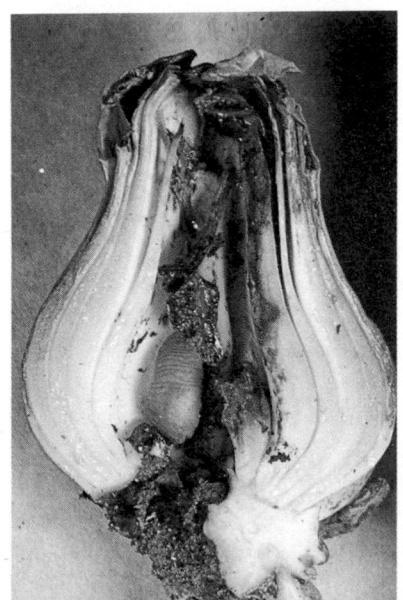

### A brown rot on fruit

This can affect most fruit trees and bushes and is caused by a fungus which produces a ringed spore over the surface of the fruit. It affects the fruit during the summer and can also affect fruit in store. That is why it is always wise to check through stored fruit regularly during the storage period and remove and destroy those which are affected, even though slightly.

**Control:** Pick and destroy infected fruit. Spray as your state recommends.

### White grubs found in soft fruit

This affects loganberries and raspberries, and the culprit is the grub of the raspberry beetle, which is found from June to late August.

**Control:** Spray with derris, malathion or Sevin when the fruits begin to color.

### Fruits rotting and covered with gray mold

This affects all soft fruits and is caused by the gray mold fungus. The trouble is not often seen until the fruit is well on the way to becoming ripe.

**Control:** The treatment is to spray as soon as the first flowers begin to open, repeating the spray at 14 day intervals. Use whatever is recommended by your state. Badly affected fruit should be removed and destroyed.

### A circular black or brownish area at the base of tomato fruits

This usually affects the outdoor tomatoes and is caused by a fungus disease. It is more prevalent in bad wet summers and usually affects the fruit when it begins to ripen.

**Control:** Remove and destroy badly affected fruits and spray at 14 day intervals with maneb or whatever your state permits.

### Brown area on tomato fruits

This unfortunately can be rather common and is known as blossom end rot. It is seen when the fruit is beginning to swell.

**Control:** Prevent fluctuations in the water supply to the plants and also avoid plants drying out before they receive a watering.

### White grubs in pea pods

This is an irritating discovery and ruins whole crops of peas. It is caused by the maggot of the pea moth caterpillar and is seen usually in late spring or summer.

**Control:** The plants should be sprayed when the flowers begin to open, as recommended by your Extension Service. It may be necessary to apply a second spray about two or three weeks after the first one.

### Rotten bulbs

Quite often when bulbs such as daffodils are lifted the bulb is soft and rotten and a little maggot is found inside. This is the grub of the narcissus fly and it attacks between April and late June.

**Control:** The affected bulbs must be destroyed and the soil should be dusted with a locally permitted dust as a precautionary measure before more bulbs are planted.

### Holes and tunnels in tubers

This is a sign of attacks by slugs, and plants such as potatoes are particularly affected.

Control: The slugs can attack at any time of the year, and as they are usually prevalent in wet badly drained soils one control is to improve drainage by deeper digging. Proprietary slug baits are very effective and most of those in use today are harmless to birds and domestic animals, though they can be covered with slate or a seed tray if desired.

### Brownish discoloration of potatoes

Blight disease is the trouble and can affect potatoes especially in a wet season. The potatoes which are badly affected should be destroyed, and any doubtful potatoes should not be stored away for winter use.

Control: Earth up the potatoes to prevent infection entering around the root area. The control for blight is to spray at fortnightly intervals from June onward with a recommended fungicide.

### Brownish–red area on the top or crown of parsnips

This is caused by parsnip canker and it can affect the plants during the entire growing period.

Control: The parsnips should be kept covered with soil and a more resistant modern variety should be grown.

### Maggots in carrot roots

These are the grubs of the carrot fly and are usually seen in the main summer period.

Control: Water plants with diazinon or whatever your state permits in late August. Another way of avoiding the trouble is to sow in late May.

### Cabbage plants collapsing

This is a result of attack on the root system by the cabbage root fly maggot. The time to look out for trouble is from late April until the end of September.

Control: The ground should be treated with a solution of diazinon—or other recommended material. Affected plants must be lifted and burnt. Collapsing cabbages can be caused by the attacks of the leather jacket maggot which is a fat gray brown color. It is usually active between April and late June.

Control: Protect the plants by working Sevin into the soil.

### Distorted enlarged roots

This usually affects the brassicas (members of the cabbage family) and is discovered when plants begin to collapse. This is caused by the disease club root.

Control: Affected plants must be lifted and destroyed. The affected ground must be given a good liming in the autumn and winter using ground limestone. It is interesting to note that if the fertility of the ground is built up with plenty of organic matter the disease can be reduced over the seasons. It is important also to practise a strict rotation of vegetable crops, and members of the brassica family must not be grown in affected ground for two or three seasons at least.

It is as well to remember that although plants can show signs of distress by discoloration of foliage this may not always mean that pests and diseases are affecting the plants. It could well be that plants, especially young ones, are chilled through cold winds or poor hardening off. It could also be that the soil is in a poor way as far as drainage is concerned, or even that the plants are not receiving sufficient feeding. Healthy plants will always be produced if the ground is well manured and the plants given an occasional tonic or feed during their growth. Liquid feeds are especially good because these are assimilated so quickly by the plants that a rapid recovery often follows.

Finally, never put diseased plants on the compost heap: wherever possible leave them in a neat heap until they can dry out and be burnt later on.

*Below, top: there is no cure for potato blight. Affected plants must be dug up and burned. Bottom: club root on a cabbage plant. Again, there is no cure, and affected plants must be destroyed.*

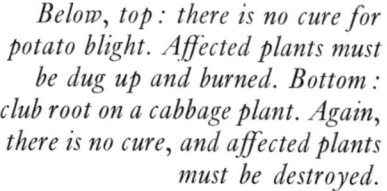

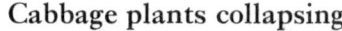
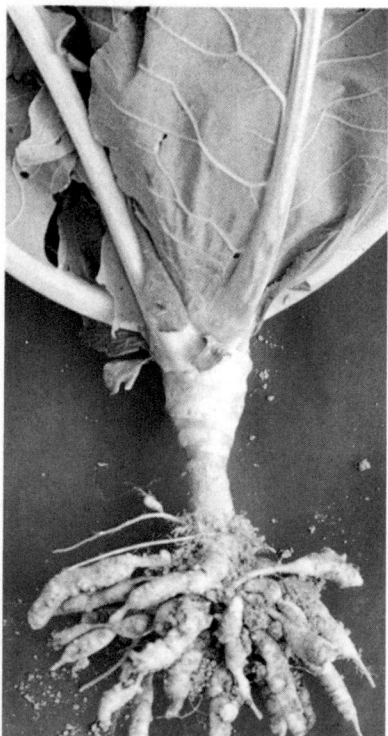

# GARDEN TOOLS & EQUIPMENT

No garden can be prepared and maintained without a basic set of equipment and once this basic set has been acquired it is possible to add to it during the course of the seasons until a comprehensive array of tools and gadgets is available in the garden shed. Most of those listed here are essential, and others you may wish to acquire as you go along.

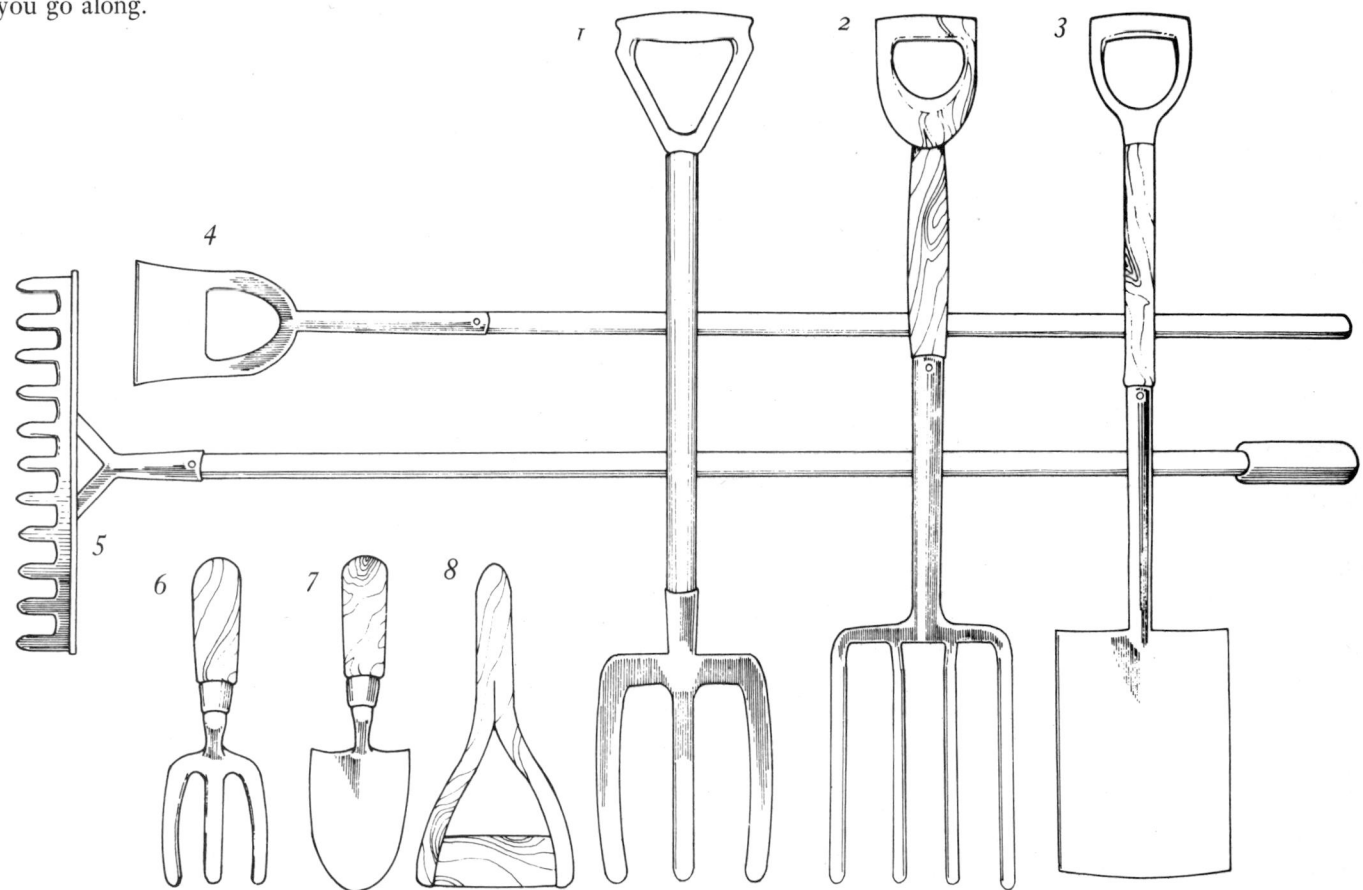

**Digging spade and fork**  The most important basic tools are those related to soil cultivation and planting. Two important tools are the digging spade and the digging fork, and there are several designs available ranging from the relatively inexpensive items to those which cost considerably more because they have stainless steel heads or tines and lightweight but strong tubular handles, which may be polyethylene or plastic covered and with very comfortable contoured handle grips.

**Border spade and fork**  There is a smaller and lighter type of spade and fork known as the border spade and fork, and these are very handy for working in more confined areas. They are especially useful tools for the woman gardener to use. In a small garden the border spade and fork may be sufficient for all requirements.

**Garden rake**  Another essential tool is the garden rake, which should have at least ten teeth. There are rakes with more teeth than this, and the more teeth a rake has the easier it is to break down and prepare the surface or tilth of the soil.

**Hoe**  A dutch or D-shaped hoe is important, for this is the tool for keeping weeds and weed seedlings under control. The hoe is worked down the rows between the plants, and this action slices off young weeds just below the surface and uproots seedlings.

**Hand trowel and fork**  These are also essential for planting out and for working in very confined situations.

**Garden line**  Do not forget the garden line which is essential where one has a vegetable garden in order to keep the rows nice and straight. It is also useful for trimming straight lawn edges.

KEY
1 border fork
2 digging fork
3 digging spade
4 hoe
5 garden rake
6 hand fork
7 hand trowel
8 dibber made from a cut-down spade handle

# Terms, tools & techniques

KEY
*1 all-purpose watering can with interchangeable rose for fine or coarse spray*
*2 shears*
*3 pruners*
*4 pruning knife*

**Dibber**   A dibber or dibble will be useful for making plant holes. This tool can vary from a small stick for pricking out small seedlings to a cut-down spade or fork handle for larger plants.

**Lawn mower**   The type of lawn mower to purchase will depend on the size of the lawn, and of course the type of grass it has to cut. For the small lawns the hand mower is quite sufficient and for powered assistance the small electric mowers are also very handy. For larger areas the bigger electric mowers are excellent and so too are gasoline engined machines which are the most popular as the operator is not restricted by a wire. In this category there are cutting widths from 30cm (12in) to about 75cm (30in) and the latter would be ideal for large areas of grass. For really big areas there are the riding mowers to consider.

The type of cut is important too. The rotary mower, where the blades revolve parallel to the grass, gives you the best of both worlds. They will cut the domestic garden quite well, giving a reasonably close cut and good finish, and they will also cut the taller tougher grasses. For really tough work there are special rotary mowers available for jobs like cutting rough grass in orchards. For the best quality cut there is no doubt that the reel-type mower is the best, and the more blades it has the larger the number of cuts and the finer the finish.

**Edging shears and edgers**   A lawn is only as neat as its edges, and edging shears are essential. One should also have a half moon edger to keep the edges cut cleanly so that the edging tool can be used more efficiently.

**Shears**   There will also be the need to cut hedges with a pair of shears. Electric hedge-cutters can save a lot of effort if the garden has a lot of hedges to be kept trimmed.

**Pruning shears**   The cutting of blooms and the cutting of stems during pruning will require the use of a good pair of pruners. This is an item you will use a great deal, and it is worth paying more for a really top quality pair.

**Sprayer**   Do not forget the war to be waged against pest and disease. A sprayer should be included as an essential part of the tool kit. The size of sprayer will depend on the size of garden but usually a pneumatic 5 liter (one gallon) sprayer is adequate, with a small hand sprayer for work in the greenhouse or for spraying indoor plants.

**Hoses, sprinklers and watering cans**   Also essential for a garden of any size is a good quality hose, and a sprinkler and a watering can will not go amiss either.

**Wheelbarrows and carts**   Where a new, large or neglected garden is being taken over, a wheelbarrow or garden cart is an essential item.

**Potting requisites**   If one has a greenhouse or a frame a selection of plastic pots and seed trays should be included in the range of essential equipment for the garden, and do not forget to keep a stock of seed labels so that a check can be kept on the names and types of plants being grown.

# GLOSSARY OF GARDENING TERMS

Like many other hobbies gardening has developed its own peculiar language and it is useful to know some of the gardening terms which you will encounter in this book and elsewhere. Here is a selection of the most common.

**Blanch**   This is a term used in vegetable growing which means to make the plant or part of the plant white by excluding light. Two examples arc in the case of celery and leeks where paper collars or soil is drawn up around the stems to exclude light. The purpose of blanching celery is to remove the sometimes bitter taste of the green plant, although in the U.S. green celery is preferred.

**Bolt**   This is the early or premature flowering or running to seed of a plant.

**Compost**   This can be a misleading word because it has two meanings. Compost can refer to the ingredients of the compost heap where material is rotting down. Compost is also a British term for special soil mixtures used in the growing of plants such as seed composts and potting composts, meaning seed or potting mixes.

**Crown**   The area or part of a plant which is at soil level or just below it.

**Drill**   A fairly shallow trench or furrow made for the sowing of seeds.

**F1 Hybrid**   This is a term used for the new generation of plants where a variety is obtained by a controlled fertilization or breeding of two different plants. Usually two different parent plants are used, and the point must be made that seed from the resultant plants cannot be saved as the progeny of these will not run true to the original seed or variety.

**Harden off**   Getting plants used to cooler conditions or atmosphere in a gradual process. Plants raised in a greenhouse in heat or in a frame should be hardened off before they are planted outside in their permanent quarters. This is usually done by placing the plants in a frame from the greenhouse or, if plants are already in a frame, the frame lights are gradually opened a bit each week until finally they are removed completely to allow the plants to become fully accustomed to outside conditions.

**Haulm**   This refers to the top growth or foliage on stems of plants and is particularly used with reference to vegetables such as peas, potatoes and beans.

**Heel in**   To place plants temporarily in the ground until they can be planted out finally in their permanent quarters in the garden.

**Laterals**   These are the side growths of plants.

**Maiden**   This refers chiefly to fruit. A maiden is a fruit tree which is one year old.

**Mulch**   A layer or covering of manure, peat, vegetable waste (composted or otherwise), or even black polyethylene around plants and over the soil surface, applied to conserve moisture and also in many cases to suppress small weed seedlings.

**Pinch out**   The stopping of a growth by tenderly nipping out or pinching out the growing center. This causes the plants to branch out also.

**Prick out**   To transfer seedlings either from seed trays into individual pots, or spaced wider apart in new seed trays. It must be carried out carefully to avoid damaging the young plants or their root systems.

**Set out**   This means to plant out.

**Spit**   Refers to the depth of digging and usually refers to the length of the spade blade which is approximately 25cm (10in).

**Stopping**   The prevention of further growth or extension of growth by pinching out the growing center or laterals.

**Thinning**   The reduction of the number of young plants or seedlings in a row. This refers chiefly to vegetable and annual flower growing and can refer for example to where a row of lettuce has been sown and the young seedlings are thinned out to a few inches apart to give them more room for expansion. Thinning can also take place where seed such as seed of annual plants has been broadcast over a bed. Thinning can also refer to fruit growing, where some fruits which develop in trusses such as apples and pears are carefully thinned in their young stage to allow the remaining fruit to have plenty of room to swell and mature.

**Tuber**   A swollen underground stem, as for example a potato or dahlia.

# Index